PRAISE FOR *DEALING WITH THE URGENT EDUCATIONAL CHALLENGE: PROMOTING SOCIAL-EMOTIONAL WELL-BEING AMONG TEACHERS, STUDENTS, AND FAMILIES*

"In education, we often refer to and discuss ACEs or 'Adverse Childhood Experiences' and their impact on student learning. The experience of COVID-19 has made ACE now a major part of the makeup of every student in every school across the county. When you add a national 'Common ACE' to the multifaceted challenges students faced in our nation's schools and globally before COVID-19, as educators, we have an even greater need for a practical, solution-based work from the foremost thinkers and writers during this time that requires an even braver new world view of teaching and learning. Polka, McKenna, and VanHusen have once again crafted a pragmatic and significant read that should be on the desk of every educator."

—**Mark Laurrie**, superintendent of schools, City School District of the City of Niagara Falls, New York.

"*Dealing with the Urgent Educational Challenge* is focused on addressing the social emotional problems and issues that our students face in the post-COVID-19 years. The authors of this book make meaningful suggestions and strategies to help students, their parents, and their teachers overcome these difficulties. The negative impact of COVID-19 on student social-emotional learning was projected and monitored by many. This projection and monitoring approach of educational planning as fully explored in this book facilitates the launch of specific strategies, techniques, and pragmatic activities to help students with social emotional problems after COVID-19."

—**Tak Cheung Chan**, PhD, professor emeritus of Educational Leadership, Kennesaw State University, Kennesaw, Georgia, editor of *Educational Planning*, International Society for Educational Planning

"*Dealing with the Urgent Educational Challenge* fills a void for preservice and practicing educators regarding strategies to meet the varied needs of students, teachers, and caregivers. While facing a variety of challenges during COVID-19, educators found new strength and confidence in their abilities to effectively teach students who were dealing with their own challenges, which most often resulted in disruptions in academic as well as social-emotional growth. I plan to incorporate the concepts contained in this edition in my work, and I believe that it is imperative that other educators do the same!"

—**Kelly A. NewVine**, PhD, associate professor, director of the School of Health, Education, Sustainability, and Society, Hiram College, Hiram, Ohio

"The authors of this insightful, soon-to-be-seminal book on COVID-19 social-emotional well-being have envisioned and produced evidence of what has become a necessary movement toward the well-being of the children, students, educational facilitators, and caregivers to our nation and the world community of education. Each chapter in the edited volume demonstrates the need to promote healing for all stakeholders in our educational communities—P–12 and higher education."

—**Noran L. Moffett**, EdD, professor, Department of Educational Leadership and School Administration, Fayetteville State University, Fayetteville, North Carolina; past vice chair (2019–2023) of the Council for the Accreditation of Educator Preparation (CAEP)

"*Dealing with the Urgent Educational Challenge* illuminates the urgency and responsiveness needed in a post-COVID-19 world to authentically foster social-emotional well-being within our school communities. This book provides a blueprint for implementation with illustrative examples highlighting purposeful leadership, peak moments, and methods to maintain vision alignment while adapting to real-world challenges. Moreover, this book positions leaders to think beyond reacting to the individual challenges of the day to lead true organizational change by promoting comprehensive social-emotional well-being of the entire school community."

—**Daniel Walh**, PhD, principal, Transit Middle School, New York, 2021 School Administrators Association of New York State Secondary School Principal of the Year (SAANYS) and National Association of Secondary School Principals (NASSP) New York State Principal of the Year.

"The pressures and problems on schools have deeply affected the physical and mental health of teachers, students, and parents and, unfortunately, made them pessimistic. In this book, the authors examined *'social-emotional well-being among teachers, students, and families'* in all its aspects and offer valuable alternative solutions."

—**Selahattin Turan**, PhD, professor of educational leadership and policy, Bursa Uludağ University, Turkey; member of the Board of Directors of *International Society for Educational Planning* (ISEP).

Dealing with the Urgent Educational Challenge

Promoting Social-Emotional Well-Being among Teachers, Students, and Families

Edited by

Walter S. Polka
John E. McKenna
Monica J. VanHusen

ROWMAN & LITTLEFIELD
Lanham • Boulder • New York • London

Published by Rowman & Littlefield
An imprint of The Rowman & Littlefield Publishing Group, Inc.
4501 Forbes Boulevard, Suite 200, Lanham, Maryland 20706
www.rowman.com

86-90 Paul Street, London EC2A 4NE, United Kingdom

British Library Cataloguing in Publication Information Available

Library of Congress Cataloging-in-Publication Data

Names: Polka, Walter S., 1945– editor. | McKenna, John, 1963– editor. | VanHusen, Monica J., 1980– editor.
Title: Dealing with the urgent educational challenge : promoting social-emotional well-being among teachers, students, and families / Edited by Walter S. Polka, John E. McKenna, and Monica J. VanHusen.
Description: Lanham, Maryland : Rowman & Littlefield, [2024] | Includes bibliographical references. | Summary: "Dealing with the Urgent Educational Challenge provides readers with key research-based and pragmatically tested approaches and processes to deal with the unprecedented mental health issues prevalent in today's schools, families, and communities"— Provided by publisher.
Identifiers: LCCN 2024015970 (print) | LCCN 2024015971 (ebook) | ISBN 9781475870190 (cloth) | ISBN 9781475870206 (paperback) | ISBN 9781475870213 (epub)
Subjects: LCSH: Affective education. | Social learning. | Teachers—Mental health. | Students—Mental health. | Parent-teacher relationships. | Teacher-student relationships. | Emotional intelligence (Psychology)
Classification: LCC LB1072 .D42 2024 (print) | LCC LB1072 (ebook) | DDC 370.15/34—dc23/eng/20240501
LC record available at https://lccn.loc.gov/2024015970
LC ebook record available at https://lccn.loc.gov/2024015971

Contents

Foreword

Social-Emotional Learning: "A Serious Matter"

Having been an educator for over thirty years on both P–12 and Higher Education levels serving as a teacher, leader, administrator, and mentor, I deem that the intentional infusion of social-emotional learning is a *serious matter* for education. As a *matter* of fact, I grasped the need for social-emotional learning and well-being before the term *social-emotional* learning became a prominent reiteration in today's educational system. From the mid-1970s to the late 1980s, I was a student in a rural Mississippi school district where there was a community of educators who nurtured, disciplined, mentored, molded, and exposed students to an interesting world of learning, creating, synthesizing, and evaluating. Perhaps, this was my introduction to social-emotional learning without me really knowing it.

Social-emotional learning is a strategic approach for student personal development and application of "life-long" attitudes and knowledge that provides skills to help students manage anger, control emotions, achieve goals, and show empathy and respect. Now that I think about it, the teachers of the era when I was a student were practicing social-emotional learning as they engaged students in activities as simple as encouraging them to recite with confidence; to apologize when warranted; to be proud of a grade that moved from a *D* to a *C*; to embrace their own talents and celebrate the talents of others; and to respect protocol and leadership. With such nurturing, the natural stresses that came with being a student—eventually a teenager—were minimized and not overwhelmingly stressful. In recent conversations with some of those teachers of that era, the concept was never introduced as *social emotional learning*; yet the practices were exemplified through their love for their students and their passion for teaching and learning, without the pressure of standardized testing and evaluations of courses or schools.

I can vividly remember an act of social-emotional learning when I was in first grade in 1975 at Tchula Attendance Center. I was excited that I could tell time on the clock (digital clocks were not present in our schools). When I got off the bus, I ran straight to Principal Gladys Walker's office and enthusiastically shared with her that I could tell time on the clock. She pointed to the big "school-day" wall clock and asked, "Young, what time is it now"? I confidently stated the time. Mrs. Walker smiled and said, "That is correct; you are truly a smart student, and you are going to achieve many great things in life."

I remember thinking to myself that Principal Walker called me "smart," and if she said it, it was true. From that day forward, I just knew that I was smart! Nothing or no one was going to change my confidence in my ability. I felt a sense of self-awareness and commitment because I was "smart." Therefore, I had a responsibility to act accordingly. A positive word at an early age impacted my whole academic trajectory, and as a result, I have excelled academically throughout my life. One may ask, "Was that social-emotional learning"? For me, it gave me hope for a bright academic future, and it put me on a path to life-long success. Personally, it was social-emotional learning at its best!

Dealing with the Urgent Educational Challenge: Promoting Social-Emotional Well-Being among Teachers, Students, and Families reminds one of the importance of experiences with educators like Principal Walker. It also reiterates the concept of social-emotional learning (SEL) and therapy and its importance to student behavior, academic success, teacher efficacy, teaching practices and approaches, positive impact, community care, and students with special needs during a crucial era in the world. Primarily, this book reemphasizes the need for implementation, practice, and embracement of social emotional learning, thus reminding us that without the balance of belonging and well-being, learning and teaching can become deficient, prompting an urgency to intervene, orient, recalibrate, and support.

As we know, the effects of COVID-19 induced the promotion of social-emotional learning. Because of the sudden transition to virtual learning, isolation, and discouragement from social engagement during COVID-19, many students, educators, family, and friends suffered a lack of mental equilibrium, whether minor or severe. Now that schools are still trying to heal from the academic atrocities caused by COVID-19, it is equally important that they support social-emotional well-being for all.

The Collaborative for Academic, Social, and Emotional Learning (CASEL) framework postulates that SEL is the center of five competencies: self-awareness, self-management, social awareness, relationship skills, and responsible decision-making. Each chapter of this book reflects at least one of those competencies. Further, the research embedded in each chapter is a reiteration that social-emotional learning promotes well-being, resilience, positivity, and academic achievement. The chapters highlight the issues and provide insights that empower educators with testimonies, research, and content to implement SEL with precision and passion. When you read the chapters in this book, you will clearly observe the relevance to one or more of the five competencies of SEL as defined by CASEL. Though each chapter includes several competencies, I have observed and cogently articulated below the most prevalent competency in each chapter that provides a broader understanding of SEL with specific content based on research.

Chapters 8 and 9 have a particular representation of self-awareness. Chapter 8 focuses on helping students with disabilities to understand their emotions due to the effects of COVID-19, with instructions on how to assess their behavior. Through the story of Samuel, chapter 9 provides application of a multi-tiered system of academics and behavior in leading educators to help students assess their behavior and engagement. Self-management is obvious in chapters 1 and 10. In chapter 1 the focus is on promoting well-being for happy teachers, emphasizing the ability of teachers to manage their emotions, thoughts, and behavior through a strong support system. Chapter 10 suggests a need for social emotional intelligence with an aim to help teachers and parents help the children manage fear, stress, and other inhibiting emotions. Chapters 2, 6, and 11 reiterate social awareness. They focus on students' and teachers' ability to understand others, foster a sense of belonging through best practices and collaboration, and rid educational silos to enhance multiple learning environments. Chapters 3, 7, and 12 highlight healthy relationships and the approaches to creating SEL programs that impact student skills and community care services. Through developing relationship skills, districts and the community can move from "caring how much you know" to "knowing how much you care." Chapters 4 and 5 present the need for responsible decision-making in making behavior referrals and reorienting how educators think about the decisions they make with an urgency to provide the appropriate professional development for effective implementation.

Based on my personal research and the chapter authors' research in this book, I conclude that my philosophy of social-emotional learning persists: *Social-emotional learning is a matter of paramount importance to successful teaching and learning.* Principal Walker changed my life at a very early age and established my "mind-set" for future personal and academic success. She told me that I was "smart," thus, I believed it, and I never forgot it. Further, she held me accountable academically, socially, and personally as she often drafted me and others for student-leadership roles in the school. If our behavior was not representative of leadership, she and the educators she empowered would apply what we now call *social-emotional learning skills* through fostering self-awareness, self-management, social awareness, relationship skills, and responsible decision-making.

Dealing with the Urgent Educational Challenge: Promoting Social-Emotional Well-Being among Teachers, Students, and Families insists that we continue to reorient our minds and behavior to embrace, exemplify, and intentionally execute the concept of social-emotional well-being in the home, school, and community. In each chapter, the author(s) reiterate the urgency of the challenge, thus promoting, through research, the need for support, collaboration, professional development and intentionality of implementing pragmatic social-emotional learning/well-being in the curriculum. This is a serious matter.

Jennifer Young Wallace, PhD
Tenured Associate Professor/Coordinator of the Doctoral Program of Educational Leadership for the College of Education and Human Development at Jackson State University
Association of Teacher Educators President, 2025–2026

Preface

Walter S. Polka, John E. McKenna,
and Monica J. VanHusen

Opportunities are like sunrises: if you wait too long, you miss them.

—William Ward

The COVID-19 pandemic has exponentially increased the social-emotional problems and issues that our students face today. According to the National Center for Education Statistics (NCES), 87 percent of public-school officials reported that the COVID-19 pandemic has negatively impacted student social-emotional development and 84 percent of public school officials agreed or strongly agreed that students' behavioral development has also been negatively impacted (NCES, 2022).

These are staggering statistics that have caused educational leaders to make social-emotional wellness a top priority in every school across the country. The twenty-three authors of this book's twelve chapters have addressed these issues head on and have provided research-based and practical solutions that school leaders can utilize to support the social-emotional and mental health needs of everyone in their school communities.

This book is the third book in a trilogy that the editors assembled after the COVID-19 pandemic to assist school leaders to reconstruct, revise, and create new policies, programs, and practices to meet the ever-changing needs of people in our global village of today.

The two other books in the trilogy are *Managing Yourself and Others during Crises: Key Leadership Visions, Approaches, and Dispositions to Survive and Thrive* and *Coping with Educational Crises: Approaches from School Leaders Who Did It.* In both books, the editors worked with authors, including researchers and practicing school leaders from across the globe, to determine the best-fit solutions to the real-world problems of the time and provide tested examples of applying theory into leadership actions for the expedience of personal and organizational survival and thriving in the future.

All three books emphasize the point that with crises come opportunities, and school leaders must seize this moment and change the way they deliver programs and services to students and staff to be effective, now and well into the future. This is especially true in the areas of mental health and social-emotional well-being where people are struggling with unprecedented levels of stress, anxiety, and fear. This is the major educational challenge of our post-COVID-19 time!

The editors of this book worked intensively with the twenty-three different writers to capture their pragmatic and research-based thoughts and recommendations and compile them into this volume for ease of reference. Each of the authors has had considerable experiences in developing, implementing, or evaluating programs and practices related to social-emotional wellness. The resultant twelve chapters of this book, based on the authors' diverse backgrounds and experiences, provide an analysis of the causes and acute solutions to a myriad of student-related social-emotional and mental-health issues from a wide range of local, regional, and global perspectives including but not limited to: PreK–16 education, special education concerns, early childhood practices, after-school programming, community services, multi-tiered support systems, and the role of artificial intelligence (AI) in supporting teachers and students.

The book offers a comprehensive and eclectic view of the programs and practices available to school leaders related to social-emotional learning now and well into the future. It serves as a practical guide and resource to help school leaders make the best decisions to support the social-emotional needs of their students, staff, parents, and school communities at this time of greatest need and greatest opportunity. Don't miss this historic moment in education!

REFERENCES

National Center for Education Statistics (2022). "More Than 80 Percent of U.S. Public Schools Report Pandemic Has Negatively Impacted Student Behavior and Socio-emotional Development." July 12. https://nces.ed.gov/whatsnew/press_releases/07_06_2022.asp.

Acknowledgments

The editors of this book wish to thank the chapter authors who have provided outstanding examples and insights related to their experiences with social-emotional learning and well-being issues in their respective schools and communities. Their dedication and expertise, as well as their leadership, knowledge, and wisdom add significantly to the quality of this publication. Accordingly, the editors appreciate their efforts and those of their colleagues in making our world safer, kinder, and more empathetic for all.

Introduction

John E. McKenna, Walter S. Polka,
and Monica J. VanHusen

We cannot always build a future for our youth, but we can always build our youth for the future.

—Franklin D. Roosevelt (1940)

The social-emotional well-being of students and staff has always been a concern of school leaders. Since the COVID-19 pandemic it has become a major priority for most every school district throughout our global village. The pandemic has shined a bright light on the importance of addressing the social-emotional needs of students, staff, and parents in order to more appropriately prepare our youth to live in their future.

This book was developed as a compendium reference volume that includes the analysis and sage advice of twenty-three writers with very diverse educational leadership backgrounds and robust research experiences. It is designed to provide current and aspiring school leaders with proven strategies, methods, and programs that they may implement and utilize to meet the various social-emotional needs of everyone in their respective school communities. The chapter authors are practitioners who have utilized these methods in their own practice and researchers who have dedicated their careers to searching for the best programs and practices to meet the ever-evolving needs of students. All of the book chapter authors agree that schools must act aggressively *now* and develop an intentional "full-court press" approach to meet the diverse needs of students and combat the mental health crisis that is prevalent in our schools and society.

The twelve chapters in this book review, describe, and recommend practical, real-world applications, based on research, that school administrators can pilot and implement to support the social-emotional well-being of all stakeholders in their school districts. At the conclusion of the book the editors summarize the material into "Ten Key Pragmatic Leadership Takeaways." These recommendations for implementing more and better-quality social-emotional programs, projects, and activities may be used as guides for school district leaders to follow to develop classroom, school building, and school district plans that meet the unique needs of their respective learning contexts.

The following is a summary and description of the information presented in each chapter:

Chapter 1. This chapter is written by international researchers with a vast array of practical teaching and leadership experiences. They provide theoretical and conceptual frameworks associated with positive psychology approaches to coping with changes and implementing programs designed to improve mental health. The authors present strategies for personal and professional well-being in schools to promote happier teachers, students, and parents who are focused on bringing back the "joy" in teaching and learning for *all*. They explore the root causes of teacher, student, and parent burnout and offer specific strategies school leaders may employ to satisfy personal, professional, and organizational coping needs.

Chapter 2. The authors of this chapter, who possess outstanding building and school district experiences in diverse contexts, analyze the best practices to promote and support social-emotional learning and wellness in K–12 schools. The authors separate best practices into two categories: (1) classroom strategies and methods and (2) school-wide programs and practices. The authors provide research of proven, practical strategies that school leaders can explore and implement with ease. The chapter offers a wide menu of choices and methods that can be used as a resource for school district leaders who are searching for best practices to meet the various needs of their students, staff, and communities.

Chapter 3. In this chapter a practicing superintendent takes readers through the process that was utilized to unite the faculty and staff with a common vision and mission regarding social-emotional learning in the school district. The chapter author describes the steps taken to review programs and practices and develop a program and plan to meet the unique needs of students, staff, and community. After a thorough analysis of multiple programs, it was decided in this school district to implement the Positivity Project (P2). A program developed by two West Point graduates. This chapter reviews the importance of building capacity and implementing the program with fidelity. The program has been very well received and is making an extremely positive difference in the lives of students, teachers, and parents.

Chapter 4. This chapter is written by three practicing high school principals who worked together on a joint doctoral dissertation, at a major public university, to study the impact of the COVID-19 pandemic on their students and explore possible programs and practices to provide social-emotional support to their school communities. The three schools had very different demographics and wide variations in poverty rates, special needs students, and English-language learners. The authors were surprised that all three schools yielded similar results regarding the COVID-19 effects on students and recommendations for support from the staff. It is a fascinating study with practical recommendations that all school leaders will find helpful.

Chapter 5. This is a comprehensive chapter with intentional strategies that school leaders can adapt and apply in a variety of teaching-learning situations. It consists of a "real-world personal narrative" from an experienced building principal who spent part of the COVID-19 pandemic as a middle school principal in an affluent district and then transferred to an elementary school in a rural setting. This chapter's author chronicles the leadership journey of reorienting faculty and staff mind-sets, moving from transactional transformational thinking, and developing a homegrown SEL program. The author also describes the steps taken to unify the entire school community around a common purpose and empower the staff to work in collaborative groups. The lessons learned, modifications made, and adaptations employed to successfully transfer social-emotional programs, projects, and activities from the middle school level to the elementary level are evaluated.

Chapter 6. This chapter is written by a team of educators in a large suburban school division in Virginia. They worked together through the pandemic and are now implementing new plans, methods, and strategies throughout the district to intentionally shatter silos and foster collaboration and belonging to support the well-being of all stakeholders in the K–12 organization. The authors examine the causes of "silo mentality" and how leaders can implement intentional strategies to break down silos and create safe places for teachers and administrators to work together to address the social-emotional needs of students and their fellow colleagues.

Chapter 7. This chapter's author, a Canadian researcher with various international experiences in diverse organizations, including schools, analyzes the importance of providing community care services that extend beyond the school day. This experienced researcher investigates the importance of before- and after-school programs and how they are necessary to meet the comprehensive learning needs of students. The author recommends that instructional settings need to reduce their staffing ratios to provide more individualized support and instruction to students, and school leaders must work with community assistance programs to meet the complex social-emotional needs of students.

Chapter 8. The author of this chapter possesses over twenty years' experience as a special education teacher and program coordinator and focuses on the extensive social-emotional needs of students with special needs. It is widely accepted that the COVID-19 crisis impacted all students, but it was especially difficult for special needs students who had preexisting emotional concerns and required counseling and social worker assistance. It was difficult to deliver special education services during the pandemic, and many students did not receive the specific programming attention required by their Individual Education Plans (IEPs). The author reviews how districts must deliver all required IEP services for special needs students and offers suggestions and strategies school leaders can utilize to meet requirements, especially in times of crisis.

Chapter 9. This chapter was written by a team of authors who study social-emotional wellness at Florida International University. The authors do a deep dive into the applications of multi-tiered support systems (MTSS) to promote social, behavioral, and academic success for students with attention deficit/hyperactivity disorder. They provide an overview of how to successfully develop and implement an MTSS system that meets the unique needs of the ADHD population. They stress the importance of staff collaboration and the utilization of a multidisciplinary teaming that meets regularly to review and develop plans to meet the individual needs of students.

Chapter 10. This chapter's author, a Canadian higher education professor and child development researcher, examines the concept of social-emotional intelligence (SEI) often referred to as emotional intelligence (EI). The author of this chapter stresses that emotional intelligence can be nurtured and taught by applying well-established child growth and development research on social-emotional learning including, Gardner's multiple intelligences, Maslow's hierarchy of needs, and Erickson's stages of psychosocial development. The author also provides practical tips that educators and parents can apply to enhance the emotional intelligence of students and foster their social-emotional development, especially in early childhood.

Chapter 11. The authors of this chapter, who possess practical teaching experiences in the K–16 real world and have also conducted various research studies, explore the cutting-edge concept of integrating artificial intelligence in supporting teacher well-being and reducing burnout. The authors explore the role of artificial intelligence in schools and identify specific ways that AI could be used to support teachers in the classroom. Those strategies include: personalized learning; differentiated, tiered instruction; cultivating twenty-first-century skills; incorporating technology; embracing cultural competence; assessment, data-driven decisions; and effective classroom management. The authors claim that AI can alleviate workload burdens, promote personalized learning, and provide educators with valuable tools for enhancing instructional effectiveness and increasing teacher resiliency now and well into the future.

Chapter 12. In this final chapter the editors provide a summary of the main themes and ideas that the various chapter authors present in their respective chapters. They consolidate the information into ten key leadership pragmatic takeaways designed to facilitate the incorporation of more comprehensive and better-quality social-emotional learning programs, projects, and activities into current education contexts. These concepts may be used as a guiding framework for current or aspiring school district leaders that want to most appropriately and effectively address the social-emotional well-being of everyone in their organization.

The editors of this book hope that readers will find practical ideas as well as multiple programs and practices, based on research, to explore and utilize to meet the social-emotional needs of every stakeholder in their respective school context, including: students, staff members, parents, and community members. This book is designed to be a resource that can be used again and again to find the right methods and develop a highly effective plan of action to address the most significant issue facing our schools today: the social-emotional well-being of our students. The editors of this book believe that the following letter from a former concentration camp prisoner captures the "Sense of Urgency" and the *why* of providing more comprehensive and better social-emotional learning in today's educational experiences:

> *Dear Teacher,*
> *I am a survivor of a concentration camp. My eyes saw what no man should witness:*
> *Gas chambers built by* learned *engineers.*
> *Children poisoned by* educated *physicians.*
> *Infants killed by* trained *nurses.*

Women and babies shot and burned by high school and college *graduates.*
So I am suspicious of education.
My request is: Help your students become human. Your efforts must never produce learned monsters, skilled psychopaths, educated Eichmanns.
Reading, writing, arithmetic are important
Only if they serve to make children more humane.

Author Anonymous

Chapter 1

Promoting Personal and Professional Well-Being in Schools for Happier Teachers, Students, and Parents

Insights from Positive Psychology

Roselle C. Aranha and Walter S. Polka

> *I am a teacher at heart, and there are moments in the classroom when I can hardly hold the joy. When my students and I discover uncharted territory to explore, when the pathway out of the thicket opens up before us, when our experience is illumined by the lightning-life of the mind—then teaching is the finest work I know.*
>
> *But at other moments, the classroom is so lifeless, or painful, or confused—and I am so powerless to do anything about it that my claim to be a teacher seems a transparent sham.*
>
> —Parker Palmer (2017)

Learning in school classrooms is often an adventure speckled with shades of mystery, magic, joy, patience, challenge, and grandeur. Committed teachers find fulfillment in their profession through these epiphanies. The beauty and joy of teaching transcends mastery over method and content, grades, and audits. Authentic teaching lies at the confluence of the mind and the heart. Schools were intended to be homely places where the individuality of each student and teacher was treasured, where diversity marked strength, and where educators and students felt a deep connection as students discovered their unique talents and gifts while learning valuable life skills.

A school classroom is supposed to be a safe, lively, and encouraging space that nurtures the unfolding of creativity through eureka moments that may be subtle or profound. It is a two-way street. While students incrementally discover their vocation, passion, and potential under the careful guidance of their teachers and in the company of their classmates, teachers keenly invested in their students discover the joy of their professional calling as they witness precious moments of illumination when students successfully move to their zone of proximal development.

The zone of proximal development, as envisioned by Vygotsky in his writings (published posthumously) in 1978, is the next near point of achievement for students, which they can reach with some encouragement, direction, and scaffolding provided by their teacher. Teachers and students learn alongside each other, and care and trust are reciprocal (Noddings, 2003; Meier, 2002). It was precisely this sense of wonder and fulfillment that attracted young people to become school educators who generally stayed in the profession for their entire careers.

In recent years, however, the idea of schools being joyful places and the view that teaching is a fulfilling profession has suffered a jolt. The teaching profession is adapting to the demands of the new world order. The focus is on audits, protocols, service targets, standardized testing, grades, and competition. Schools are becoming more commercial and impersonal. The struggles besetting education systems and professionals today reflect the gaps in these adaptive changes.

Negative repercussions from such struggles also impact student and community well-being. Focusing on bridging gaps and fixing issues is important to create a new vision that inspires hope for teachers and students. This chapter aims to identify some causes for the challenges within the teaching profession and presents potential solutions to support the well-being of teachers drawn from the realm of positive psychology. These solutions can be executed by school leaders and administrators within their scope of influence.

FROM SURPLUS TO SHORTAGE: THE GRIM REALITY OF TEACHER ATTRITION IN NORTH AMERICA

The teaching profession in North America has seen dwindling numbers in its workforce, particularly in the last decade. This is due to the loss of early-career teachers leaving within the first five to seven years of their initiation into teaching and mid-career teachers experiencing burnout and leaving the profession before retirement. The following paragraphs provide insight into the chaotic circumstances from a Canadian and an American viewpoint.

When Early Career Teachers Decide to Opt Out of Teaching: A Canadian Perspective

Teaching is a regulated profession in Canada. A teacher with a permanent employment position in Canada's publicly funded schools enjoys the benefits of a tenured career, job security, promotions within the system, a unionized workforce, and enrollment in government pension plans, among other perks.

The attractiveness of the profession made the employment market for teachers very competitive. For example, in the province of Ontario, the unemployment rate for early-career teachers stood at a significantly high range of 29–45 percent in 2014 (Mindzak, 2019). This was due to a teacher surplus in the market. The present-day picture, though, is very different. According to the latest *Transition to Teaching* Report released by the Ontario College of Teachers in 2022, the unemployment rate for first-year teachers is now down to 1 percent.

While these figures might seem to represent a positive outlook on the prospects for teachers in Ontario, the fact is that a teacher's journey to full-time employment in the province's publicly funded schools is often long and meandering. During the years of a teacher surplus (from 2005 to 2014), it could sometimes take teachers more than ten years to land a permanent teaching position.

Job satisfaction was elusive as most new teachers were assigned "precarious education work." This term describes employment that includes temporary teaching certifications, being on the daily roster for supply teaching positions, and term contracts for long-term occasional teaching positions (Mindzak, 2019). It is only after a new teacher has passed through these hoops that the possibility of a permanent teaching position emerges. The independent school sector has its own rules for hiring teachers, which are often unique to each school's size, location, legacy, and administrative discretion. Job security and tenure in this sector are not always assured.

The teacher surplus began to decline after the government, in 2015, increased the length of the teacher education program from two to four semesters. Many teachers also chose to leave the province and work overseas, where they could obtain a full-time teaching position without waiting for long years on the daily supply rosters. This stiff competition discouraged young people from being enthusiastic about teaching.

Less than ideal working conditions, low salaries, and uncertainty can mark the first five years of a teacher's career. According to Frank McIntyre (2021), an Ontario College of Teachers researcher, early-career teachers assigned precarious education work have few opportunities for professional development, mentoring, collaborative learning, teacher inquiry, and feedback from their principals and colleagues to hone their skills and craft.

This adds to the loneliness and struggle of new teachers, which negatively impacts a teacher's sense of self-efficacy. Bandura (1997) defined self-efficacy as the individual's belief in personal capabilities "to organize and execute the course of action required to produce given attainments" (p. 11). The factors contributing to an individual's self-efficacy are mastery experiences, vicarious experiences, verbal persuasion, and physiological arousal.

A teacher on the supply list of the daily roster of a school has little opportunity to acquire mastery experiences. The absence of connection with colleagues and mentorship from the *more knowledgeable others* in the workplace constrains the potential to obtain vicarious experiences and positive encouragement from verbal persuasion. The uncertainty about the future due to job insecurity might often leave new teachers with an aftertaste that makes them feel disconnected from their careers, students, and professional community.

In a Canada-wide survey on the reasons for teacher attrition, researchers Karsenti and Collin (2013) highlighted four major factors for young teachers quitting the profession. These were task-related factors, individual factors, social environment factors, and socioeconomic conditions. The task-related factors included managing difficult classrooms, unsatisfactory work conditions, low salaries, inappropriate teaching subjects, and restrictive administrative policies. The individual factors pointed to emotional and psychological strain. The social environment factors were the lack of strong relational bonds with colleagues and administrators. In fact, some teachers reported they were hesitant to discuss student discipline problems with administrators and colleagues because it might give the perception that they are not yet ready to take on a permanent teaching position at the school.

This account provides some perspective on why Canada's new teacher pipeline is drying up. According to the census data released by Statistics, Canada (2022), the total employment numbers for teachers in publicly funded elementary and secondary schools from the 2021 census have declined in the provinces of Alberta, Yukon, and Nunavut compared to the 2016 census. In Alberta, the decline was 0.35 percent; in Yukon, it was almost 21 percent; in Nunavut, it was 4.51 percent. Data figures from the provinces of Ontario, Saskatchewan, and Manitoba also indicate a shortage of teachers.

Teacher Loss Due to Burnout in the United States

Teacher burnout is real and present. It poses a significant threat to the long-term sustainability of the workforce. Data from three recent surveys across the United States have pointed to this distressing trend. The 2022 Gallup poll that studied U.S. workers' burnout rates by industry showed that more than four in ten K–12 teachers reported feeling burned out at work "always" or "very often." This is higher than any other profession

(Carstarphen, 2022). The Merrimack College Teacher Survey (2022) reported that 44 percent of the 1,324 K–12 teachers interviewed across America were likely to leave teaching as a profession in the next two years.

Among the reasons cited by the teachers for their professional frustration were low salaries, too many demands put on them, lack of respect from the general public, and lack of sufficient autonomy with respect to personal scheduling time on the job. Results from the National Education Association (NEA) survey for 2022 revealed that 55 percent of K–12 teachers indicated they would leave the profession earlier than expected. The NEA press release further pointed out that nationally in the United States, the ratio of hires for job postings in education is at 0.59. Post the pandemic, the number of school-teachers across America's public schools has declined by 567,000 (Walker, 2022). In an interview with Yahoo! Finance Live (2022), the American Federation of Teachers president, Randi Weingarten, said, "We have about 300,000 teachers who actually leave every single year, many before retirement. It's not just about new teachers. It's also a retention issue. . . . We need to retain teachers. And we're facing a retention crisis as well as a recruitment crisis."

The COVID-19 pandemic has definitely added to the professional challenges for teachers. The uncertainties of online teaching, experimenting with hybrid models, following back-to-school regulations for students, ensuring school hygiene, personal health concerns from the risk of COVID infections in school settings, filling in for absent colleagues, and prioritizing student safety, mental health, and well-being have spread teachers thin. As a result, many teachers feel vulnerable, confused, uncared for, and under pressure.

In addition, the rising number of school shootings across America has made teachers feel defenseless. According to an *Education Week* report (August 16, 2023), there have been twenty-four school shootings recorded across the United States for 2023, and there were fifty-one shootings in 2022. These unfortunate and mindless incidents of violence have resulted in injuries and death and also perpetrated a fear psychosis among students, teachers, parents, and the general community. No wonder the K–12 teaching community across America is reporting the highest rates of burnout compared to other occupations.

The World Health Organization (WHO) identified burnout as an occupational phenomenon. In its updated 2019 definition, WHO described burnout as a "syndrome conceptualized as resulting from chronic workplace stress that has not been successfully managed. It is characterized by feelings of energy depletion or exhaustion, increased distance from one's job, or feelings of negativism or cynicism related to one's job and reduced professional efficacy. Burnout refers specifically to phenomena in the occupational context and should not be applied to describe experiences in other areas of life" (World Health Organization, 2019).

Maslach and Leiter (1997) described burnout as "the index of dislocation between what people value and what they have to do. It represents an erosion in values, dignity, spirit, and will—an erosion of the human soul. It is a malady that spreads gradually and continuously over time, putting people in a downward spiral from which it is hard to recover" (p. 33). Burnout has three dimensions:

1. Physical and emotional exhaustion;
2. Cynicism, which causes individuals to have minimal involvement in work to safeguard personal interests;
3. Personal feelings of ineffectiveness, which manifest in a growing sense of self-inadequacy and an erosion of confidence in oneself and in one's environment.

In their 1997 book, *The Truth about Burnout*, Maslach and Leiter identified the following six causes for employee burnout.

1. Work overload
2. Lack of control
3. Insufficient reward
4. Breakdown in community
5. Absence of fairness
6. Conflicting values

Work overload shows up when work becomes more complex, demanding, and intense. In the teaching sphere, cuts in education budgets, which result in larger class sizes, more systems of accountability, audits, standardized testing, coping with social pressures, the intrusion of social media, the stresses of incorporating inclusivity through individualized education plans for students, teaching mixed-grade-level students in the same class, increasing protocols, paper-work, balancing administrative demands and parental concerns along with the regular teaching load makes a teacher's workday overwhelming.

The feeling of *lack of control* results when teachers perceive that they do not have the autonomy to schedule their planning time according to their own needs. They might work in an environment where they are subject to micromanagement from the administrators, and a teacher might not have the creative freedom to engage with work tasks. The domino effect arising from too much control is a perception by individual teachers that the management lacks confidence in their skills and abilities. This further depletes the culture of cohesion, compassion, and trust within a school.

Insufficient reward has two aspects: extrinsic reward and intrinsic reward. The extrinsic reward may most often revolve around teachers' remuneration package from the government and the apparent respect teachers receive as professionals in society. This is something that teachers have foreknowledge and acceptance of. It might not contribute to the proverbial "straw that breaks the camel's back," but the insufficient intrinsic reward often breaks teacher morale. The lack of fulfillment in work, the loneliness along the journey in schools bereft of a culture of collaboration, and the changing nature of student-teacher relationships contribute to the insufficiency of intrinsic rewards. Many students and parents today are more entitled and focused on grades. Teachers are considered mere service providers or employees overseeing the flow of manufactured goods across a conveyor belt.

Breakdown in community happens when schools become impersonal, teacher turnover is high, and competition is rife among employees. In the book *The Courage to Teach*, Palmer (2017) deplores the academic culture we find prevalent in many educational institutions today—one that builds barriers between colleagues with its focus on myopic goals like teacher evaluations and peer competition, which fuel professional distrust and isolation. Shared practice and honest dialogue are elusive in the presence of fear, insecurity, and fragmented relationships.

In workplaces where nepotism and suspicion are commonplace, it's unfortunately all too common to see *the absence of fairness*. School leaders are responsible for ensuring that every employee feels valued and respected. Distrust breeds cynicism, which further leads to disengaged employees. This is certainly not the mind space we want our teachers to operate from.

Conflicting values reflect the incongruence between a teacher's personally espoused values and those in practice at the organization or within the profession. A teacher's entry into the profession begins with idealism. When dedicated teachers feel defeated by systemic values that conflict with their personal ideals, it causes them to lose heart. The conflict between the value of faithfulness to one's professional calling and the values of time management and increasing efficiencies causes teachers to find a lack of personal meaning in their work, leading to burnout (Schaufeli et al., 2008).

THE TRIPLE STRIKE: FINANCIAL, PSYCHOLOGICAL, AND SOCIOLOGICAL

Socioeconomic factors and job stresses are the key reasons teachers might leave the profession. The mass exodus of teachers has far-reaching financial, psychological, and sociological impacts. Teachers often express their angst

Figure 1.1. Synthesized portrayal of contemporary teacher stressors. ***Designed by Dr. Roselle Aranha using Canva, 2023.***

about low salaries that are not commensurate with the increased cost of living standards. The government might cite budgetary constraints to raise teacher salaries, but the cost to the government to make up for losses due to teacher attrition is projected to be a staggering $8 billion a year in the United States (Garcia & Weiss, 2019). The Learning Policy Institute, in a 2017 report, estimated that the cost to replace an individual teacher was about $21,000 on average, and these expenses do not yield a return on investment until two years after the new teacher is hired.

From a psychological perspective, students are most affected when dealing with teacher turnover. Teaching is a helping profession; it is a profession where relationships matter. Teacher attrition disrupts the school's culture, climate, and social capital. Disruptions in staff cohesion and student relationships impact student achievement (Bryk & Schneider, 2002). Teacher turnover hurts high-poverty schools even more (Carver-Thomas & Darling-Hammond, 2017). These schools find it hard to recruit qualified teachers, which reflects the quality of instruction offered to students.

A sociological fallout of teacher attrition is that since society perceives the profession negatively, it is difficult to attract talent. A shortage of teachers harms students, teachers, and the public education system as a whole (Garcia & Weiss, 2019). The poor reputation of the profession in the social context has long-term consequences on the sustainability of the profession. The rise of online tutorials and artificial intelligence might give the impression that teachers are not indispensable. That would be far from true. The human side of learning cannot be replaced by algorithms. Emotions, nurture, relationships, and care play a significant role in a student's education.

It is time to do whatever we can to save the future of education for our children and our teaching professionals. The first step we can take as leaders is to care for our teachers. We do not have control over the numerous complexities that adversely affect the profession, but we can make a beginning in our circle of influence and realign the widgets within our organizations to make the culture more cohesive, respectful, and enjoyable for teachers. Here's where positive psychology can come to our aid.

Finding Flow: Rediscovering Joy in Teaching

Tracing the origins of positive psychology, Achor, the author of *The Happiness Advantage* (2010), says this branch of psychology emerged when social scientists and researchers shifted the focus from studying what is broken to studying what works. In other words, the shift was from psychopathology to the science of human flourishing. In his book, Achor posits that the formula, "success brings happiness," is flawed. It needs to be reversed to read as "happiness precedes success." "Our brains are literally hardwired to perform at their best not when they are negative or even neutral but when they are positive" (p. 15). Frankl (1946/2006) also shared the same premise in his highly acclaimed book, *Man's Search for Meaning.*

Creating work environments where employees feel happy might be key to teacher well-being and retention. Positive psychology offers many insights for school administrators and leaders in this regard. Seligman and Csikszentmihalyi are contemporary researchers widely respected as the founders of positive psychology. Seligman's theory of *learned optimism* and Csikszentmihalyi's work on *flow as the psychology of the optimal experience* can pave the way for a better understanding of how we can work to bring back the joy in teaching.

The Autotelic Self

Csikszentmihalyi (1990) described flow as the optimal experience, in which individuals are deeply involved in an activity, they are invested in realistic goals, their skills match the challenge they have at hand, the experience of engaging attentively with the task itself is so enjoyable that the individual's psychic energy is harmoniously ordered. Finding meaning in the chaos and stresses of life requires an individual to be in control of their subjective reality. It does not by any means suggest imperviousness to external challenges; rather, it emphasizes the wonder in looking for opportunities amid adversity, driven not by self-pity or self-centeredness but by the *autotelic self.*

The autotelic self relates to the individual who is immersed in an activity for the joy within the activity itself; the rewards from the activity are secondary. While this disposition and focus might often be an outcome of one's personality and upbringing, Csikszentmihalyi says it is possible to cultivate the autotelic self just as one would work to acquire a new skill.

The key for school leaders and administrators here is to facilitate the conditions within the school culture that can take employees on the path of discovering their individual autotelic selves. The conditions to develop the autotelic self are:

1. The existence of clear goals that one can strive for. Keen attention to monitoring the feedback from one's striving, adjusting the course of action when needed, and having a feeling of ownership and dedication to the chosen goal.
2. The ability to concentrate deeply on the task at hand.
3. Strong attention to the incremental progress achieved toward attaining the chosen goal. This depth of attention and involvement shuts off the distractions brought on by self-consciousness.
4. The ability to sustain enjoyment in the task, even in the simple things that one might often take for granted.

One does need a community of congruence to build the autotelic self. The autotelic self finds a parallel in Bandura's (1997) concept of individual self-efficacy. The factors contributing to self-efficacy also play a significant role in nurturing the autotelic personality.

The Science of Learned Optimism

Seligman first wrote about the "Science of Learned Optimism" in 1990. He said learning optimism is a skill, and one can train for it by revisiting our self-talk each time we encounter a difficult situation or "find ourselves hitting a wall." Each time an individual encounters a setback, they tend to believe that the tide is against them, and the endeavor to overcome the challenge might not be worth the effort. Seligman contends that if an individual learns optimism, it can help in acquiring resilience and hope in the face of adversity.

Again, there is a caution note that learned optimism is not the best solution when the cost of failure is high. He gives the example of driving under the influence of alcohol. The cost of failure, in this case, is very high, and optimism is not the solution. But when it comes to workplace trials, learned optimism can help. Seligman proposes using Albert Ellis's *ABCDE Model.* In the model, *ABCDE* is an acronym where *A* = Adversity, *B* = Beliefs, *C* = Consequences, *D* = Disputation, and *E* = Energizing.

Accordingly, each time one encounters *Adversity*, the individual should write down the adversity and the *Beliefs* that accompany it. Then introspect on the *Consequences* that result from those beliefs. The next step is to analyze the merit of the held beliefs and consequences through *Disputation.* In *Disputation*, one weighs the pros and cons of the beliefs and consequences through reliance on evidence, alternatives, implications, and usefulness. Successful disputation of the originally held beliefs and consequences brings in the last piece of the model—*Energizing effect*. The individual can now move ahead and face the next trial with increased resilience. Seligman (2011) says, "Learned optimism works not through an unjustifiable positivity about the world but through the power of 'non-negative' thinking" (p. 289).

Learning to use the *ABCDE Model* requires some mentorship and coaching from colleagues at the workplace. Having optimistic people in the workplace helps keep the morale of the organization high. The key for administrators and leaders is that hiring practices should not solely focus on the attributes of achievement but also on the attribute of optimism.

While optimism and flow are subjective constructs, they can be nurtured within organizations that care for their employees. Bringing back the joy in teaching is a high and lofty goal, but it can be achieved incrementally through cultivating a collective consciousness of care in our school communities. The process might be slow, but it can yield increasing returns over time. In recent years, there has been a thrust on finding interventions that support and encourage teachers in the workplace.

Through the rest of this chapter, the authors explore two different models from positive psychology and their potential benefits to support teacher and student well-being for authentically happier schools, families, and communities. The models are: *PERMA* and the *Effective Change Zone.*

MODELS OF PROMISE FOR IMPLEMENTING MORE EFFECTIVE SOCIAL-EMOTIONAL ACTIVITIES

There exist several different conceptual models, manufactured programs, professional pragmatic strategies, and personal approaches employed by educators at all levels of the instructional spectrum, from PreK to Terminal Doctoral Degrees, to incorporate social-emotional learning into various teaching-learning settings and curricula. This book contains numerous examples of such diverse applications in education to improve and sustain social-emotional growth and development. The authors of this chapter contend that the following two models encapsulate the key theoretical and conceptual frameworks associated with those examples and provide immediate actions that educators may take to infuse a greater degree of social-emotional learning into their classrooms and organizational activities via specific personal and professional behaviors when interacting with others.

The *PERMA Model*

The *PERMA Model* was introduced to the world by Seligman in 2011 through his book *Flourish*. *PERMA* is an acronym for *P* = Positive emotion, *E* = Engagement, *R* = Relationships, *M* = Meaning, and *A* = Accomplishment.

Positive emotions come through the experiences of joy, happiness, gratitude, and fulfillment in the daily and routine tasks at school. While there is much emphasis on making classrooms happy spaces for children, the necessity of creating a work culture where employees feel positive emotions of joy, happiness, and gratitude can be woven into the cultural fabric at the school. Common celebrations, special events, and rituals to institute gratitude, respect toward teachers and other members of the school community, and kindness as a general rule within the school can go a long way in helping positive emotions to become self-reinforcing within the school culture.

Engagement is being in a state of flow. It is the ability to engage with a task at a level that holds challenge, with concentration and attention compatible with one's signature strengths. Time is of secondary consideration when a person is in a state of flow because psychic energy is harmoniously ordered on the task at hand. Matching teachers' responsibilities to their core character strengths can be one way to improve engagement. To understand one's character strengths, teachers and students can take the VIA Character Strengths Survey (2023) online for free from https://www.viacharacter.org/.

Relationships are the ability to feel secure within a community of congruence at the workplace. Relationships between teachers and administrators, between teachers and their peers, and their students and parents are based on mutual respect and appreciation for the value and goodness the other brings to the enrichment of the school community. There is a strong sense of interdependence within the community.

Meaning is the realization that one is connected to a higher purpose; it is a feeling of being part of a bigger collective vision, similar to a strand of yarn woven into the tapestry of a beautiful design. One can think of Maslow's concept of self-actualization here. When teachers feel their strivings are for a higher purpose, they are able to transcend the adversity of the present moment. Finding meaning in work stalls the onset of burnout. It brings in resilience and learned optimism.

Accomplishment is the sense of self-efficacy through mastery in spite of the inherent challenge at hand. It requires grit, self-discipline, and delayed gratification. It is the force that drives excellence, and it is the stuff that makes champions out of ordinary folks. Seligman says great teachers possess a stronger sense of humor and zest. These are teachable qualities that can be engrained into the school culture.

The *PERMA Model* holds promise for happier schools, happier teachers, happier students, and happier families. Teachers can also use it to design their curriculum and assessments and even organize cocurricular events at school. Parents can reinforce the key components of the *PERMA Model* at home on a regular basis via focused interactions and varied experiences with their children.

The High-Touch Model for Effective Change

The high-touch model for effective change, represented by the *Effective Change Zone Figure* (see figure 1.2), is based on literature reviews and research about the micro-contextual needs of people participating in organizations within a dynamically evolving social culture. The micro-context is a

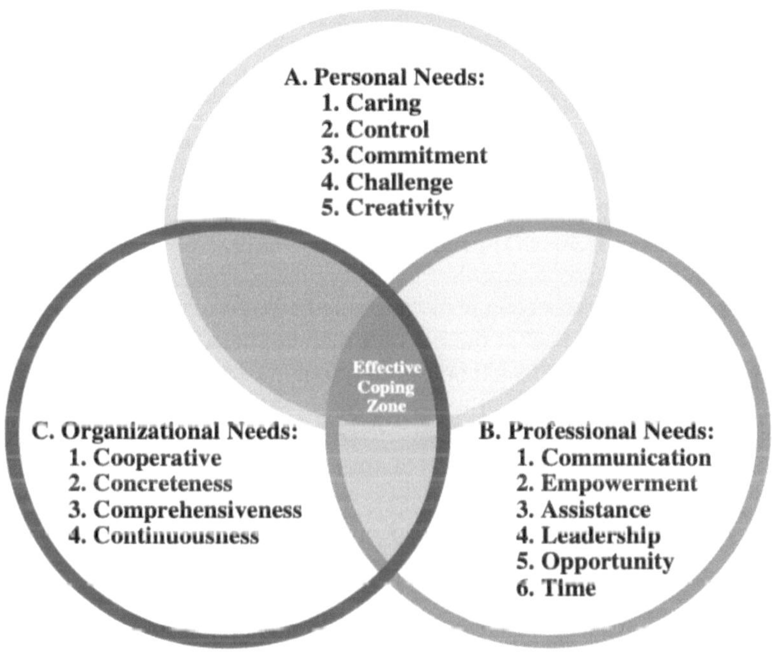

Figure 1.2. The effective change or coping zone. ***Previously published in W. Polka, J. McKenna, and M. VanHusen, eds. (2023), 94.***

particular organization, including schools, where the individual is a key actor. The organizational needs of individuals are also relative to the macro-context, which correlates with the region or state within which the organization operates, as well as the mega-context, which connects to the national or global context of the organization at any given time.

Educational leaders and their followers have been caught in multiple crosscurrents for the past three decades. With the pervasive intrusion of social media, technological innovations, and the pressures related to several organizational and professional demands including increasing audits, hiring, retention and dismissal protocols, and standardized testing, organizational leaders need to cautiously balance the trifold overlap between the organizational needs of people in their respective organizations as well as the personal and professional needs of individuals functioning in the organization to help them cope with change, including within themselves. Polka developed the initial conceptual framework for this "high-touch" approach to managing people (Polka, 1997; Polka, 2007) and, subsequently with several colleagues, conducted research studies that illustrated the practical applications of each of the various components within this model in diverse organizational settings. The components of those three "high-touch need" categories are identified as follows:

- Four components of the *organizational need category*: (1) Cooperativeness, (2) Comprehensiveness, (3) Continuity, and (4) Concreteness.
- Five components of *personal need category*: (1) Challenge, (2) Commitment, (3) Control, (4) Creativity, and (5) Caring.
- Six components of the *professional need category*: (1) Communication, (2) Empowerment, (3) Assistance in decision-making, (4) Leadership, (5) Opportunity for professional growth, and (6) Time.

Accordingly, effective change or "sustained effective coping with changes" occurs in the "sweet spot" at the nexus where the individual's organizational needs, as well as their personal and professional needs are addressed and met (Polka, 2009; Polka, 2010; Polka & Kardash, 2013; Lewis & Polka, 2014; Polka et al., 2014; Polka & McKenna, 2016; Polka, Wolfgang, & Mete, 2017; Polka, VanHusen, & Carlson, 2021; Polka, 2023; Polka & VanHusen, 2023).

Figure 1.2 depicts the "high-touch effective change or coping zone," which is conceptually congruent to Vygotsky's vision of the *zone of proximal development* and is also consistent with the *PERMA Model* that was introduced by Seligman in 2011.

School administrators who can effectively address and provide for the fifteen components contained in those three categories of needs (organizational, personal, and professional) have met success in achieving job satisfaction and higher productivity in their employees (Polka, 2023). It must be noted that attending to these needs adequately requires leadership acuteness to observe and adapt based on the hierarchy of the pressures and demands for these needs within their specific contexts at any given time. Subsequently, organizational leaders, including school leaders at all levels of the educational spectrum, must adopt the constructivist "high-touch" approach to supervising people, things, and ideas within their span of control. This requires sensitivity to the individual needs and individual differences of all people within the micro-context and an astuteness to read the signs of change within the macro- and the mega-context.

The high-touch model for effective change is congruent with the principles associated with the positive psychology constructs of flow and learned optimism. When in a state of flow, individuals experience *challenge* that stimulates their *creative* acumen, the ability to concentrate with resolve is spurred by the individual's perceived *control* of the situation. When people feel that the responsibilities assigned to them at their workplace or school are in keeping with their signature strengths, there is reason to believe there is an atmosphere of *caring* within the school. There is also increased assurance that the school administrators are *committed* to the teacher's well-being. Attention to teachers' personal needs creates an environment of greater optimism and collaboration within the school.

Addressing the professional needs of teachers through clear and unambiguous communication and assigning teachers work where they experience autonomy provides the scaffolding for an increased sense of empowerment and leadership. Individualized professional development and coaching address teachers' unique needs, including leadership, time constraints, and opportunities for growth. In effect, an organization with well-thought-out systems and strategies to attend to teachers' organizational, personal, and professional needs will find greater success in teacher retention, self-efficacy, and well-being.

Table 1.1 is an adaptation of previously published tables (Polka et al., 2017; Polka et al., 2021; Polka, 2023). It provides specific definitions for each of the five personal needs and includes strategies that educational leaders may employ to address and facilitate satisfying each personal need to help their followers incorporate more positive social-emotional behaviors in their respective contexts.

Table 1.2 is an adaptation of previously published tables (Polka et al., 2017; Polka et al., 2021; Polka, 2023). It provides specific definitions for each of the six professional needs and includes strategies that educational leaders may employ to address and facilitate satisfying each professional need to help their followers incorporate more positive social-emotional behaviors in their respective contexts.

Table 1.1. Personal Coping Needs for Effectively Dealing with Social-Emotional Implementation Related Challenges

A. Personal Needs	*Strategies to Satisfy Personal Coping Needs*
1. **Caring**—*need to perform expected roles and operations in comfortable work settings and to feel safe, supported, and productive.*	Promote peer mentoring and group interactions to debrief reactions to evolving situations. Encourage a culture of nurturance and respect for all. Balance the importance of individual, group, and organizational behaviors. Encourage "family-reunion"-type activities and "high-touch" personal fun with each other.
2. **Control**—*need to internalize the value of planned activities and procedures and feel a sense of ownership in making changes.*	Seek input from stakeholders to make modifications in planned activities and procedures. Provide opportunities for personal choices. Emphasize the various degrees of freedom that may exist in plans and procedures. Create a strong "climate of belief" in the process that individuals can personally exercise their control over activities and procedures.
3. **Commitment**—*need to believe in the purpose of the educational organization and the WHY of operations.*	Encourage dedication to the vision, mission, and procedures of the organization. Facilitate interactions between all organization stakeholders about short-term and long-term goals. Frequently acknowledge and celebrate "achievements and small wins" of individuals, classes, and schools.
4. **Challenge**—*need to learn and master new activities to address crises situations for the survival and continuation of the organization.*	Encourage all members of the organization to work collectively to initiate social-emotional changes in their behaviors and actions. Encourage all to individually accept this opportunity for positive social-emotional change in the context. Promote the belief that this is a "significant test" of individual engagement and be a cheerleader for the cause!
5. **Creativity**—*need to reflect about multiple options that may be employed to promote social-emotional learning.*	Demonstrate and promote enthusiasm and interest in diverse thinking about applications of social-emotional learning. Support new ways for followers to reinvent their thinking and actions. Reinforce "boundless opportunities" thinking among individuals in the micro-context to express their creativity.

Table 1.3 is an adaptation of previously published tables (Polka, Wolfgang, & Mete, 2017; Polka, VanHusen, & Carlson, 2021; Polka, 2023). It provides specific definitions for each of the four organizational needs and includes strategies that educational leaders may employ to address and facilitate satisfying each organizational need to help their followers incorporate more positive social-emotional behaviors in their respective contexts.

Table 1.2. Professional Coping Needs for Effectively Dealing with Social-Emotional Implementation Related Challenges

B. Professional Needs	*Strategies to Satisfy Professional Coping Needs*
1. Communication—*Need to interact with others and share views regarding incorporating social-emotional learning behaviors and actions into the learning contexts.*	Present a variety of information sessions to stakeholder groups and encourage discussion between and among various organizational actors to the impact of incorporating more positive social-emotional learning activities. Provide "user-friendly" feedback mechanisms to disseminate and collect relevant information regarding social-emotional learning in education.
2. Empowerment—*Need to have regular and meaningful dialog and input with supervisors and peers about the implications of operational changes and personal role expectations.*	Keep all faculty and other stakeholders well informed about the various applications of social-emotional learning in classroom and school contexts. Disseminate information and continuously collect input from all stakeholders. Provide opportunities for stakeholders to see how their input has been considered and/or used in implementing social-emotional activities and programs.
3. Assistance—*Need to know that additional services, including personnel, supplies, and materials, are available to facilitate the incorporation of social-emotional learning in contextual teaching-learning settings.*	Provide resources, including personnel, equipment, supplies, and materials as needed to implement social-emotional learning. Stockpile key supplies and materials as soon as practicable to demonstrate commitment to implementation. Be sure that all personnel are notified of plans to deal with unplanned outcomes or events related to the people, things, and ideas associated with implementation plans in the local and regional contexts.
4. Leadership—*Need to know that mega (national and international actors), macro (state and regional actors), and micro (district office and building supervisors) are committed to the proposed implementation of social-emotional learning and are philosophically and financially committed to it.*	Demonstrate the financial and material commitment to provide adequate human and technical resources to facilitate the implementation of social-emotional learning programs and activities. Demonstrate cooperation with other macro-context and mega-context school governance agencies that may be able to provide additional leadership advice and financial assistance to facilitate implementation.

5. Opportunity for Growth—*Need to be aware of both short-term and long-term personal and professional benefits that may accrue to individuals directly involved in developing, implementing, and evaluating social-emotional innovations in curriculum and instruction.*	Leaders emphasize the ample possibilities that implementing social-emotional learning presents to organization members and encourage key personnel not to wait too long to engage, or they may miss the personal and professional opportunities! Help all context stakeholders to reflect on the importance of nurturing and sustaining positive social-emotional values in classrooms and schools of the context. Promote the sense of accomplishment associated with the cooperation, faculty, community unity, and personal satisfaction that should result from successfully implementing social-emotional programs.
6. Time—*Need to understand the "real-time" commitments of involvement in social-emotional program development in classes and schools of the context. And the potential personal and professional impacts on work-family balance.*	Educational leaders must be specific and candid with colleagues and subordinates about time demands to successfully develop, implement, and evaluate plans for implementing social-emotional learning behaviors and programs. Encourage reflection on the impacts of necessary time commitments and provide cautions to actors about the burnout and stress associated with functioning in an unhealthy physical and mental "out-of-balance" work life. Recognize that time constraints impact individuals differently at their different stages of life. Be sure to customize time requirements for implementation based on time factors for all actors, including the leaders.

FINAL THOUGHTS

The teaching profession today is weathering a storm. External controls, demands, and apathy toward the profession have discouraged and disillusioned teachers. The tectonic shift is seen in the failure of the profession to attract new talent as well as retain existing talent. Fatigue, fear, and burnout are endemic to the profession. Our schools need committed, dedicated, and gifted teachers. While school leaders and administrators might have limited leverage to balance the external force fields that threaten the stability of the profession, they do have the trim-tab advantage to transform schools into happy places by focusing on building work cultures that are supportive and encouraging to teachers. Positive psychology offers solutions of promise that can be creatively and strategically woven into the work routines at school. As educators and leaders who care for our craft and community, we must take up this challenge to make our schools microcosms where our teachers feel

Table 1.3. Organizational Coping Needs for Effectively Dealing with Social-Emotional Implementation Related Challenges

C. Organizational Needs	*Strategies to Satisfy Organizational Coping Needs*
1. Cooperativeness—*Need to feel that everyone in their micro-level of the organization is working together and collaborating to effectively implement social-emotional learning goals and objectives.*	Encourage all organization members, especially key communicators, to "buy into" working together to implement and evaluate the various programs and activities associated with improving the degree and quality of social-emotional learning in classrooms and schools of the context. Encourage formal and informal organization leaders to continuously interact with all stakeholders about implementing and evaluating social-emotional programs and activities. Ensure that individuals and teams of the school contexts are continuously encouraged to actively interact with each other to propose innovative adaptations to the social-emotional plans and activities.
2. Concreteness—*Need to see, experience, and internalize "real-world" examples or models of social-emotional programs and activities.*	Be aware of the impact of social-emotional learning plans and specific modifications to them. Provide specific examples for faculty reference and review using data-based models implemented elsewhere. Make readily available examples of social-emotional learning plans for "real-time/real-world" classroom and school context use.
3. Comprehensiveness—*Personal and collective need to know the WHY of implementing social-emotional-learning-proposed changes in school policy, procedures, and operations in the organization caused by crises reactions.*	Assure that all stakeholders know the WHY for implementing social-emotional learning in educational contexts. Recognize that both internal and external micro and macro factors impact the need to deliver effective social-emotional learning experiences to all students and faculty. Incorporate SWOT (Strengths, Weaknesses, Opportunities, and Threats) analyses into initial and subsequent implementation plans and actions regarding social-emotional learning in schools.
4. Continuousness—*Need to be acutely aware and updated about changes occurring throughout the organization as a result of the crisis, as well as leadership's short-term and long-term plans for survival during the crisis and organizational development after the crisis.*	Promote the acceptance in the organizational culture of the schools and school district that change is inevitable and will occur, sometimes rapidly and/or sometimes slowly, but that it is imperative to prepare for all possible, probable, and preferable options, including modifications to well-established plans for the incorporation of social-emotional learning. Encourage all stakeholders to stay updated and acutely aware of the organizational implementation and evaluation status of social-emotional learning plans and programs.

valued, respected, and cared for and where the joy of teaching is reclaimed and celebrated. In the words of Sir Ken Robinson (2020):

> *"There is an opportunity; it takes bravery and imagination, and we have plenty of that in store."*

KEY PRAGMATIC LEADERSHIP TAKEAWAYS

- *School leaders must endeavor to create work environments where teachers feel valued and respected as professionals.* Using insights from positive psychology, leaders can foster a school culture where positive emotions, engagement, relationships, meaning, and accomplishment for all stakeholders are carefully structured, with a special focus on the well-being and happiness of teachers. The PERMA Model is a good guide to building a better school culture.
- *School leaders need to balance the organizational needs within the macro- and the mega- context while considering the professional and personal needs of their teachers within the micro-context.* Effective change occurs at the confluence of these three types of needs. The High-Touch Model for Effective Change, with its fifteen checkpoints, is an excellent and pragmatic guide for school leaders looking to support their employees while navigating change amid the dynamism of the challenges posed by globalization, evolving government rules, protocols, and so on.
- *School leaders may have limited influence over the external forces of change that contribute to the shortage of teachers, but they can work within their own learning communities to build a future that holds hope for happier teachers, students, and parents.* It is the micro-interventions that matter. Small acts of kindness, concern, genuine feedback, transparent and clear communication, and authentic empowerment go a long way in bringing a renewed sense of optimism and interest to schools as assets to the communities in which they operate and to teachers as treasured professionals who touch the future as they teach.

REFERENCES

Achor, S. (2010). *The Happiness Advantage*. New York: Crown Publishing Group.

Bandura, A. (1997). *Self-Efficacy: The Exercise of Control*. New York: Worth Publishers.

Bryk, A. S., & Schneider, B. (2002). *Trust in Schools: A Core Resource for Improvement*. New York: Russell Sage Foundation.

Carstarphen, M. (2022). "Putting Out Teacher Burnout." Gallup Blog, September 8. https://news.gallup.com/opinion/gallup/400670/putting-teacher-burnout.aspx.

Carver-Thomas, D., & Darling-Hammond, L. (2017). *Teacher Turnover: Why It Matters and What We Can Do about It.* Palo Alto, CA: Learning Policy Institute.

Csikszentmihalyi, M. (1990). *Flow*. New York: Harper Perennial.

Education Week. (2023). "School Shootings This Year: How Many and Where." January 6. https://www.edweek.org/leadership/school-shootings-this-year-how-many-and-where/2023/01.

Frankl, V. (2006). *Man's Search for Meaning*. Boston: Beacon Press. (Original work published in 1946).

Garcia, E., & Weiss, E. (2019). *The Teacher Shortage Is Real, Large and Growing, and Worse Than We Thought: The First Report in 'The Perfect Storm in the Teacher Labor Market' Series*. Economic Policy Institute, March 26. https://www.epi.org/publication/the-teacher-shortage-is-real-large-and-growing-and-worse-than-we-thought-the-first-report-in-the-perfect-storm-in-the-teacher-labor-market-series/.

Karsenti, T., & Collin, S. (2013). "Why Are New Teachers Leaving the Profession? Results of a Canada-Wide Survey." *Education 3*(3), 141–49.

Lewis, M., & Polka, W. (2014). "Planning to Change Student Behaviors in a Small City School District: A Case Study of Managing in the Effective Change Zone." *Educational Planning 21*(2), 4–18.

Maslach, C., & Leiter, M. P. (1997). *The Truth about Burnout: How Organizations Cause Personal Stress and What to Do about It.* Hoboken, NJ: John Wiley & Sons.

McIntyre, F. (2021). *Transition to Teaching 2021: 20th Annual Survey of Ontario's Early-Career Elementary and Secondary Teachers*. Ontario: Ontario College of Teachers. https://www.oct.ca/-/media/PDF/transition_to_teaching_2021/2021T2Ten.pdf.

Meier, D. (2002). *In Schools We Trust: Creating Communities of Learning in an Era of Testing and Standardization.* Boston: Beacon Press.

Merrimack College. (2022). *1st Annual Merrimack College Teacher Survey: 2022 Results*. Education Week Research Center. https://www.baconsrebellion.com/app/uploads/2022/06/Merrimack_College-Todays_Teachers_Are_Deeply_Disillusioned_Survey_Data_Confirms.pdf.

Mindzak, M. (2019). "Precarious Employment in Education Impacts Workers, Families and Students." *The Conversation*, May 27. https://theconversation.com/precarious-employment-in-education-impacts-workers-families-and-students-115766.

Noddings, N. (2003). *Happiness and Education*. New York: Cambridge University Press.

Ontario College of Teachers. (2022). *Transition to Teaching 2022.* Ontario: Ontario College of Teachers. https://www.oct.ca/-/media/PDF/transition%20to%20teaching/2022/T2T_2022_EN_PUBLISH.pdf.

Palmer, P. J. (2017). *The Courage to Teach: Exploring the Inner Landscape of a Teacher's Life*. Hoboken, NJ: John Wiley & Sons.

Polka, W. (1997). "High-Tech + High-Touch = 21st Century Educational Success. Technology Role in the Classroom." *Educational Horizons 75*(2).

———. (2007). "Managing People, Things and Ideas in the 'Effective Change Zone': A High-Touch Approach to Educational Leadership at the Dawn of the Twenty-First Century." *Educational Planning 16*(1), 12–17.

———. (2009). "Leadership in the Effective Change Zone: A Case Study of the High-Touch Needs of Educators Implementing the Georgia Performance Standards." In C. Achilles, et. al. (Eds.), *Remembering Our Mission: Making Education and Schools Better for Students*, 187–99. The 2009 Yearbook of the National Council of Professors of Educational Administration. Lancaster, PA: *DEStech* Publications.

———. (2010). "The Art and Science of Constructivist Supervision: Transforming Schools by Applying Needs-Based Research." *Journal for the Practical Application of Constructivist Theory in Education 5*(1), 1–28.

———. (2023). "Managing Others in Crisis: Addressing the Personal, Professional, and Organizational Coping Needs of Educators." In W. Polka, J. McKenna, & M. VanHusen (Eds.), *Managing Yourself and Others During Crises: Key Leadership Visions, Approaches, and Dispositions to Survive and Thrive.* Lanham, MD: Rowman & Littlefield Education Publications.

Polka, W., & Kardash, J. (2013). "Managing in the Effective Change Zone to Implement a '1 to 1 Laptop' Program in a Rural School District: A Case Study of the Colton-Pierrepont Experience. In B. Ran (Ed.), *The Dark Side of Technological Innovation*, 323–46. Charlotte, NC: Information Age Publishing.

Polka, W., & McKenna, J. (Eds.). (2016). *Confronting Oppressive Assessments: How Parents, Educators, and Policy-Makers Are Rethinking Current Educational Reforms.* Lanham, MD: Rowman & Littlefield Education Publications.

Polka, W. J., McKenna, J. & VanHusen, M. (Eds.). (2023). *Managing Yourself and Others during Crises: Key Leadership Visions, Approaches, and Dispositions to Survive and Thrive.* Lanham, MD: Rowman & Littlefield Education Publications.

Polka, W., & VanHusen,-M. (2023). "Managing Yourself during Crises: Surviving and Thriving in the Education's Ever-Evolving Open Social System of People, Things, and Ideas." In W. Polka, J. McKenna, & M. VanHusen (Eds.), *Managing Yourself and Others during Crises: Key Leadership Visions, Approaches, and Dispositions to Survive and Thrive*. Lanham, MD: Rowman & Littlefield Education Publications.

Polka, W., VanHusen, M., & Carlson, J. (2021). "Incorporating Key 'High-Touch' Needs into eSports: The Effective Game Zone." In S. Andrews & C. Crawford (Eds,), *Handbook of Research on Pathways and Opportunities into the Business of Esports*, 270–302. Hershey, PA: IGI Global Publications.

Polka, W., Wolfgang, J., & Mete, R. (2017). "Serendipitous Educational Planning: Expeditiously Applying Effective Change Zone (ECZ) Mindset Concepts." *Educational Planning 24*(3), 25–44.

Polka, W., Wolfgang, J., Mete, R., Ayaga, A., & Khokhar, A. (2014). "Planning to Effectively Motivate Digital-Age Learners by Addressing Their 'High-Tech' Interests and Their 'High-Touch' Needs." *Educational Planning 21*(4), 51–68.

Robinson, Sir Ken. (2020). "My Thoughts for the Call to Unite" [Video]. YouTube, May 7. https://www.youtube.com/watch?v=QU4Q17t4muY.

Schaufeli, W. B., Leiter, M. P., & Maslach, C. (2008). "Burnout: 35 Years of Research and Practice. *Career Development International 14*(3), 204–20.

Seligman, M. E. P. (2011). *Flourish: A Visionary New Understanding of Happiness and Well-Being*. New York: Simon & Schuster.

———. (2011). *Learned Optimism: How to Change Your Mind and Your Life.* New York: Knopf Doubleday Publishing Group.

Statistics Canada (2022). "Educators in Public Elementary and Secondary Schools." February 9. https://www150.statcan.gc.ca/t1/tbl1/en/cv.action?pid=3710015301.

VIA Institute on Character. (2023). "The VIA Character Strengths Survey." https://www.viacharacter.org/survey.

Vygotsky, L. S. (1978). *Mind in Society: The Development of Higher Psychological Processes*. Cambridge, MA: Harvard University Press.

Walker, T. (2022). "Survey: Alarming Number of Educators May Soon Leave the Profession." *NEA News*, February 1. https://www.nea.org/nea-today/all-news-articles/survey-alarming-number-educators-may-soon-leave-profession.

World Health Organization. (2019). "Burn-Out an 'Occupational Phenomenon': International Classification of Diseases." May 28. https://www.who.int/news/item/28-05-2019-burn-out-an-occupational-phenomenon-international-classification-of-diseases.

Yahoo! Finance. (2022). "More Than Half of U.S. Teachers Are Considering Leaving the Profession: Survey" [Video]. June 14. https://ca.finance.yahoo.com/news/more-than-half-of-us-teachers-are-considering-leaving-164708586.html.

Chapter 2

Best Practices to Promote and Support Social-Emotional Learning and Wellness in PreK–12 Schools

John McKenna and Lori Jonas

Social-emotional wellness has always been part of school programming but was usually reserved for students who were identified through the Committee on Special Education to have emotional difficulties that needed the support of school counselors or social workers. The COVID-19 crisis has made it evidently clear that schools must prioritize and address the social-emotional wellness needs of their students, staff, and parents. Whether it's from stress, anxiety, depression, or thoughts of suicide, the mental health of America's adolescents and teens has grown steadily worse for more than a decade, with the COVID-19 pandemic exacerbating the trend (Stone, 2023). The pandemic brought to light that social-emotional wellness and support is a universal issue that affects everyone in a school community and school leaders must develop and implement programs and practices to support the entire school community. When schools returned to fully in-person teaching and learning, both students and staff returned to brick-and-mortar buildings with anxieties and fears that hadn't existed prior. Not only were students and teachers mustering through digital learning and the skyrocketing, necessary use of technology, but the isolation that they all had survived for over a year when school was solely digital, left emotional debris that was not going to be easy for school leaders to handle. Nonetheless, it absolutely needed to be handled. Three-plus years past the pandemic, we can now look back and realize what we did well, what we need to improve on, and how we can support all students and staff with their social emotional learning and growing.

Focusing on social-emotional wellness for students and staff after the COVID-19 pandemic is critically important for several reasons:

1. *Mental Health Impact:* The pandemic has taken a toll on the mental health of individuals worldwide. Students and staff have faced increased stress, anxiety, isolation, grief, and trauma due to the disruptions caused by the virus. Prioritizing social-emotional wellness helps address these mental health challenges.
2. *Academic Performance:* Social-emotional well-being is closely linked to academic performance. When students and staff are emotionally and mentally healthy, they are better equipped to engage in learning and teaching effectively. Neglecting mental health can lead to a decline in academic outcomes.
3. *School Climate:* A positive school climate is crucial for the overall well-being of everyone in the educational community. When principals prioritize social-emotional wellness, they create an environment where students and staff feel safe, supported, and valued, which in turn fosters a more conducive learning and working environment.
4. *Resilience:* Developing social and emotional skills helps students and staff build resilience, enabling them to cope with future challenges. The pandemic has shown that the ability to adapt and manage stress is essential in times of crisis.
5. *Relationships:* Strong, positive relationships are at the core of effective education. Principals who focus on social-emotional wellness help nurture these relationships among students and between students and staff. This can lead to increased trust, collaboration, and a sense of belonging.
6. *Equity:* The pandemic has disproportionately affected marginalized communities. Prioritizing social-emotional wellness is crucial for addressing these disparities and ensuring that all students and staff have equal access to the support and resources they need to thrive.
7. *Long-Term Outcomes:* Investing in social-emotional wellness today can have long-term benefits for both students and staff. It can improve the overall quality of life, increase job satisfaction, reduce burnout among educators, and set students on a path for success beyond their academic years.
8. *Holistic Development:* Education is not just about academic achievement; it's also about personal growth and development. Focusing on social-emotional wellness acknowledges the importance of nurturing the whole person, not just their cognitive abilities.
9. *Legal and Ethical Responsibilities:* Schools and educational institutions have a legal and ethical responsibility to provide a safe and supportive

learning and working environment. Neglecting social-emotional wellness can lead to legal issues and ethical concerns.

10. *Community Well-Being:* Schools are central to communities, and the well-being of students and staff has a ripple effect on the broader community. Prioritizing social-emotional wellness can help strengthen the social fabric of the community.

Principals and staff play a pivotal role in promoting social-emotional wellness among students and communities after the COVID-19 pandemic. Doing so not only addresses immediate mental health needs but also contributes to a more resilient, equitable, and successful educational ecosystem.

The authors of this chapter were practicing school administrators who faced the challenge of providing social-emotional support to a school district with approximately ten thousand students and over two thousand staff members during the COVID-19 crisis. The following methods, programs, and strategies are ones that have been utilized directly, or learned from fellow educators, who were charged with addressing social-emotional needs during the crisis. These methods were identified by administrators, staff, students, and parents as the most beneficial and impactful in successfully supporting others during this turbulent time. These programs and practices are also essential in building a proactive foundation for the future to ensure that school districts provide the proper support for all students and cultivate a culture of caring where social-emotional programming is intentionally embedded across the curriculum and throughout the school.

The first step that a district must take is to establish a committee structure at the district and building level to address social-emotional concerns. Every district should create a district-level "School District Social-Emotional Wellness Committee" to identify district-wide needs and set annual goals. This committee should consist of district administrators, building administrators, teachers, counselors, social workers, psychologists, students, and parents. The authors suggest that this district team meet at least three times per year to establish goals, monitor goals, and assess goals.

Each school building should also have a "Building Social-Emotional Wellness Team" to ensure the district goals are consistently applied to the schools and to develop school specific goals, programs and initiatives that meet the individual needs of each school. These teams should include the building principal, teachers from different grades and departments, a school counselor, social worker, psychologist, key parent representatives, and students when appropriate. Diverse members from the building teams should be selected to participate on the district committee to ensure continuity and articulation with district goals. The building teams should meet on at least a monthly basis to monitor progress and ensure programs are consistently being implemented and goals are being met.

School districts must also develop a plan for professional learning to provide the proper training and support so staff can successfully implement Social Emotional Learning (SEL) programs and practices. Districts can provide a needs assessment, with SEL as the focus, to gain data on what areas of professional development are needed for staff to understand SEL, the need for SEL and the intended goals. It is imperative that districts intentionally provide ample opportunities for in-service and coaching to ensure staff is prepared to appropriately plan and apply the new programs and methods. The professional development learning plan should be developed by the District Social Emotional Wellness Committee in conjunction with the Building Wellness Teams to ensure vertical articulation as well as horizonal articulation, consistent implementation, and appropriate evaluation. The plan should have specific goals, action steps and a clear timeline to monitor the progress and effectiveness of the plan. Consistently monitoring the progress of the plan also allows for the administration and the committees themselves to adjust if necessary. The district plan should designate specific staff in each building to receive turnkey training so they can serve as leaders and provide support to the entire staff as needed. It is important that each school has people on site who can give immediate help and assistance as needed.

It is also necessary that each school have a fully functioning and readily accessible student support team where staff can go daily to receive guidance and specific ideas to provide intervention strategies to support students who are experiencing social emotional difficulties or triage emergency mental health situations. These teams should consist of counselors, social workers, psychologists, speech therapists, occupational therapists, physical therapists, reading specialists, math specialists, classroom teachers, and building administration. Not all school environments have all of these professionals in their building. Therefore, the building principal should ensure that those who are student centered and in touch with families are on the team. The individuals who work with students closely and have the knowledge of their needs, struggles and battles will offer incredible insight into support students when they are having difficulty. In addition to the student support team, a clear process is needed so that all staff can access the team and create an intervention plan that is individually tailored to the specific needs of each student. It is also extremely important for students and families to be aware of who the team is and how they can contact these individuals. Building relationships with someone at school is often a lifeline for students and families when they are struggling.

Having the appropriate district and building level teams and structures in place to address social emotional issues is imperative to be proactive with the social emotional needs that we already know exist within our schools. They are needed to diagnose needs, provide appropriate interventions, and ensure the consistent delivery of programs. These teams are also important for securing training and professional development for the staff. The author of this chapter recommends that districts should take the time and set up and establish these structures before implementing programs to guarantee that students, staff, and families receive the highest-quality services and best practices that meet their social emotional needs.

Once a district and their schools have their teams and procedures in place, they can move forward with developing and implementing programs. The following practices and methods were identified by the authors, via personal district leadership experiences during the COVID-19 crisis, as being highly effective in addressing social-emotional concerns with all stakeholders. The authors of this chapter have utilized many of these programs and had discussions with other school administrators to identify the methods that practitioners felt were most effective and beneficial.

BEST PRACTICES TO PROMOTE SOCIAL-EMOTIONAL WELLNESS

The following "Best Practices" are separated into two categories: (1) Classroom Strategies and Methods and (2) Schoolwide Programs and Practices.

Classroom Strategies and Methods

Daily/Weekly Check-Ins

The strategy that has been very successful in proactively identifying social-emotional issues in students and staff was the utilization for daily or weekly check-ins. This is a very simple, straightforward strategy that can easily be implemented in all PreK–12 classrooms. Checking in with students frequently and consistently is extremely important in developing trusting relationships and creating a safe and supportive environment. It should be done daily or as much as possible and built into the structure of a classroom community. The most significant benefit of daily emotional check-ins for students is the consistency it brings. Not only does the action help teachers create a solid routine, but it also ensures SEL is a part of everyday learning (YouHue, 2022). Teachers should make it a goal to begin each day or class period with a personal connection. This is a very simple procedure that can be done as soon as students enter the classroom, in small groups, morning meetings or individually.

Each teacher can sculpt a system that works best for their classroom. The check-ins consist of asking the students some simple but powerful questions such as "How are you feeling?" "What can I do for you?" "What emotion are you feeling the most today?" "What are you proud of?" A school can develop check-in questions that they feel are most relevant to a particular situation. Check-ins can also differ by level. For example, a primary check-in may be based on pictures that depict emotions of how students feel, and check-ins can be done in person or virtually. They help to build trusting relationships between students and teachers and provide students with a voice and resources to access immediate help and support. Teachers know that undesired and disruptive behaviors stem from basic human needs that aren't being met. Setting aside time each day to hear what is on students' hearts and minds allows the teacher to quickly gather feedback and insights from students. If educators know that a student is having a particularly difficult day, that knowledge can help deescalate a situation quickly (Rodgers, 2023). Some educators have added Check Out to the process, creating a system where they touch base with individual students at the start and end of each day. This is most helpful for students who struggle more than most or for students who are returning from a disciplinary suspension because it builds in an accountability for the student.

Community Circles

This is a technique that teachers can use to foster positive relationships and build supportive communities in classrooms. The community circle is a tool where teachers have students sit alongside them in a circle and talk about a prompt that the teacher gives. Students then pass around a certain object and share their thoughts and feelings about that prompt. This tool is helpful in a classroom because it gives the class the opportunity to express their thoughts, feelings, and ideas about the topic at hand (Stinger, 2018). They are used to freely express thoughts, build trusting relationships, provide support, foster positive communication, create shared values, and develop respect and understanding for everyone in the classroom. These circles are to be developed to be a safe place where students and teachers can share their thoughts and gain understanding and empathy for others. Community circles should be used frequently to become part of the culture where students feel comfortable sharing their thoughts, feelings, and suggestions with others.

Encourage Expression through Art and Music

Incorporating art activities into the curriculum can have a very powerful effect on a student's well-being. Much like intentional breathing and rhythmic movement practices, the integration of art activities and practices can create a sense of safety and comfort, reducing stress (Desautels, 2022). Many students are shy and fearful to express themselves to adults or other students verbally or in writing. Teachers should intentionally create art activities that help students develop self-awareness and express their inner feelings. Artistic expression also helps students expand their coping strategies to manage stress and visualize positive outcomes. Drawing and creating art are powerful ways to help students express their sensations, feelings, thoughts, strengths, and preferences (Desautels, 2022). Art teachers must develop lessons that tap into students' thoughts, hopes, fears, concerns, and joys. These are the kinds of activities that help students cope and work through issues and find strength to persevere through difficult times.

Similarly, incorporating music into the curriculum can make a positive impact on students' lives and help them overcome social emotional challenges they are facing. According to the National Association of Music Education (Edgar, 2019), music is an authentic vehicle to teach social emotional skills to students. Music is also an excellent way to foster leadership skills, self-expression, and creativity. Music education teaches and encourages students to set their own musical goals, develop solutions for individual and group dynamics, overcome performance anxiety, and understand the power of music to influence personal and social change. It is a healthy way to teach our students how to persevere, be resilient, work together and experience joy!

Buddy Up with an Older or Younger Class

Having older students work with younger students is a simple way to build positive relations and create a sense of community in a school. Creating buddy or partner classrooms helps the older students feel a sense of responsibility and mentorship and the younger students feel special and cared for. These partnerships can be utilized in a variety of ways including reading and writing buddies, art projects, science experiment teammates, lunch bunch, and peer encouragement and support during difficult situations when appropriate. To maximize the effectiveness of these partnerships the classes need to plan regularly scheduled meetings on at least a weekly basis. This will allow for students to create bonds and form trusting relationships.

Utilize Journaling and the Writers Workshop

Researchers have shown that journaling in the classroom can help students in setting and achieving goals, boost memory and comprehension, improve communication skills, provide organization practice, and lead to a reduction in stress (Merrow, 2020). Every teacher in each subject, and at all levels, should find a way to incorporate journaling and free writing into their lesson plans.

Students need time to reflect and process information and express their thoughts, fears, triumphs, and questions in a safe nonjudgmental place. Many students will not express themselves openly in a classroom and teachers will assume that everything is fine when the student may be struggling, frustrated and confused, and afraid to speak up in class. Teaching students how to share, develop empathy for partners, excel in challenging situations, accomplish goals, and control impulsive behavior are just as important as academic skills (Anderson, 2015). Teachers should keep journaling as free and unrestrictive as possible to allow the freedom of personal expression.

Utilizing the writers workshop model is also a great way to engage students in self-reflective and creative writing. Mulvahill (2018), defines the writer's workshop in the following way: "Writing workshop is a student-centered framework for teaching writing that is based on the idea that students learn to write best when they write frequently, for extended periods of time, on topics of their own choosing."

The writers workshop model empowers students to take control of their own writing, gives them opportunities to work cooperatively with others, and allows them the chance to share their writing with others.

Integrating meaningful, relevant, and reflective writing assignments are also great ways to help students express themselves and gain an understanding of the world and their own personal circumstances. Teachers can utilize the writer's workshop model to sculpt critical and creative writing assignments that foster self-reflection, ideas, and solutions to problems. This will allow students to build confidence daily and foster positive relationships with their teachers and peers.

Establish Partner Activities and Cooperative Learning Projects

Designing activities where students work together as partners or in cooperative groups is essential in building positive relationships and showing the importance of working together to achieve a goal. This is a great way for students to get to know each other and form friendships. When teachers rotate the groups and mix or "jigsaw" the students on a regular basis, it helps students connect with each other and meet people they may never have known before. Cooperative activities also help to foster new relationships, tolerance, and understanding for different people from different backgrounds.

There are many cooperative learning activities that teachers can utilize to foster teamwork and cooperation among students, but cooperative learning makes a powerful impact on student well-being when implemented consistently throughout a school. Kagan Structures (Kagan, 2009) is one of the most popular and effective school-wide cooperative learning programs that have been adopted by schools throughout the world.

Kagan developed over two hundred different cooperative learning structures to create active engagement across all grade levels. Utilizing Kagan Structures, every student interacts with each other and has a chance to share with each other. All students are engaged simultaneously in brief small-group activities to create teamwork. Students develop self-esteem, social skills, leadership skills, and communication skills. They become teammates while learning the curriculum, collaborating, and bouncing ideas off one another (Sanders, 2022). Kagan Structures (2009) help students build positive relationships, increase confidence, lower anxiety, and achieve common goals.

Utilize Literature and a Clear Curriculum That Promotes Empathy, Caring, Respect, and Resilience

Selecting and integrating literature that emphasizes caring, kindness, empathy, and other social-emotional traits is a simple yet powerful strategy that every K–12 teacher can implement daily has and have a direct impact on students' thoughts, feelings, and understanding of resilience (Ginsburg & Jablow, 2015). Teachers can integrate literature that promotes respect, understanding, and personal leadership into their guided reading, shared reading, and read-aloud lessons. When reading aloud to students, teachers create an opportunity to have open discussions about the plot, characters' feelings, and setting. These conversations often lead to classroom community building as these discussions allow for students to make personal connections with what is happening in the book. This type of classroom collaboration builds empathy in students as they learn and discuss differences (Savas, 2023). Literature can be integrated into all subject areas and can be an essential tool for providing students with positive role models and the skills they need to cultivate confidence and increased self-esteem to navigate difficult situations.

Social-emotional learning helps to ready students with skills that they need throughout life. Therefore, teachers should be encouraged to be mindful and intentional with the books they make available for students for independent reading. When students have access to literature that is culturally diverse, this provides an opportunity for students to see others who are different than them and their own experiences. Encouraging students to explore and learn from the viewpoints of book characters who are different than they are, allows for their emotional capacity to grow (Wellesley Centers for Women, 2022). Students should be encouraged to read literature that promotes a range of topics such as diversity, caring, respect, leadership, and resilience. Reading meaningful literature can teach critical life lessons, foster personal growth, and inspire students to have hope and confidence in themselves.

Similarly, schools need to be intentional in the planning of reading and writing assignments. Each school should have a clear and viable curriculum that integrates literature and writing assignments that promote the social and emotional well-being of students. Schools need to develop vertical and horizontal cooperative teams of teachers and provide time during the school year for teachers to create and align these activities to ensure that all students are receiving quality instruction to support their mental health.

Utilize Anchor Charts in Classrooms and Signs throughout the School

When part of a larger SEL focus, behavior charts and anchor charts can promote the behavior that will lead students toward success (Epperson, 2021). Creating charts that clearly show class rules and expectations for behavior should be in every classroom. Classroom charts can also be created that highlight steps for mindfulness and how to defuse a conflict. Anchor charts are simple to make and can be customized to communicate almost any message the teacher feels is important for the students. The key is that the teachers need to discuss and explain the reason and meaning for the chart for it to be an effective resource for students. Students need to know why there are rules and why they need to follow them. It comes down to safety, both physical and emotional. Students and staff need and deserve to feel safe in their school and classroom in order to learn.

Similarly, the school administration should develop signs and charts that are posted throughout the school that promote positive behavior and good citizenship. The principal needs to make sure that school rules and behavior expectations are understood by all students and staff. The administration must spend time with the student body explaining the behavior expectations and why it is important to treat others with respect and kindness in school and throughout the community. School administration's role in developing schoolwide behavior expectations and following through to ensure they are being enforced by all is enormously important. Teachers and staff need to feel supported by their administration with student behavior.

Begin and End Each Day with Intentional Reflection

All teachers should begin and end each day intentionally, bringing the class together with positive, motivational activities. It is simple and powerful to begin each day reviewing positive ways to treat and support each other, talking about strategies to reduce stress and release emotions positively, reviewing personal, class, and schoolwide goals, and brainstorming things to accomplish to make it a great day. These lessons and strategies can be very short in time and impactful at the same time. They can be done in conjunction with Community Circles or on their own.

Principals should also intentionally plan the opening announcements to be filled with positive, inspirational messages to teach, reinforce, and motivate students to treat each other with kindness. Opening announcements can highlight acts of kindness, empathy, caring, and good citizenship that the students and staff showed toward each other. Principals need to intentionally embed real-life examples of empathy, caring, understanding, and personal responsibility into their daily announcements to create a culture of caring. This is also a great way for principals to reinforce the school goals and expectations for citizenship and leadership. According to Noddings (1999), as educators acquire more knowledge about our students and their needs and we realize how much more than standard curriculum is needed, we should be inspired to increase our own competence.

Teachers and principals also need to intentionally end each day on a positive note because it is important for students to leave the school day in a positive way so that they are excited to return the next day. Teachers should bring the class together at the end of the day to review what went well, celebrate successes, and address things that need to be changed for tomorrow. This researcher suggests that each teacher intentionally rewards at least five students daily for positive behavior toward others or achieving goals. These awards can then be reported to the principal who can showcase them for tomorrow's opening announcements.

When these intentional and empathetic strategies are embraced by the school community and utilized consistently over time, they create a culture where all feel seen, valued, and safe to express themselves. When students and staff know that they are cared for, empowered to have a voice and celebrate, there can be a positive culture shift that happens, filled with kindness, compassion, and hope. Sometimes, leading with empathy can be quite simple: when you can, offer to cover a classroom while a teacher takes a quick break, or gets a cup of coffee—small ways to offer support and acknowledge just how demanding teaching can be (Tutt, 2022).

Build in Recess, Team Games, and Fun Time

Recess is a time for students to let loose and simply enjoy being children for a while. It provides a crucial period of respite in a heavily structured routine that involves lots of sitting still and listening. It also plays an important role in children's social-emotional learning (Mindful Practices, 2018). It is essential that schools intentionally build in time daily for recess, team games, and fun collaborative activities. These activities are necessary to let students blow off steam, cultivate friendships, and relieve stress. School leaders must prioritize these activities and build in times in their master schedules.

At the elementary level, school leaders should schedule a daily recess block where students are given the opportunity to play outside or participate in fun, team-building activities indoors. Elementary students need this time daily to positively let out pent-up energy and to foster relationships and form positive bonds with other students.

This time is also essential for middle and high school students. Finding time for cooperative games, mindfulness, and teambuilding activities can be challenging at the middle and high school levels, but it is imperative that teachers find this time because all students at all levels need to blow off steam and have fun!

Schoolwide Programs and Practices

Restorative Practices

Restorative practices—also known as restorative school discipline practices—are procedures or structures that foster a sense of community to prevent conflict, that act on misconduct, or that mend the harm caused by another student by accepting responsibility and restoring relationships (Ferlazzo, 2023). These practices help students see and understand how their actions have impacted and affected others. They also focus on actions that repair the situation and identify future behavior that could proactively be applied to create a different and positive result.

Restorative practices can be implemented either formally or informally. Formal practices include but are not limited to restorative justice, community conferencing, community service, restorative circles, peer juries, and peer mediation.

Restorative justice in schools focuses on repairing relationships that have been damaged by the harmful behavior of one student toward another. Restorative practices programs for schools highlight accountability in a system of nonpunitive reconciliation and community building (Prutzman et al., 2022). The students work together with a trained facilitator, often a teacher or counselor, to find ways to heal the situation and find ways to coexist and respect each other moving forward in the future.

Community conferencing is a technique where the facilitator brings in stakeholders who are familiar with a particular situation to weigh in and offer suggestions and help contribute to the conflict resolution process. This strategy should only be used in certain situations when the facilitator believes the input from others would be helpful. If a student who acted in ways that are unacceptable, is not willing or in a space where they can mediate, conferencing should not occur. Both parties, the one who did harm and the one who was harmed, need to be open to this process or it will not be successful for anyone.

Restorative circles allow students to listen to each other and work together to solve problems and offer proactive solutions to avoid conflict in the future. Our students come to school with many issues on their minds and in their hearts. As educators, we can help them process their thoughts and feelings so they can better handle their situations and be more present in class. Restorative circles are a useful practice to do just that. While frequently used to replace punitive forms of discipline, restorative circles are equally important in proactively building the relationships and skills students need to support one another and collectively address the challenges they face (Van Woerkom, 2018).

Peer juries and peer mediation are both techniques that actively engage specially trained students to help other students resolve conflicts. These methods should only be used when approved by the trained facilitators or the administration.

Informal methods of Restorative Practices include affective statements by people to communicate their feelings and affective questions that are asked to foster critical thinking and self-reflection. These methods are designed to be proactive measures to foster awareness of other feelings and prevent potential issues by teaching tolerance and understanding.

Mindfulness Training

Mindfulness is the basic human ability to be fully present, aware of where we are and what we are doing, and not be overly reactive or overwhelmed by what's going on around us (Mindful.org, 2023).

Our schools today need caring and compassion now more than ever. According to the National Association of Secondary School Principals (NASSP) 2022 Survey of America's School Leaders and High School Students, "3 out of 4 of school leaders (73%) and students (74%) report they needed help with their mental and emotional health" (NASSP, 2022). Research conducted by the *EdWeek* Research Center in 2021 concluded that 60 percent of teachers say they experience job related stress frequently or always (Will, 2021).

These statistics are alarming and represent a crisis that must be directly addressed. Mindfulness training for staff and students is one way that schools across the country have been addressing this problem. Mindfulness training helps to create a school culture where students and staff feel safe, supported, comfortable, focused, and relaxed. This allows them to learn and reach their maximum potential in a healthy, caring environment.

Shardlow (2015) provides four keyways that staff can be trained to incorporate mindfulness and foster calm and confidence in a classroom: *Mindfulness through Breath*, *Mindfulness through Sensory Experiences*, *Mindfulness through Guided Imagery, and Mindfulness through Movement.* These practices have shown many benefits to students including increased focus, attention, self-control, and positive classroom participation. They have also improved academic performance and the ability to resolve conflicts. Mindfulness's popularity has been bolstered by a growing body of research showing that it reduces stress and anxiety, improves attention and memory, and promotes self-regulation and empathy (Mineo, 2018).

The key to implementation is to start with the teachers. They are the ones who work directly with the students daily and can plan to ensure that the mindfulness strategies get integrated daily into their lessons. Training teachers in mindfulness methods is also very beneficial and helpful to them in controlling their own stress and classroom environments. Jennings (2015) highlights seven specific ways that mindfulness training directly benefits teachers. Mindfulness helps teachers: understand their own emotions better, communicate more effectively with students, manage students who are difficult, set up a positive learning environment, strengthen relationships with students, slow down when they need to, and build community. Mindfulness training, when implemented correctly, can have a dramatically positive impact on the culture of a school by transforming the mindset of a school to a more caring and compassionate place that benefits all.

Collaborative Academic Social-Emotional Learning (CASEL)

The Collaborative for Academic, Social, and Emotional Learning (CASEL) framework is a program that was created to support the social-emotional growth of students. In their framework for systemic schoolwide SEL, CASEL defines social-emotional competence (SEC) as intrapersonal and interpersonal knowledge, skills, and behaviors across the five interrelated domains of self-awareness, self-management, social awareness, relationship skills, and responsible decision-making (Weissberg et al., 2015). The CASEL framework is designed to embed and integrate social-emotional learning activities into all disciplines. Schools and districts have used the CASEL framework to foster knowledge, skills, and attitudes across five areas of social-emotional competence. These areas are referred to as "The CASEL 5" and include self-awareness, self-management, social awareness, relationship skills, and responsible decision making (CASEL, 2023).

These five areas can be specifically taught to staff and applied at all levels PreK–12 and into adulthood. Many school districts have used the framework to establish SEL standards, competencies, and curriculum to clearly identify what students should know and be able to apply to be successful and secure in school and life. The program facilitates the intentional designing of explicit instruction to integrate SEL competencies in daily teaching. The program also shows administrators how to design a schoolwide SEL program that includes planning, implementation, and evaluation components.

Trauma and Trauma-Informed Care Training

Up to two-thirds of U.S. children have experienced at least one type of serious childhood trauma, such as abuse, neglect, natural disaster, or experiencing or witnessing violence (Minahan, 2019). Trauma can be a parent's divorce, loss of family income, or health struggles. Many students deal with trauma each day of their lives and educators need to be aware of such. Neurobiologically, students can't learn if they don't feel safe, known, and cared for within their schools (Aupperle et al., 2012). It is therefore essential that teachers and staff are aware of trauma-informed approaches to use with their students.

Trauma informed care is a way to treat social-emotional and mental health concerns that acknowledges the need to understand a child's life experiences to deliver effective instruction and care. A trauma-informed approach attempts to construct a complete picture of a person's life both past and present to provide comprehensive care and inner healing. Experiencing trauma, especially as a child, significantly increases the likelihood of mental health problems and social emotional issues. Trauma-informed care is designed to help people heal from negative past experiences and move forward constructively.

With so much pain in the classroom, educators should be mindful that traumatic life experiences can sometimes emerge as behaviors that we might otherwise label as challenging (Venet, 2018). Teachers do not need to know each and every trauma in a student's life, but they do need to be aware that trauma has happened. Approaching every student as if there was trauma is a great practice because there most likely has been trauma in that child's life.

How a child behaves in the classroom may be a response to trauma. At school, a child who has experienced trauma may have unpredictable or explosive emotions. They may have out-sized reactions to even small events. Or they may shut down and become "zoned out." Any of these behaviors can impact their learning and relationships at school (Cleaver, 2023).

Levings (2020) explains that there are simple steps that educators can follow in order to be more trauma informed in their classrooms and schools. Instead of having a classroom arranged with the traditional rows of desks, teachers can create a space with dimmed lights, a cool-down corner, warm colors on the walls and flexible seating. Flexible seating can include wobble stools, yoga balls, or other alternate seats so that students are able to move their bodies if they feel the need. Levings also explains that students benefit when teachers specifically teach and model empathy and active listening. This helps to build a classroom of care and one that feels safe to students so that they are able to learn at their highest level.

Multi-tiered Systems of Support (MTSS)

MTSS is a framework to provide academic and behavioral support for all students based on their individual needs. MTSS is a multi-tiered system that uses data to match specific interventions to the unique needs of students. Tomko and Pendharkar (2023) explain that Tier 1 is universal support for all students and the general classroom instruction. Tier 2 is targeted support for some students who are identified as at risk. Small-group instruction is a support provided for Tier 2 students. The smallest tier is the last; Tier 3. Tier 3 is considered individualized support for students who struggle the most. The tiered system needs to be accompanied by data collection for students and reevaluation on performance and behaviors so that plans can be adjusted as needed.

MTSS is considered an umbrella framework that includes other tiered systems including Positive Behavioral Interventions and Supports (PBIS) and Response to Intervention (RTI). PBIS is generally considered a multi-tiered framework to provide behavioral support, whereas the RTI framework is designed to provide academic support. Each school district must develop and design a MTSS system that meets their unique needs. The following presents a brief overview of differences between PBIS and RTI programs.

Positive Behavioral Interventions and Supports (PBIS)

Positive Behavioral Interventions and Supports (PBIS) is a schoolwide systems approach aimed at establishing positive student culture and individualized behavioral supports necessary to create a safe and effective learning environment for all students (Sugai & Horner, 2009).

According to the Center on PBIS (n.d.), PBIS is an evidence-based, tiered framework for supporting students' behavioral, academic, social, emotional, and mental health needs. Their research claims that if PBIS strategies are implemented with fidelity, social-emotional competence, academic success, and school climate will improve. They also assert that successful implementation also has a positive effect on teachers' mental health and well-being. When implemented consistently, a PBIS system provides support for all students and staff. PBIS emphasizes five inter-related elements: equity, systems, data, practices, and outcomes (Center on PBIS, n.d.). The PBIS framework consists of a three-tiered model of support. Tier 1 is primary prevention that is universally implemented across the school for all students. In this tier schoolwide positive behavior expectations and procedures are explicitly taught. Positive reinforcements and consistent consequences for behavior are established and applied throughout the school. Consistent instruction and classroom management systems are developed that align with school wide expectations. When implemented with fidelity, Tier 1 supports enable approximately 80 percent of the student population to experience success (Center on PBIS n.d.).

Tier 2 support is targeted, secondary prevention strategies for some students who need extra support and assistance. These supports include specific adult mentors who check in and monitor student progress on a daily basis, counseling with targeted social skills instruction, additional academic support, and home/school plans. Approximately 10–15 percent of the students will need this form of extra support.

Tier 3 support is individualized and intensive support for a few students who have extensive needs. These are for students who need functional behavioral assessments and comprehensive academic support. These students require wrap-around services and affect 1–5 percent of the student population (Center on PBIS, n.d.).

Response to Intervention (RTI)

RTI is a multi-tiered approach to the early identification and individualized support to specific students with learning or behavioral needs. According to the RTI Action Network (2023) the RTI process begins with high-quality instruction and screening of all students in the regular classroom setting. Struggling learners are identified and provided interventions at specific levels of intensity depending on the needs of the students. The intervention services are provided by multiple staff including classroom teachers and RTI specialists. Learning progress is constantly monitored and evaluated, and intervention levels are adjusted as necessary depending on student needs.

Similar to PBIS, RTI is generally designated as a three-tiered system with Tier 1 being characterized as universal high-quality instruction and screening for all students. Tier 2 methods are referred to as targeted interventions for some students identified as at risk. Tier 3 strategies are targeted interventions for students who have extensive learning and behavioral needs.

Responsive Classroom

This program is an evidence-based approach to teaching that focuses on the strong relationship between social-emotional learning and academic success. This approach to teaching and discipline creates the conditions for social, emotional, and academic learning using practical strategies in four domains: positive community, effective management, engaging academics, and developmentally responsive teaching (Responsive Classroom, 2022).

The program is based on four key domain areas: Engaging Academics, Positive Community, Effective Management, and Developmentally Responsive Teaching. Responsive Classroom has established a core belief that students must learn the following social emotional competencies: cooperation, assertiveness, responsibility, empathy, and self-control.

They must also learn the academic competencies of academic mindset, perseverance, learning strategies, and academic behaviors if they are to be successful in school and in life (Responsive Classroom 2022). To achieve these competencies, teachers are trained in specific classroom practices and strategies. These strategies include but are not limited to morning meetings, interactive modeling, student choice in learning experiences, establishing rules, interactive learning structures, and closing circles.

The Leader in Me

Leader in Me is an evidence-based, social-emotional learning process—developed in partnership with educators—that empowers students with the leadership and life skills they need to thrive in the twenty-first century (Leader in Me, 2021). Leader in Me helps students learn how to become self-reliant, take initiative, plan ahead, set and track goals, do their homework, prioritize their time, manage their emotions, be considerate of others, express their viewpoint persuasively, resolve conflicts, find creative solutions, value differences, and live a balanced life. The process helps students develop the skills and self-confidence they need to lead their lives and succeed in school and beyond (Leader in Me, 2023).

The program is a whole-school transformation process for students, staff, and parents to create a positive culture and common language throughout the school community. The goals are to create a culture of trust and engagement, empower students to be leaders of their own lives, help and support others, provide students tools to set and achieve personal goals academically and socially, and develop student voice.

Teachers are taught how to integrate and embed the leadership principles into daily instruction and administrators learn how to cultivate and incorporate Stephen Covey's *7 Habits of Highly Effective People* throughout the school community, making it part of the culture and traditions of the school.

Sources of Strength

This is a comprehensive program designed to influence everyone in a school community. It is based on the premise that everyone experiences emotional ups and downs and if a person knows their strengths, they can lean on those strengths in times of anxiety, fear, sadness, anger, and hopelessness. The program provides curriculum, training, and activities that work to increase overall well-being, coping skills, self-advocacy and belonging (Sources of Strength, 2023).

The Boomerang Project's Link Crew and WEB programs

The Boomerang Project (2023) developed Link Crew and WEB (Where Everybody Belongs) programs to facilitate smooth transition programs for middle school and high school students. The programs focus on character development and service learning through professional learning for teachers, student to student mentoring, school safety practices, and anti-bullying training programs (Boomerang Project, 2023).

Link Crew is a transition program for high school students designed to welcome freshmen, make them feel comfortable, and provide social emotional and academic support to them throughout their first year of high school. Juniors and seniors are trained to be mentors and provide continuous guidance and support to freshmen. The older students are trained to be student leaders who meet with the freshmen on a regular basis and check in with them often to see how they are doing and offer advice and help them through any difficulties they may be experiencing. More and more studies show that if students have a positive experience their first year in high school, their chance for success increases dramatically. Link Crew provides the structure for freshmen to receive support and guidance from juniors and seniors who have been through the challenges that high school poses, and understand that the transition to a larger school can sometimes be overwhelming (Boomerang Project, 2023).

The WEB program stands for "Where Everybody Belongs" and is a middle school transition and orientation program designed to support students as they enter middle school. Similar to the Link Crew, the WEB Program trains older middle school students to be mentors to the incoming students to make them feel comfortable and supported. The mentors meet with the younger students regularly throughout the year and check in with them often to see how they are doing socially, emotionally, and academically.

Both WEB and Link Crew programs provide a structure where students make positive connections with other students. They also act as anti-bullying programs where student leaders are trained to recognize negative behavior and empowered to help stop it. These programs build positive relationships between students and let the younger students see that people care about them and are there to help and support them through difficult transitions.

FINAL THOUGHTS

When planning, implementing, and evaluating classroom strategies or schoolwide programs it is imperative that the administration and staff make social-emotional learning a top priority in the school. There is real data and research on the benefits not just to students but the entire school body when social-emotional learning is a focus in school. They must work together to establish a common mission and goals and create a collaborative team structure that develops a strategic plan to implement the programs and strategies with fidelity.

School programs must be well planned to be successful. It is also critical that school districts provide appropriate professional development to support the staff in learning and implementing new strategies. Programs, strategies, and methods to improve social-emotional learning are important, but it is imperative that the entire school community become actively engaged in the process to maximize the results of these efforts. Two areas the authors of this chapter find especially key in the successful implementation of SEL programs are: family engagement with parents and direct involvement from the administration and staff.

Family Engagement and Collaboration with Parents

To engage families in social-emotional development, teachers and school administrators can't just send home packets and to-do lists. They need to create strong relationships, partner with families on goals for their children, and receive and provide ongoing support (Shafer, 2018). It is essential that school officials work cooperatively with families as partners to ensure students receive the support they need at school and home. Students spend most of their time at home, and it is important that the home environment is working in harmony with the school to maximize the positive effects on students. If a student receives social-emotional counseling, it is imperative that they receive the services at home and school to ensure continuity of support.

Comprehensive support plans and behavioral intervention plans for students need to be developed in cooperation with parents and the school must provide the proper help to assist families successfully implement and navigate through the process.

An excellent way that schools can offer support to families is to create a *Family Support Center*. These centers are designed to provide services to families and strengthen students and families through collaboration and building strong home/school relationships. Family Support Centers provide a variety of services including but not limited to individual and family counseling, support groups, parenting groups, restorative justice, mediation, mentoring, specialized training, and referrals and information regarding community resources and wrap-around services. The Family Support Center does not have to be an entirely separate building. If space limitations exist, the counselor's office, school library, or a conference room could house many of the meetings and trainings.

Direct Involvement by Principals and Support Staff

The key to feeling connected is forming positive relationships at school with students, staff, parents, community, and family members. According to the National Center on Safe Supportive Learning Environments, caring adults play a key role in creating connectedness at school. Accordingly, they conclude that "the relationships formed between students and school staff members are at the heart of school connectedness. Students who perceive their teachers and school administrators as creating a caring, well-structured learning environment in which expectations are high, clear, and fair are more likely to be connected to school" (National Center on Safe Supportive Learning Environments, 2023).

Given this research it is imperative that schools develop and implement intentional programs to foster direct positive relationships between students and caring adults working in the school. These adults can be certified staff, classified staff, administrators, or any adult connected with school. The key is to develop one-on-one personal relationships that meet consistently to build trust, have honest dialogue, and help students feel safe and supported at school.

Where to Start

In the ever-changing and multifaceted roles of being a teacher or school administrator, it can be overwhelming for one to understand and believe in the need to improve their current practices but struggle to know where to begin. Needs assessments are valuable tools for principals and schools as they provide essential insights into the strengths and weaknesses of the educational institution. Following are several ways in which needs assessments can benefit principals and schools:

Strategic Planning: Needs assessments help principals and schools identify their specific strengths and weaknesses. This information is crucial for developing strategic plans and setting priorities for improvement. It ensures that resources are allocated effectively to address the most pressing needs.

Resource Allocation: By understanding the needs of students, teachers, and the school community, principals can allocate resources such as funding, staff, and materials more efficiently. This helps in optimizing the use of available resources.

Improved Instruction: Needs assessments can highlight areas where instructional practices can be enhanced. Principals can use this information to provide targeted professional development opportunities for teachers and implement evidence-based instructional strategies.

Curriculum Development: Schools can use needs assessments to identify gaps in their curriculum and make necessary adjustments. This ensures that the curriculum is aligned with educational standards and meets the needs of the student population.

Staff Development: Principals can identify areas where staff members may need additional training or support. Needs assessments can inform decisions about professional development programs and opportunities for staff improvement.

Student Support Services: Schools can use needs assessments to identify students who may require additional support, such as special education services, counseling, or interventions. This helps in ensuring that students' individual needs are met.

Parent and Community Engagement: Needs assessments can include input from parents and the community, fostering a sense of ownership and involvement in the school's improvement efforts. This engagement can lead to stronger partnerships and support for the school.

Data-Driven Decision-Making: Principals can make informed decisions based on data gathered from needs assessments rather than relying on assumptions or anecdotal evidence. This promotes data-driven decision-making, which is essential for continuous improvement.

Accountability: Needs assessments can serve as a basis for accountability. They provide a benchmark against which progress can be measured, allowing principals to track improvements over time and be accountable to stakeholders.

Grant and Funding Applications: Many grant applications and funding requests require evidence of need. Needs assessments can provide the necessary data and documentation to support these requests, increasing the school's chances of securing additional resources.

School Improvement Plans: The findings from needs assessments often form the basis for developing school improvement plans. These plans outline specific goals, strategies, and timelines for addressing identified needs.

Legal and Regulatory Compliance: Needs assessments can help schools ensure compliance with legal and regulatory requirements, particularly in areas such as special education, school safety, and equitable resource allocation.

In summary, needs assessments play a critical role in helping principals and schools identify areas for improvement, allocate resources effectively, and make data-driven decisions to enhance the overall educational experience for students, teachers, and the school community.

KEY PRAGMATIC LEADERSHIP TAKEAWAYS

- *Leaders must establish a clear moral purpose for the work and make social emotional wellness and learning a priority for the entire school community.* The staff must know what they are doing and why they are doing it. If leaders do not take the time to establish the importance of the mission, the staff will not buy into the process.
- *Leaders must create wellness teams at the district and school levels to establish common goals and practices to implement with fidelity.* There must be a common team structure to articulate goals and practices from the district level to the building and most importantly to the classroom where teachers directly implement the strategies.
- *Leaders must develop schoolwide multi-tiered support systems (MTSS) to evaluate student needs and monitor progress.* There must be a structure to diagnose problems and issues, a clear system to apply interventions, and a way to monitor and evaluate progress. If this is not in place, programs become haphazard and must rely on luck to be successful. Our students, staff, and families deserve a clear, structured process that maximizes our success.
- *Leaders must decide on what schoolwide programs and classroom strategies they want to utilize and then ensure they are implemented with fidelity.* This chapter provides practical examples of many of the programs, methods, and strategies that school administrators must consider when adopting practices for their schools. It is imperative that they identify those strategies that are nonnegotiable and are expected to be implemented with fidelity. This will direct their staff development efforts and allow staff to work together vertically and horizontally to consistently implement programs.
- *Leaders must ensure that they develop and provide an appropriate professional learning plan to support their staff.* Professional learning must be provided to ensure the staff has the training and tools to successfully implement any program that is adopted by the school. No program will be successful if this is not provided.
- *Leaders must enlist parents as partners and actively engage them in the process of providing social-emotional support to their children.* Parental involvement is key to the success of all programs to support social-emotional wellness. Students spend a significant amount of time at home and this environment is critical to the positive mental health and

well-being of students. The research is clear that when home and school work together, the students benefit greatly.

- *Leaders must be directly involved in the process, and they must ensure their staff is actively engaged.* When the administration gets on the front lines and works with the students and staff it is a game changer. Leaders must be good role models and be the change they want to see in the world. This motivates and inspires the entire school community to take social-emotional wellness and learning seriously.

REFERENCES

Anderson, M. (2015). "Social-Emotional Learning and Academics: Better Together." *Educational Leadership 73*(2). https://www.ascd.org/el/articles/social-emotional-learning-and-academics-better-together.

Aupperle, R. L., Melrose, A. J., Stein, M. B., & Paulus, M. P. (2012). "Executive Function and PTSD: Disengaging from Trauma." *Neuropharmacology 62*(2), 686–94.

Boomerang Project (2023). "You Get Back What You Give." https://www.boomerangproject.com/.

CASEL. (2023). "What Is the CASEL Framework?" https://casel.org/fundamentals-of-Fsel/what-is-the-casel-framework/.

Center on PBIS (n.d.). "Positive Behavioral Interventions and Supports." https://www.pbis.org/pbis/what-is-pbis. www.pbis.org.

Cleaver, S. (2023). "What Is Trauma-Informed Teaching?" We Are Teachers. https://www.weareteachers.com/what-is-trauma-informed-teaching/.

Desautels, L. (2022). "Using Art to Help Students Find Their Calm." *Edutopia*, April 20. https://www.edutopia.org/article/using-art-help-students-find-their-calm/.

Edgar, S. (2019). Music Education and Social-Emotional Learning. NAfME. https://nafme.org/blog/music-education-social-emotional-learning/.

Epperson, A. (2021). "Is It Time to Reconsider the Behavior Chart?" PBIS Rewards. https://www.pbisrewards.com/blog/reconsider-behavior-chart/.

Ferlazzo, L. (2023). "How Do Restorative Practices Work? Educators Share Implementation Tips (Opinion)." *Education Week*. https://www.edweek.org/leadership/opinion-how-do-restorative-practices-work-educators-share-implementation-tips/2023/11.

Ginsburg, K. R., & Jablow, M. M. (2015). *Building Resilience in Children and Teens: Giving Kids Roots and Wings*. Itasca, IL: American Academy of Pediatrics.

Jennings, P. (2015). "Seven Ways Mindfulness Can Help Teachers." *Greater Good Magazine*. https://greatergood.berkeley.edu/article/item/seven_ways_mindfulness_can_help_teachers.

Kagan, S. (2009). "Kagan Structures: A Miracle of Active Engagement." *Kagan Online Magazine*, Fall/Winter 2009. https://www.kaganonline.com/free_articles/dr_spencer_kagan/281/Kagan-Structures-A-Miracle-of-Active-Engagement.

Leader in Me. (2021). "Questions & Answers about The Leader in Me." FranklinCoveyCo. Leaderinme.org. https://www.leaderinme.org/faqs/#:~:text=Leader%20in%20Me%20is%20an,thrive%20in%20the%2021st%20century.

———. (2024). FAQs. https://www.leaderinme.org/faqs/.

Levings, K. (2020). "Trauma-Informed Classroom: Creating a Trauma-Sensitive Classroom." Insights to Behavior, June 23. https://insightstobehavior.com/blog/trauma-informed-classroom-creating-trauma-sensitive-classroom/.

Merrow, C. (2020). "Journaling as a Social Emotional Practice." Empowering Education. https://empoweringeducation.org/blog/journaling-as-a-social-emotional-practice/.

Minahan, J. (2019). "Trauma-Informed Teaching Strategies." ACSD. https://www.ascd.org/el/articles/trauma-informed-teaching-strategies. ascd.org.

Mindful.org. (2023.). "Mindfulness: Getting Started. Mindful." https://www.mindful.org/meditation/mindfulness-getting-started/.

Mindful Practices. (2018). "The Role of Social-Emotional Learning in Recess." May 11, 2018. https://mindfulpractices.us/2018/05/11/the-role-of-social-emotional-learning-in-recess/.

Mineo, L. (2018). "Less Stress, Clearer Thoughts with Mindfulness Meditation." *Harvard Gazette*, April. https://news.harvard.edu/gazette/story/2018/04/less-stress-clearer-thoughts-with-mindfulness-meditation.

Mulvahill, E. (2018). "What Is Writing Workshop?" We Are Teachers. https://www.weareteachers.com/what-is-writing-workshop/.

National Association of Secondary School Principals. (2022). "2022 Survey." https://survey.nassp.org/2022/.

National Center on Safe Supportive Learning Environments. (2023). "Relationships. Safe and Supportive Learning." https://safesupportivelearning.ed.gov/topic-research/engagement/relationships.

Noddings, N. (1999). "Caring and Competence." *Teachers College Record 100*(5), 205–20. https://doi.org/10.1177/016146819910000509.

Prutzman, P., Roberts, E., Fishler, T., & Jones, T. (2022). "The Story of a Model Restorative School: Creative Response to Conflict at MS 217 in Queens, NY." *Journal of Aggression, Conflict and Peace Research, 14*(4), 346–62. https://doi.org/10.1108/JACPR-02-2022-0690.

Responsive Classroom. (2022). "Schoolwide Responsive Classroom." https://www.responsiveclassroom.org/schoolwide-responsive-classroom/.

Rodgers, C. (2023). "Yays, Nays and Hip Hip Hoorays: A Daily Check-In Practice in Which Students Share Their Ups and Downs Can Have a Big Impact on Their Well-Being." *Edutopia*, September 6. https://www.edutopia.org/article/daily-student-check-in-strategy/.

RTI Action Network. (2023). "What Is RTI?" RTI Network. https://www.rtinetwork.org/learn/what/whatisrti.

Sanders, S. (2022) "What Are Kagan Strategies? Building a Caring and Kind Classroom Environment to Help Students Thrive." We Are Teachers. https://www.weareteachers.com/what-are-kagan-strategies/.

Savas, V. (2023). "Using Read-Alouds to Support Social and Emotional Learning." *Edutopia*, September 20. https://www.edutopia.org/article/social-emotional-learning-read-alouds-can-support-literacy/.

Shafer, L. (2018). "Family Engagement and SEL." Harvard Graduate School of Education, July 5. https://www.gse.harvard.edu/ideas/usable-knowledge/18/07/family-engagement-and-sel.

Shardlow, G. (2015). "Integrating Mindfulness in Your Classroom Curriculum." *Edutopia*, November 18. https://www.edutopia.org/blog/integrating-mindfulness-in-classroom-curriculum-giselle-shardlow.

Sources of Strength. (2023). "Our Vision Is to Empower a Well World: Who We Are." https://sourcesofstrength.org/.

Stinger, H. (2018). "Community Circles." Classroom Management Toolbox, November 26. https://inside.ewu.edu/managementtoolbox/community-circle/.

Stone, M. (2023). "Why America Has a Youth Mental Health Crisis, and How Schools Can Help." *Education Week*, October 16. https://www.edweek.org/leadership/why-america-has-a-youth-mental-health-crisis-and-how-schools-can-help/2023/10.

Sugai, G., & Horner, R. H. (2009). "Defining and Describing Schoolwide Positive Behavior Support." In W. Sailor, G. Dunlop, G. Sugai, & R. Horner (Eds.), *Handbook of Positive Behavior Support*, 307–26. New York: Springer Publishing Company.

Tomko, G, & Pendharkar, G. (2023). "The Essential Components of MTSS: A Downloadable Guide." *Education Week*, October 13. https://www.edweek.org/teaching-learning/the-essential-components-of-mtss-a-downloadable-guide/2023/10.

Tutt, P. (2022). "How to Lead with Empathy." *Edutopia*, February 4. https://www.edutopia.org/article/how-lead-empathy/.

Venet, A. S. (2018). "The How and Why of Trauma-Informed Teaching." *Edutopia*, August 3. https://www.edutopia.org/article/how-and-why-trauma-informed-teaching/.

Van Woerkom, M. (2018). "Building Community with Restorative Circles." *Edutopia*, March 12. https://www.edutopia.org/article/building-community-restorative-circles/.

Weissberg, R. P., Durlak, J. A., Domitrovich, C. E., & Gullotta, T. P. (2015). "Social and Emotional Learning: Past, Present, and Future." In J. A. Durlak, C. E. Domitrovich, R. P. Weissberg & T. P. Gullotta (Eds.), *Handbook of Social and Emotional Learning: Research and Practice*, 3–19. New York: Guilford.

Wellesley Centers for Women. (2018). *Women Change Worlds* (blog), January 23. "Five Ways to Support Social and Emotional Learning with Children's Books." https://www.wcwonline.org/WCW-Blog-Women-Change-Worlds/Five-ways-support-social-emotional-learning-childrens-books.

Will, M. (2021). "Teachers Are Not OK, Even Though We Need Them to Be." *Education Week*, September 14. https://www.edweek.org/teaching-learning/teachers-are-not-ok-even-though-we-need-them-to-be/2021/09#.

YouHue. 2022. "How Daily Emotional Check-Ins for Students Can Benefit Your Classroom." Medium, September 29. https://youhue.medium.com/how-daily-emotional-check-ins-for-students-can-benefit-your-classroom-da976ca568a3.

Chapter 3

One School District's Upstream Approach to Creating Successful Initiatives

The Journey of a Social-Emotional Learning (SEL) Program

Paul M. Fanuele

In order to successfully create and implement an educational initiative it is important to consider many factors before, during, and after implementation. This chapter highlights how a district located in the Hudson Valley of New York State embarked on a journey to successfully start a much-needed Social-Emotional Learning (SEL) program. The following statement from a recent district plan sums up the district's belief in the importance of SEL education:

> *Our work is grounded in our beliefs that the most equitable opportunities for educational success rely upon the comprehensive support for students and families provided in our schools with our professionals and the systems of support we have built. These supports include academics as well as the social and emotional well-being of our students. We are committed to prioritizing social-emotional well-being and emotional space to access rigorous academic content with confidence.*

Clearly, the district's goal was to implement a SEL program that would provide academic and social-emotional support to its students. In order to effectuate change and initiate a sustainable program that would impact students

across all grade levels, the district followed simple steps to create and implement its vision.
These steps are:

1. Set the Stage
2. Create the Need/Urgency
3. The Search Is On!
4. Build Capacity
5. Implementation
6. Stay Aligned
7. Vision for the Future/Next Steps

SET THE STAGE

The task for the district was to set the stage so that any new initiatives, either centered around SEL education or other educational needs, would have a chance to survive implementation. Any program, despite its importance, needs the soil to be prepped (just like plants do) before laying down the seed (let alone watering and fertilizing). A district needs a core set of known beliefs that will guide it especially during difficult times—in other words, a set of priorities that are easy to understand and decipher.

The setting of the stage began a year before the initiative was introduced. At that time, a new superintendent was hired who looked to instill his philosophy into the district. This philosophy meshed well with the already established beliefs within the district but created a simple approach to ensuring student success. Simply put, the philosophy aimed to meet students where they are by focusing on a growth mindset.

The superintendent created a visual to depict this philosophy to aid the coherence and alignment within the district's four schools. As seen in figure 3.1, the most important belief is in a growth mindset. This belief, championed by author and psychologist Dr. Carol Dweck (2006), puts the focus on learning and growing as a learner. Dr. Dweck posits that students with a fixed mindset tend to give up sooner rather than stick with the learning process. In order to ensure that a growth mindset prevailed among teachers, in the hiring process the superintendent made a point of asking potential teaching candidates to explain their thoughts on a growth mindset. Fortunately (or unfortunately, depending on your perspective), all answered that they had more of a fixed mindset as students but then shifted to having a growth mindset as educators. This sentiment echoes the importance for teachers to focus on a growth mindset in the classroom to help shape students into motivated learners at an earlier age.

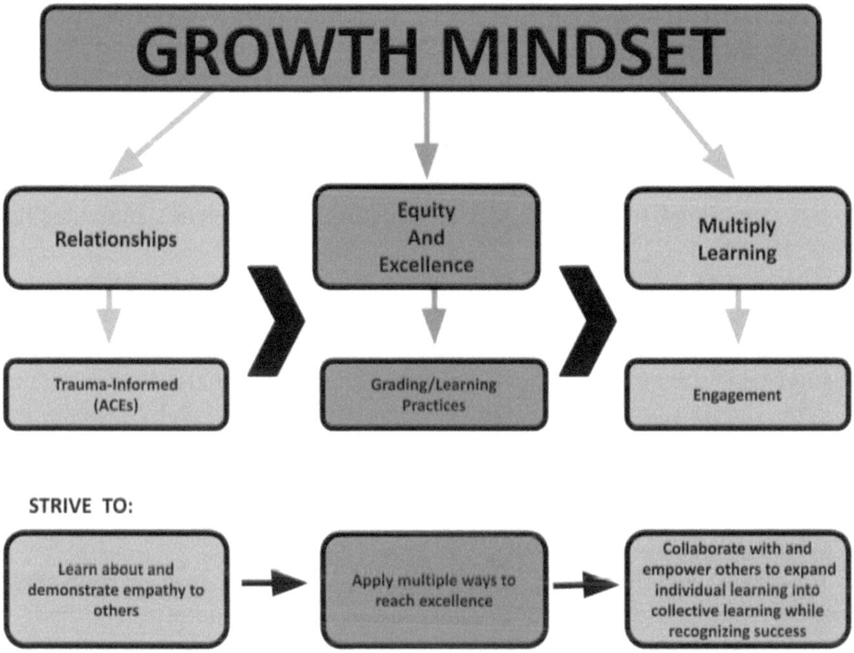

Figure 3.1. Growth mindset chart.

Three other beliefs (seen in figure 3.1) that encompass a growth mindset are also important to the district philosophy: Build Relationships—Learn about and demonstrate empathy to others; Equity and Excellence—Apply multiple ways to reach excellence; and Multiply Learning—Collaborate with and empower others to expand individual learning into collective learning while recognizing success.

Building relationships is at the foundation of this district's success and has been an intensive focus of the superintendent from the time that he assumed his position. Essentially, the district administration not only sought to build relationships internally—such as between students and teachers—but also to strengthen connections between all four of its buildings, *as well as* the community. The goal was to learn all they could about students by becoming trauma-informed and demonstrating empathy to others, from teachers to stakeholders.

In the process, it was important that the superintendent embraced the work of *equity and excellence.* Note that it is not equity *or* excellence: it is both. In short, this means that educators need to meet their students where they are. By building relationships and learning about each student's life circumstances and trauma, the district could tailor an education to each student.

This individualized approach occurs by applying multiple ways for students to reach excellence.

The district also emphasized *multiplying learning* by engaging the workforce with its initiatives. This created a synergy by empowering and inspiring people to lead in their own classrooms and buildings. With a staff so fully engaged, the district approached the new school year with renewed vigor, committed to ensuring and recognizing each student's individuality and success.

The growth mindset philosophy and use of the chart help to keep the district focused on what matters throughout the school year, especially when adversity hits. Another important way to set the stage is by reshaping district-wide thinking. Two books and philosophies that helped set the stage for the district were *Think Again* by Adam Grant (2021) and *Upstream* by Dan Heath (2020). The messages of both these books meshed well with the superintendent's philosophy and provided a foundation to enable leaders in the district to successfully navigate challenges that arise. Administrators regularly met to discuss the tenets of these books.

Creating a successive SEL initiative, as well as navigating new challenges, requires a way of thinking that differs from the norm established in prior years. This responsiveness to ever-changing circumstances is crucial, as today's educational challenges are adaptive challenges as opposed to technical challenges, a concept popularized by Heifetz Linsky, and Grashow (2009). Technical challenges are known and have tried-and-true methods to solve the issue. For example, if the copy machine does not work, we can add paper, find the jam, or add toner. An adaptive challenge is a new challenge without previously created possible solutions. This is where thinking differently comes into play. As an example, navigating the pandemic was clearly an adaptive challenge.

Finally, a focus of the superintendent's philosophy is to think upstream. Heath emphasized this concept by retelling a popular anecdote often used to discuss public health. Many people in education have heard the classic parable of the children floundering in the stream. It goes something like this: A family and friends are picnicking near a stream. They see a child coming downstream struggling in the water and shouting for help. They save the child and bring her ashore. Then another child appears. Again, they rescue the child. When even more children appear in the stream in danger of drowning, the picnickers rescue them, too. Amid this chaos, one of the family members abruptly starts running away. His brother shouts, "Why are you going in that direction? We need your help here." The reply: "I'm going upstream to help stop the crazy person who's throwing all these children in the water."

This parable illustrates the importance of thinking upstream. The development of the district's SEL program is a product of thinking differently and thinking upstream. It was important for the team to develop their skills in these departments before embarking on creating the SEL program. Whatever the philosophy or focus, a district needs to set the stage before moving forward. Moving too quickly only increases the chances of failure.

CREATE THE NEED/URGENCY

Once the stage is set, a district needs to articulate the reason why such an initiative is being sought. Some change agents call this part "creating an urgency." John Kotter (2012) championed this concept in his seminal work *Leading Change*. For this district, establishing a sense of urgency was easy to create coming off of a pandemic not seen in a hundred years.

The pandemic created negativity and uncertainty. The district needed to find a way to counter both. However, even though the crisis of the pandemic helped to create an urgency, the need for an SEL program had certainly existed prior to it. In fact, the pandemic highlighted the importance of SEL as a fundamental component of school districts, both during the best of times and during a crisis. Also, as bad as it sounds, it is never a good idea to waste a crisis, so founding an SEL program on the heels of the pandemic was a silver lining.

As was so common in the United States during pandemic times and beyond, the district was facing a mental health crisis, national social unrest, and political polarization. On top of all that, US Surgeon General Dr. Vivek Murthy declared that the country was in the grip of a "loneliness epidemic." In his Surgeon General's Advisory on Our Epidemic of Loneliness and Isolation, Dr. Murthy wrote, "Loneliness is far more than just a bad feeling—it harms both individual and societal health. . . . And the harmful consequences of a society that lacks social connection can be felt in our schools, workplaces, and civic organizations, where performance, productivity, and engagement are diminished."

Added to these complications, there was also a change in demographics resulting in different needs of the community, reflected in an uptick in students qualifying for free-or-reduced meals. It was important to be proactive and stop issues before they become issues. In other words, it was essential to think upstream.

The need for a proactive SEL program became clear to administration, teachers, and staff. Teachers had witnessed the community issues mentioned and were ready to take action. All staff saw the ramifications of remote learning on students. Socialization had been reduced and students became disconnected from peers and adults. It was important to move forward, and that involved keeping a growth mindset and finding new ways to positively impact students. The negativity and uncertainty needed an antidote. It was time to take advantage of this multipronged crisis and search for a program that would meet the district's needs.

THE SEARCH IS ON!

Once this urgency became apparent, the search for a program was on. There are all kinds of SEL programs out there. It is a sea full of creatures big and small, to say the least. Each program is different from the others. The district's task was to find one to fit with its larger goals and that aligned with the "setting of the stage" beliefs. Finding a program is easy, but finding one that meshes with your specific needs and wants is much more difficult. Nevertheless, this was the task. Also, essential was finding a program that did not add to the plate of our educators on what seems to be a plate already piled quite high. Kotter (2012) emphasized the importance of removing barriers when leading change.

In previous years, the district reacted to mental health issues and other fires as they occurred. The response had been piecemeal and certainly not proactive. Though the district had access to a bevy of social-emotional resources, none had been applied in an aligned fashion. This was a key finding as administrators assessed their current situation and options. Though they were satisfied with their response to individual students in need, they also wanted a whole system approach that would do more.

It turns out part of the solution had been available to them the whole time. Their previous work with behavioral consultant Dr. Donna Riter had helped them in the past, and it could help them bring SEL to the next level. Dr. Riter got her start as a teacher in New York. She suggested SEL programs that she had experienced and implemented throughout her career. Because Dr. Riter had worked in each of the district's buildings and with its teachers in previous years, she was fully versed in its philosophy and culture. She was, in fact, an extension of the district. Reciprocally, the district reflected many of her philosophies and multiplied learnings from her. This team approach has aided the district during its journey to implementation of the SEL program.

Fortuitously, one of the district's principals also had experience working with an SEL program in his previous job. He was tasked with reconnecting with the directors of the program and presenting his findings and thoughts to the district's administrators and the Board of Education. The program, the Positivity Project (P2), had the team's attention from the beginning of its search. P2 was created by two West Point graduates and had an impressive track record.

A key tenet of the district, not mentioned in the "set the stage" step, was to tap into the intrinsic motivation of its students and staff. One of the first books the superintendent asked the administrative team to read and discuss was Daniel Pink's *Drive* (2009). This work clearly illustrated the importance of intrinsic motivation as opposed to extrinsic motivation. The principal who had exposure with P2 was also intrinsically motivated and passionate about his experiences with P2. There was no extrinsic reward for whatever program that would be chosen.

While the district eventually chose this program, it did so only after exploring a variety of other ones, including Rachel's Challenge and Second Step. The two parameters that stood out during the search were that the program had to align with the district's philosophy, and it had to create minimal additional work for its teachers. After an extensive search, many meetings, and much discussion, P2 emerged the clear winner.

Impressed by the personalized attention from the creators of P2, the administrator team recognized that the program clearly was aligned to the district's philosophy. It came with highly developed lessons and videos that eased the burden on teachers. Most initiatives are viewed by teachers as additional work. However, P2's focus was readily—even eagerly—accepted. A main reason (other than the program itself) was that the district took the time to build the capacity of its staff and buildings in general.

BUILD CAPACITY

Each building in the district houses different grades (Princeton model). This, along with other differences and personalities, had each of the district's four buildings in different places of readiness. It is important to understand that this is quite normal, but needs to be planned for. Some buildings need more time for the seeds to root than other buildings, including the requirement for more water and fertilizer. Meeting the staff of buildings where they are is equally important as meeting students where they are.

The district began the process by building the capacity of the district overall. An opportunity to build capacity for the whole district came on Superintendent's Conference Day in November, post-pandemic, early enough in the school year to put the process in motion. In meetings with administrators over the previous summer, the superintendent had asked, "How can we continue our work with the growth mindset and remain aligned to our work in building relationships?" The idea of showing *Paper Tigers*, a documentary that explores at-risk teens but also applies to children at all stages of development, came out of these conversations.

On Conference Day, the superintendent addressed teachers and staff with these words:

> *Our teachers and staff are doing a great job of meeting children where they are and helping them stay on track to develop these skills. So, we show this documentary not because we are deficient here, but instead to stimulate conversations about how we can help children succeed even more. Since every child is different, there is no one-size-fits all approach. But if we put our heads together, we can make even greater progress and spread more positivity in the lives of children. These efforts are worth it because their effects will last a lifetime.*

Next, staff watched a short video clip from Dr. Riter. She introduced and embraced the message of the documentary. Because of the staff's high esteem and respect for Dr. Riter due to her previous work in the district, she was well received as an advocate for meeting students where they are. In the coming months, she continued to work with staff and provide effective strategies for working with students with traumatic backgrounds and/or behavioral challenges.

Fast-forward six months: At the district's March Superintendent's Conference Day, Dr. Riter built on her previous work on Adverse Childhood Experiences (ACEs). She encouraged teachers and staff to continue "being courageous and stepping forward" when it comes to making school a better place for students and provided them with readings to deepen their understanding of ACEs and the role of adults in helping children. In a private meeting with the superintendent, she commented on how "cohesive" the district was in its collective vision, with all buildings sharing a common goal.

Showing the documentary and following up with visits from Dr. Riter proved to be an effective way to build capacity. Staff recognized the level of commitment involved outside of academics in getting to know students and building relationships with them while also fostering a sense of community.

This was a great start to building capacity, but the district still had to meet each building where they were while staying aligned to its focus. From the beginning, it was clear that the two elementary buildings were ahead of the secondary buildings in their acceptance of this new initiative. Accordingly, the search for the new program was primarily led by the elementary principals, and they were able to build capacity at a quicker rate. However, the Board of Education was looking for the implementation to occur at the K–12 level. Pressure started to mount, but administration felt it was important to build up the capacity of the secondary buildings before starting the program at that level.

IMPLEMENTATION

Part of the district was now set for implementation. It was decided to start the initiative at the elementary level first while continuing to build capacity in the middle and high schools. The success of the implementation stage was based on the success of all of the previous stages. A tiered implementation schedule was a key component to the district's implementation success. Although a tiered approach can create other implementation issues, it's important to note, as this district learned, that *more* work and time given up front can lead to *less* work overall (even if it causes its superintendent stress!).

Administrators recognized that buy-in from the district and buildings was needed for a successful implementation. They acted as what Fullan (2014) would call "lead learners" and helped to create an atmosphere of learning. The elementary schools utilized the end of the school year before implementation, as well as the summer, to train staff. The two elementary principals collaborated with immense enthusiasm during this period. They did a great job of talking with key teacher leaders before discussing the program with the entire faculty and staff. However, the faculty and staff were ready because of the previous steps that had been put into motion well in advance: setting the stage, creating an urgency, finding an appropriate program, and building their capacity.

The superintendent attended an end-of-the-year elementary-level meeting where staff members spoke on the need for implementing the Positivity Project the next school year. It was beautiful to witness teachers wanting an initiative instead of just administrators making the decision. They were making statements like, "Maslow before Bloom" to show their enthusiasm. Proactively, following the work with Dr. Riter, the viewing of *Paper Tigers* and discussion, and the P2 Training, the district was able to move the elementary staff from "how can we find the time?" to "how can we *not* find the time?" The elementary schools were off and running.

The secondary schools were a different story. They weren't ready for implementation. They needed more time to build capacity. The middle school was further along than the high school. So, the district focused on how to get the middle school started with the program by the mid-point of the school year. The success of the elementary program helped out in this endeavor. Teachers were able to visit the elementary schools and talk with colleagues about the program and its success. The middle school had been searching for an SEL program for a few years before the superintendent arrived but never really gained any momentum. Momentum was now beginning to build, a direct result of following the stages previously discussed.

One issue kept emerging at every meeting was how to schedule P2. At the elementary level, the main teacher in each classroom has the students for most of the day, which makes it easier to find time for implementation. At the secondary level, students change classes, with each period lasting approximately forty minutes. Inevitably, questions emerged: Who should teach the program? Which subject area? What time of day? These questions were hard to answer, but the middle school principal had a great idea: "Take" two minutes from the six non-lunch periods to create a twelve-minute block. Then add the twelve minutes to fourth period (middle of the day) and dub the first twelve minutes of the class "P2 instruction."

There were still some issues regarding why the fourth period teachers were the only ones providing instruction, as some teachers and support staff had fourth period as a non-teaching period. The district decided to make the P2 time an "all-in" twelve-minute period. Every available educator would team up with a fourth-period teacher and collaborate together. This move worked brilliantly and bonded the school.

To further cement the bonding, the principal and assistant principal decided to instruct the twelve-minute P2 period every Friday. They would remote into each classroom and virtually instruct the students. This gave the teachers a break and emphasized the value of the program, as all adults were part of it. It is a great example of the superintendent giving unique buildings with unique circumstances the ability to have some guided autonomy on the specifics of implementation. Without this supportive approach, the program could very well have failed at the middle school level.

The program began at the middle school at the beginning of the second semester and blossomed similarly as it did at the elementary schools. The focus was now on the high school. Remember, the Board of Education was looking for a K–12 initiative, but implementing a program such as P2 at the high school was a considerable challenge. Pressure mounted but the district stayed the course and continued to build capacity at the high school. Administrators researched and visited other districts and found that they, too, had a difficult time implementing SEL programs at the high school level. Articles in educational journals stated the same. Scheduling was a problem and a schedule change similar to the middle school was difficult due to the numerous moving parts found at the high school (more electives, singletons, late arrivals/early dismissals of seniors, students enrolled at our area tech center). On top of that, older students tend to respond better to a student-led approach, rather than having a program presented by teachers and administrators. It was time to think differently. The middle school thought upstream and differently when it developed its program. Now the high school had to do the same.

Unfortunately, the high school lagged behind. They needed another year to build capacity and see P2 in action for a full school year at the middle school. One key feature that was noticed during the building capacity stage was that the high school had a powerful student body that volunteered and helped out in the community. It became clear that the district needed to harness their power and spirit as a means of bringing the P2 program to the high school. And so, it was decided that the district would implement P2 at the high school at the start of the next school year (two years after the elementary schools and one and a half years after the middle school).

The program would center around a student-led club that would meet after school and spread the P2 character strengths (figure 3.2) throughout the school. Student leaders entering as ninth graders were tapped to lead the club. These students had experienced P2 for the previous year and a half as middle schoolers and demonstrated the leadership qualities/character strengths needed to get their peers involved.

As you can see, thinking differently and upstream paid off in order to implement the P2 program in all four of the schools. Even though each building had a slightly different approach, it was important to keep each building aligned to the district philosophy.

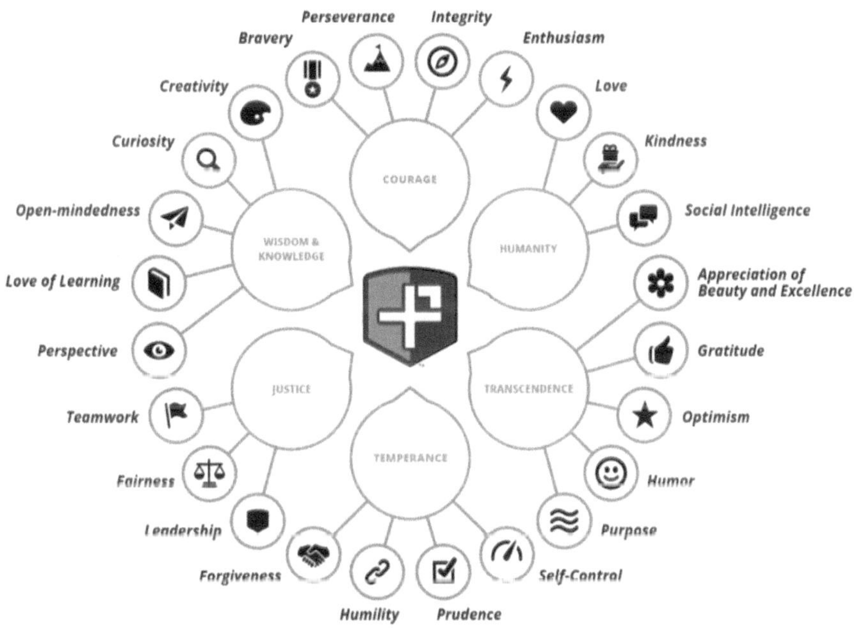

Figure 3.2. Staying aligned during the process.

STAY ALIGNED

Alignment is a key focus in the district. It's important to note that the superintendent had experiences in other districts where alignment was *not* a focus. Jumping from program to program or constantly changing professional development only frustrates all involved and brings growth to a halt. Instead, it was important to create a core philosophy and enact it in an easy-to-understand format. As mentioned previously, the chart from figure 3.1 summarizes the process and serves as a quick reminder to keep the district aligned.

Alignment is obviously important in this district and the key to its success. The SEL program it initiated is greater than just P2. While P2 serves as a nice backbone for SEL movement, it is what is implemented around P2 that comprises the full SEL program. Other initiatives that stayed aligned with the district's philosophy and P2 followed. Advancement Via Individual Determination, or AVID, also took off at the middle school in grade seven. This program dovetails with P2 and follows the same steps of implementation (that is another chapter). AVID is moving up to eighth grade next and will come to the high school the year after.

Furthering the alignment among buildings, students in the AVID program present to students in each elementary school about the power of the character traits found in P2. It is amazing to watch both sets of students light up during the presentations.

The district also started a mentoring program in which high school students are matched to elementary students. This program is as powerful to the mentor as it is to the mentee. The district even extended its connectivity to alumni: A recent graduate spoke with high school students concerning his struggle with mental health and provided meaningful strategies for how to reach out for help.

The district also invited members of the community to share stories. Following a P2 recognition ceremony led by an elementary building principal, another graduate of the district, representing the Eleanor Roosevelt Estate, presented a program on the former first lady, who dedicated her life to the cause of civil liberties and human rights. Tying into the positive character traits and virtues of P2, the ranger talked about the qualities of Mrs. Roosevelt that inspired admiration, such as her leadership, bravery, and perseverance.

All of these programs and events are aligned to the district's goals. While the SEL program and P2 are two separate entities, they reinforce one another. In particular, P2 energizes the SEL program. P2 has also inspired yet another component: book vending machines in each elementary school. Students who are "caught" using the character strengths of P2 are recognized by teachers and presented with certificates at monthly assemblies. They also receive a token for a free book from the vending machines. Students perceive this as quite an honor (which it is). Students who are chosen have often never been recognized before, as most previous awards usually involved high grades and academic achievement, not character traits.

Staying aligned allowed the district to create a powerful program that had potential to expand. The SEL program is not just P2, but a robust program centered around the P2 character strengths. Any next steps the district has regarding its SEL program, including further expansion, should be easier to implement if the district follows the same steps and most importantly, stays aligned.

VISION FOR THE FUTURE/NEXT STEPS

Staying in alignment when considering next steps is also a key component in creating a vision for the future. The district's vision is clear: continue to follow the district philosophy outlined in figure 3.1 and use P2 as a centerpiece for future enhancements to its SEL program. Following this path will help to institutionalize the program and make it part of the district's culture. A positive sign that P2 and the SEL program as a whole are becoming part of the district's culture is that in recent contract negotiations with the teachers, a segment of the contract was added to keep the middle school P2 schedule (the one with twelve minutes carved out) permanent (or at least until next negotiations).

Possible next steps are to create a district-wide recognition program for students who exemplify the P2 character strengths. Right now, only elementary students are recognized. Also, students could be recognized at Board of Education meetings. This would demonstrate the importance of the program and further institutionalize it. P2 has also recently spawned a fresh effort with the district's work to meet students where they are. This effort highlights particular diverse people for each trait. This means that the character strengths learned are applied to a person that students may have heard of through sports, politics, business, community, and so on. The goal of connecting P2 in this manner is to help visual learners relate to and remember traits better.

Next steps were a big topic at the district's summer retreat with all administrators. An idea discussed was to create a P2 community scavenger hunt that would involve area businesses and landmarks. The district is also looking to expand its mentoring program. The hope is to increase positive relationships, interconnectedness, and continue to change trajectories of students in a constructive manner. The team is also excited to present their journey at some upcoming leadership conferences. The thought is to multiply its learning while hoping to pick some ideas from conference attendees as well. Growth mindset in action.

FINAL THOUGHTS

While the importance of having a growth mindset has been part of the district's modus operandi for years, it recently actualized much of its message in unprecedented ways. On the superintendent's first conference day, he set the stage by presenting to staff about the importance of the growth mindset and how adults can help students fulfill their full potential by encouraging them to embrace challenges and also meet them where they are.

Since that time, the importance of the growth mindset has been increasingly entwined in the district's culture through such diverse avenues as the P2 initiative and through professional development that fosters an understanding of trauma and ACEs. The emphasis has been on multiplying learning by engaging the workforce with meeting students where they are and with initiatives such as P2, which creates a synergy by empowering and inspiring people to lead in their own classrooms and buildings. With a staff so fully engaged, the district was able to approach successive school years with renewed vigor, determined to meet students where they are and committed to ensuring and recognizing each student's individuality and success.

Also, it is important to note that the relationship between growth mindset and P2 is fully aligned. There is a self-survey that rates all of a person's P2 strengths from 1 to 24. Part of the P2 philosophy is teaching that character traits change throughout one's life and are not "fixed." Students can continually grow and even become character leaders.

In the final analysis, the success of the program really comes from staff. The administrators clearly utilized the framework they had been discussing and the concepts of thinking differently and upstream. Administrators were quite ingenious about what would work for their buildings, which obviously was key to meet each building where it was. The administrators were passionate about the program and deeply invested in it. The stage that was set in the district was definitely exemplified by its administrators. This was multiplied in their respective buildings and picked up by the faculty and staff and eventually the community as a whole.

The district feels that other initiatives could find success if the same process were to be followed. The seven steps create a simple yet effective way to introduce new programs. Oftentimes, districts attempt to use shortcuts to get to the implementation stage or they fail to stay aligned. There are no shortcuts if you are looking to create a sustainable program. As stated earlier, *more* work and time given up front can lead to *less* work overall. It might cause stress to move at a slower rate, but it is necessary and worth the extra effort. Hopefully, the story of this district's journey will give you the freedom to follow the seven steps, which are:

1. Set the Stage
2. Create the Need/Urgency
3. The Search Is On!
4. Build Capacity
5. Implementation
6. Stay Aligned
7. Vision for the Future/Next Steps

KEY PRAGMATIC LEADERSHIP TAKEAWAYS

The district leaders and staff members learned volumes from this endeavor. It's important to examine the trials and tribulations of what worked and what didn't as the district followed its growth mindset focus and unpacked its approach to implementing a new SEL program. There were many key takeaways learned. In sum:

- *Determine your philosophy and communicate it.*
- *Never waste a crisis.*
- *Listen to others (especially ones on your team) when searching for a new program.*
- *Tap into the benefits of intrinsic motivation.*
- *Take the time needed to build capacity. Moving too quickly increases the chance of failure.*
- *Find the balance between waiting to implement and needing to build capacity*: In other words, you can't wait forever, but you can't implement it if you are not ready. "Be quick, but don't hurry" as John Wooden has famously said.
- *Recognize the importance of staying aligned.*
- *When something works, do more of it (such as mentoring).*
- *Harness district strengths (e.g., the student community service organization).*
- *Think differently, improvise, and stay agile:* Examples include the middle school's innovative approach to scheduling and the elementary schools' book vending machines.
- *Multiply it. Pass it on and let it grow:* The program was rooted in the elementary schools but grew to the middle school and to the high school.
- *Live and think upstream!*

REFERENCES

Dweck, C. S. (2006). *Mindset: The New Psychology of Success*. New York: Random House.

Fullan, M. (2014). *The Principal: Three Keys to Maximizing Impact.* San Francisco: Jossey-Bass.

Grant, A. (2021). *Think Again: The Power of Knowing What You Don't Know*. New York: Viking/Penguin Random House.

Heath, D. (2020). *Upstream: The Quest to Solve Problems before They Happen*. New York: Avid Reader Press/Simon & Schuster.

Heifetz, R., Linsky, M., & Grashow, A. (2009). *The Practice of Adaptive Leadership: Tools and Tactics for Changing Your Organization and the World.* Boston: Harvard Business Review Press.

Kotter, J. (2012). *Leading Change*. Boston: Harvard Business Review Press.

Murthy, Vivek. 2023. *Our Epidemic of Loneliness and Isolation: The Surgeon General's Advisory on the Healing Effects of Social Connection and Community.* Washington, DC: Office of the Surgeon General. https://www.hhs.gov/sites/default/files/surgeon-general-social-connection-advisory.pdf.

Pink, D. (2009). *Drive: The Surprising Truth about What Motivates Us*. New York: Riverhead Books.

The Positivity Project. (n.d.). "Relationships, Character, Culture." https://posproject.org/.

Chapter 4

The Rise in Student Behavior Referrals and the Impact on the Social-Emotional Health of Teachers Post-Pandemic in Three Western New York High Schools

Salvatore Curella, Alan Ingraham, and Joshua Janese

The COVID-19 pandemic quickly forced significant changes to the instructional model for students starting in March 2020 through the conclusion of the 2020–2021 school year. These changes required the exclusive use of synchronous and asynchronous learning through digital platforms for students known as "remote learning." Other permissible forms of learning required students to attend in person on specific days of the week as well as engage in remote learning for the remaining portion of the week, known as "hybrid learning," to adhere to social distancing mandates. Despite the best effort from educators across the country, these nontraditional forms of learning superficially met the needs of students requiring academic, behavioral, or social-emotional support. As students reacclimated to full-time in-person schooling, building administrators and teachers began to notice a rise in behavior disruptions at the secondary level when compared to pre-pandemic norms.

Upon further investigation, research shows that special education students continue to receive more exclusionary behavior referrals than their general education peers at rates almost double of what is to be expected. Students with disabilities have faced a disproportionate rate of behavioral referrals across the country (U.S. Department of Education, 2014; U.S. Government Accountability Office, 2018). Evidence continues to mount confirming that special education students continue to be overrepresented in exclusionary discipline actions, which intensifies as students age through the education system (Green, Cohen, and Stormont 2019; Losen & Martinez, 2013). Finally, the COVID-19 pandemic has disrupted traditional school operations for students and staff from March of 2020 through the start of the 2021–2022 school year. Through our research, school district leaders should universally expect substantial student behavior and academic regression upon returning to traditional instruction.

Various research has shown that school closures due to snow days, holidays, and summer vacation can impact student progression due to the loss in instructional time. When this is compounded by longer periods of time due to environmental disasters like Hurricane Katrina, tornadoes, and earthquakes; impacts can be even more devastating. It is important that schools strategize how to successfully welcome students and staff back to traditional school settings to minimize the impacts on students socially, emotionally and academically.

One thing is for certain, ninth grade is frequently regarded as one of the most challenging years in a student's educational career. As such, schools need to consider ways to foster positive student-to-adult relationships within their buildings to help bridge the transition to high school, or a new school in general. When students make meaningful social connections with staff through a supportive and engaging academic environment, they are more likely to experience greater levels of long-term academic success than students who do not. One consequence of failing to make meaningful connections manifests in students receiving behavior referrals as they struggle to meet social and institutionalized norms.

Over the last two years, our research focused on the social-emotional health of high school students and teachers that has been impacted due to the change in instructional models from the COVID-19 pandemic. Historically, student social-emotional health plays a significant role in the behavior and academic achievement of students of all grade levels. For this reason, impacts from the school closure due to the pandemic can only potentially increase drop-out rates, credit loss, course failures, and behavior referrals.

The purpose of our study identified factors that have contributed to the drastic rise in student behavior referrals for ninth grade students in three high schools in Western New York when returning to in-person instruction after school closures due to the COVID-19 pandemic. Using a quantitative approach, data was collected on ninth-grade student behavior referrals, academic classification, and demographics, as well as teacher perceptions using a post-pandemic survey created by the researchers. The Post-Pandemic Teacher Perception survey examined 192 high school teacher responses across different schools analyzing responses by grade levels taught and student classification status.

In our findings, we could not identify specific factors associated with the rise in behavior referrals given our focus on teacher perceptions; however, results highlighted that all teachers, regardless of school, grade level, and student groups, described an increase in job-related stress and associated frustration managing student classroom behaviors. For teachers of students with disabilities, there was a twelve-point difference in reported levels of frustration compared to general education teachers in handling classroom behaviors. In addition, teachers of students with disabilities also felt less prepared than general education teachers to handle behavioral issues in their classroom. When understanding the adequacy of professional development offered post-pandemic, all teachers reported less value when compared to prior years. More specifically, teachers of students with disabilities reported lower levels of satisfaction with opportunities related to appropriately addressing student behaviors. All teachers regardless of students and grade level taught reported challenges in building positive relationships with students who are disengaged in the school community. Findings continued to reveal that teachers desire professional development offerings centered around improving student-teacher relationships and the belief that social-emotional learning, positive behavioral interventions and supports, and trauma-informed care will better prepare them in supporting students post-pandemic.

Teachers' social-emotional health and job-related stress was an important focus in our study, and because of this, our data resulted in all teachers feeling elevated levels of stress and frustration at work, particularly when addressing student misbehavior. This includes negative impacts on social-emotional health for all teachers. All teacher comparable groups also reported that they felt technology post-pandemic was making their job harder and more stressful.

Student-teacher relationships can have a significant impact on academic achievement and social-emotional development. To understand the connection between those relationships and the rise in behavior referral rates, our survey focused on understanding those relationships through student engagement, student-teacher communication, student attendance, and student behaviors during classroom instruction. Overall, the data from the survey suggested that students participate less in class, access their phone more frequently during instruction, and are more likely to speak with teachers through email versus in person regarding academic and behavioral performance. Additionally, teachers reported a rise in student absences and tardiness in the return to in-person instruction. This decreased level of engagement has shown to have a strong influence on students being able to develop a positive relationship with their school community, as well their outlook on academic achievement and social development through high school. The findings of this study also revealed teachers are more likely to write a behavior referral for students who are disrespectful to classmates, verbally argumentative to a staff member, or disruptive to the learning process. These behavior infractions can be rooted back to school engagement and a student's ability to build a positive relationship with their teacher and peers in the classroom.

Administrator support for the handling of student behavior plays an important role in the level of stress and frustration for teachers as well as the improvement of behavior for students. The results from the survey reflect positive perceptions with administrative action and follow-through when behavioral referrals are written. However, there is a belief among 65 percent of teachers that regardless of the grade level taught, harsher student consequences would change student behavior. It is expected that this is due to an increase in frustration for managing student behaviors in class and the recidivism rate for those students referred to administration.

When examining the professional development needs for teachers in the return to in-person instruction, social-emotional learning emerged as the unanimous choice for teachers of general and special education students. Closely following behind were positive behavior and intervention systems (PBIS), and trauma-informed care as the training most requested by teachers. Much like the research indicated, social-emotional practices and curricula serve as an important tool in addressing the social, behavioral, and academic needs of the students post-pandemic. Additionally, social-emotional learning practices also serve as a guide to reengage students in the school community and build positive relationships with their peers and teachers (Brown, Correll, & Stormer, 2022; Minkos & Gelber, 2020). Although restorative practices were one of the least requested trainings by general and special education teachers, our research shows that restorative justice can be very effective for students and staff that exhibit trauma following the pandemic (Brown, 2021). Due to this result, further research is needed to understand the reasons why teachers felt that restorative practices would not be beneficial for providing support in managing student behavior.

Additional findings (table 4.1) from our study show that professional development is available to teachers in all three high schools, but decreased in value during remote and hybrid learning and in the return to traditional instruction, especially for teachers who teach students with disabilities.

This finding is important as schools look to better understand how to provide teachers with the skills, knowledge, and support they need to create a positive and supportive classroom environment that can help promote positive behavior and improve student behavior and academic outcomes.

Although our problem of practice specifically recognizes both a disproportionate and increased behavior referral rate for ninth-grade students with disabilities when compared to the general education population, we feel that these recommendations can serve all students, regardless of their

Table 4.1. Perceptions of Professional Development by Student Classification Status by School

	School A		*School B*		*School C*		*Combined*	
	SWD	*Non SWD*	*SWD*	*Non SWD*	*SWD*	*Non SWD*	*SWD*	*Non SWD*
Professional development is available to me in my district	95.4	100.0	80.7	72.7	93.8	88.9	90.0	81.8
I regularly participate in professional development opportunities in my district	69.2	100.0	59.7	54.6	62.5	33.3	64.1	50.0
Professional development has been valuable to me prior to the pandemic	67.7	100.0	71.9	81.8	72.9	55.6	70.6	72.7
Professional development has been valuable to me during remote/hybrid instruction	67.7	50.0	59.7	81.8	64.6	22.2	64.1	54.6
Professional development has been valuable to me after the return to traditional instruction	66.2	100.0	54.4	72.7	41.7	0.0	55.3	45.5

From Curella, S. A., Ingraham, A. J., & Janese, J. R. (2023). "Addressing the Increase of Ninth Grade Behavior Referrals Post-Pandemic in Three Western New York High Schools (Order No. 30423592)." Available from Dissertations & Theses @ SUNY Buffalo. (2828633826). https://www.proquest.com/dissertations-theses/addressing-increase-ninth-grade-behavior/docview/2828633826/se-.

academic classification and grade level. Additionally, these recommendations also provide opportunities and support for all teachers, regardless of grade level and content area, in the areas of classroom management and social-emotional health.

Our first recommendation for managing the increase in student behavior following the pandemic is for educators and school leaders to consider prioritizing a school-wide social-emotional learning (SEL) approach. An approach in SEL can help students develop strong relationships with their teachers and peers, foster a positive and supportive learning environment, and promote student and teacher social-emotional health. It also can help students develop self-awareness, self-regulation, and empathy. Yang, Bear, and May (2018) explained that "for students to become motivated and engaged in school, their basic psychological needs for relatedness, competence, and autonomy must be fulfilled, which largely occurs in the context of positive relationships with peers and adults" (p. 47). Positive relationships are key to reducing behavior referrals, especially since the data from this study showed a strong correlation between school engagement and the behavior infractions most likely to be submitted as a referral. To understand the impacts of school engagement further, research has shown that decreased levels of school engagement are associated with a variety of negative behavioral outcomes that can result in behavior action.

Additionally, we learned that teachers' social-emotional health was negatively impacted during the pandemic in our research and findings. We also suggest that supporting the social-emotional health of teachers is essential to promoting a positive and healthy school environment. By providing teachers with the resources and support they need, we can help ensure that they are able to provide effective instruction and support for all students. This can be accomplished by providing training and professional development opportunities that focus on social-emotional learning and self-care strategies. Another important strategy to support teachers' social-emotional health is to provide counseling and mental health resources. Teachers can benefit from access to counseling and mental health resources, such as Employee Assistance Programs (EAPs) or on-site counseling services within the school or district. Providing these resources can help teachers address any mental health concerns they may have and promote positive social-emotional health.

Our second recommendation would be to foster a sense of community through positive relationships within the school and district. Many students reported feeling isolated during the pandemic, so creating a sense of community in the classroom and school can help them feel connected and supported. Educators can use strategies like morning meetings, class discussions, and team-building activities to help students connect with one another. These activities can be found using culturally responsive practices, which serve as a strong approach in the creation of community in a classroom setting, as well as supporting increased student engagement by allowing students to feel a sense of belonging regardless of their academic, cultural, and religious background. Although our findings suggested that restorative practices were not something teachers found value in, the research proves otherwise. Opportunities in restorative practices encourage students to build relationships, repair harm, and develop their personal identities. Future studies in understanding the tension between what research recommends versus what teachers value in their individual context could prove beneficial. In particular, more information is needed to understand what districts and school administrators can do to obtain teacher "buy-in" in proven programs to enhance and improve outcomes for students and teachers.

Lastly, based on the results from our data and research, we recognize the importance of providing teachers the necessary training and tools to manage student behavior in their classroom. Our data highlights that an overwhelming majority of teachers, specifically special education, do not feel they receive the necessary training to manage difficult behaviors in classrooms; this unfortunately results in additional referrals to administration. Survey responses indicate that this need is heightened for teachers who instruct ninth graders as well as those who teach students with disabilities (table 4.2).

Our recommendation is to provide training to teachers through programs such as Positive Behavior Interventions and Supports (PBIS) and Responsive Classroom (RS) for existing staff. For new staff members, it is recommended that these supports also be taught through each site's new teacher orientation or professional development program. PBIS is an evidence-based framework that focuses on creating positive school culture and preventing problem behaviors. PBIS also provides teachers with a set of strategies for preventing and addressing problem behavior. The framework focuses on teaching and reinforcing positive behaviors rather than punishing negative behaviors. The second resource for classroom management training, Responsive Classroom, is a comprehensive approach to classroom management that emphasizes building a positive classroom community, teaching social skills, and developing effective routines and procedures. This is especially important for special education students who often rely on routines and predictability to help them navigate their day. The pandemic disrupted those routines and many students have had to adjust to the new schedules and routines because of the changes in their school environment.

To connect the research to the findings, it is important to understand that prior to the COVID-19 impact, research showed that student absentee rates, behavior referrals and individual course failures are generally higher among ninth-grade students across public high schools in the country (Habeeb, 2013). Hapken (2016) believed that the increased workload and rigor of courses contributed to the challenges faced early on by ninth-grade students who entered high school with lower academic achievement rates or have prior academic and special education accommodations. We suggest future research on the evaluation of high school orientation programming for eighth-grade students entering high school, or new students entering the district post-pandemic. More specifically, how the challenges of the high school

Table 4.2. Perceptions of Administrative Support by Student Classification Status by School

	School A		*School B*		*School C*		*Combined*	
	SWD	*Non SWD*	*SWD*	*Non SWD*	*SWD*	*Non SWD*	*SWD*	*Non SWD*
Administrative support is adequate when writing a referral	66.2	50.0	54.4	81.8	83.3	77.8	67.1	77.3
Administrative response is appropriate for the behavior referral(s)	64.6	50.0	54.4	63.4	75.0	66.7	64.1	63.6
I am adequately supported to handle most student behaviors in my classroom	76.9	50.0	77.2	81.8	85.4	100.0	79.4	86.4
Harsher student consequences would change student behaviors	63.1	50.0	57.9	63.6	75.0	88.9	64.7	72.7
I contact administration more frequently regarding student behavior	30.8	100.0	26.3	45.5	41.7	22.2	32.4	40.9
Administration is progressive when handling student behavior	66.2	50.0	66.7	81.8	72.9	88.9	68.2	81.8
Administration provides adequate professional development opportunities to prepare me to handle student behaviors	35.4	50.0	29.8	63.6	45.8	55.6	36.5	59.1

From Curella, S. A., Ingraham, A. J., & Janese, J. R. (2023). "Addressing the Increase of Ninth Grade Behavior Referrals Post-Pandemic in Three Western New York High Schools (Order No. 30423592)." Available from Dissertations & Theses @ SUNY Buffalo. (2828633826). https://www.proquest.com/dissertations-theses/addressing-increase-ninth-grade-behavior/docview/2828633826/se-.

transition are compounded with the effects of the extended school closures. Our study did not investigate the orientation programs in the three high schools, but considered it to be an important factor that needs to be considered in addressing the increase in behavior referrals for ninth-grade students.

To summarize, the school closures due to the pandemic have changed high school students' academic and social experiences the past three years. These recommendations can help support a successful transition back to in-person instruction and promote the well-being and success of all students. Additionally, by providing support, professional development, and opportunities for self-care, it will mitigate the effects of stress and support all teachers' social and emotional wellness.

This quantitative study examined three similarly sized high schools in the Western New York area that experienced a significant increase in student behavior referrals for ninth graders during the 2021–2022 school year (table 4.3). The significant increase also includes a disproportionate increase in behavior referrals for students with disabilities (table 4.4). These increases were compared to the 2017–2018 and 2018–2019 school years prior to the transition of remote and hybrid instructional models. While our findings in our problem of practice were relevant and personal for our local contexts, the results can prove to be very informative in addressing similar issues in student behavior in other schools and districts.

Overall, the pandemic has had a significant impact on high school students' behavior, with many students experiencing disruptions to their academic, social, and personal lives. Additionally, our research and findings show that student and teacher experiences throughout the pandemic are important in understanding how school closures affect the learning, mental health, social development, and behavior of students. This study is limited to only one year after the return to school, so there is still much to be understood on the long-term impacts of the pandemic on our students and our school systems.

Table 4.3. Ninth-Grade Student Behavioral Referrals Pre-Pandemic vs. Post-Pandemic

	2017–2018	*2018–2019*	*2017–2018 2018–2019 Average*	*2021–2022*	*Percent Increase*
	Pre-Pandemic			*Post-Pandemic*	
School A	452	365	409	521	27.3%
School B	684	759	722	937	29.8%
School C	113	123	118	260	120.3%

From Curella, S. A., Ingraham, A. J., & Janese, I. R. (2023). "Addressing the Increase of Ninth Grade Behavior Referrals Post-Pandemic in Three Western New York High Schools (Order No. 30423592)." Available from Dissertations & Theses @ SUNY Buffalo. (2828633826). https://www.proquest.com/dissertations-theses/addressing-increase-ninth-grade-behavior/docview/2828633826/se-.

Table 4.4. Ninth-Grade Student with Disabilities Behavioral Referrals Pre-Pandemic vs. Post-Pandemic

	2017–2018	*2018–2019*	*2017–2018 2018–2019 Average*	*2017–2018 2018–2019 Average Ninth-Grade Classification Rate*	*2021–2022*	*2021–2022 Ninth-Grade Classification Rate*
	Pre-Pandemic				*Post-Pandemic*	
School A	89	55	72	10.5%	154	14.2%
School B	80	145	113	19.8%	264	21.0%
School C	25	38	32	11.6%	106	12.6%

From Curella, S. A., Ingraham, A. J., & Janese, J. R. (2023). "Addressing the Increase of Ninth Grade Behavior Referrals Post-Pandemic in Three Western New York High Schools (Order No. 30423592)." Available from Dissertations & Theses @ SUNY Buffalo. (2828633826). https://www.proquest.com/dissertations-theses/addressing-increase-ninth-grade-behavior/docview/2828633826/se-.

Our current data and research certainly provide a strong foundation in preparing and responding to similar events for the future, but it will be even more important for educators to continue to stay informed and provide support and resources for students to navigate these new challenges caused by the pandemic.

FINAL THOUGHTS

The COVID-19 pandemic has had profound academic and social-emotional impacts on high school students across the nation. Academically, students have faced disruptions in their learning routines, with shifts to remote or hybrid learning models resulting in varying levels of learning loss. Access to technology and resources has been uneven, exacerbating educational inequalities, especially for students with special needs. The isolation imposed by lockdowns and restrictions has taken a toll on students' social-emotional health, with increased rates of anxiety, depression, and stress. The disruption of normal social activities, such as extracurriculars and social gatherings, has impacted their sense of connection and belonging.

Furthermore, teachers have had to support students dealing with emotional challenges while managing their own stressors related to burnout, instructional preparedness, and the evolving educational landscape. The absence of in-person connections with colleagues and students, coupled with the pressures of delivering quality education during a crisis, has underscored the importance of providing teachers with the necessary support and resources to address students' academic and social-emotional well-being. Despite these hurdles, teachers have shown remarkable resilience, creativity, and dedication in their efforts to ensure students continue to learn and grow during these unprecedented times.

KEY PRAGMATIC LEADERSHIP TAKEAWAYS

- It is important that schools strategize how to successfully welcome students and staff back to traditional school settings to minimize the impacts on students socially, emotionally, and academically.
- All teachers, regardless of school, grade level, and student groups, described an increase in job-related stress and associated frustration managing student classroom behaviors following the return to in-person instruction.
- All teachers, regardless of students and grade level taught, reported challenges in building positive relationships with students who are disengaged in the school community.
- Findings continued to reveal that teachers desire professional development offerings centered around improving student-teacher relationships and the belief that social-emotional learning, positive behavioral interventions and supports, and trauma-informed care will better prepare them in supporting students post-pandemic.
- Data from the survey suggested that students participate less in class, access their phone more frequently during instruction, and are more likely to speak with teachers through email versus in person regarding academic and behavioral performance.
- An approach in SEL can help students develop strong relationships with their teachers and peers, foster a positive and supportive learning environment, and promote student and teacher social-emotional health.
- The overwhelming majority of teachers, specifically special education, do not feel they receive the necessary training to manage difficult behaviors in classrooms.

REFERENCES

Brown, C., Correll, P., & Stormer, K. J. (2022). "The 'New' Normal: Re-Imagining Professional Development amidst the COVID-19 Pandemic." *Middle School Journal 52*(5), 5–13. https://doi.org/10.1080/00940771.2021.1978787.

Brown, M. A. (2021). "We Cannot Return to 'Normal': A Post-COVID Call for a Systems Approach to Implementing Restorative Justice in Education." *RJE Laws 10*(3), 68–https://doi.org/10.3390/laws10030068.

Green, A. L., Cohen, D. R., & Stormont, M. (2019). "Addressing and Preventing Disproportionality in Exclusionary Discipline Practices for Students of Color with Disabilities." *Intervention in School and Clinic 54*(4), 241–45.

Habeeb, S. (2013). "The Ninth-Grade Challenge." *Education Digest 79*(3), 19–25.

Hapken, K. (2016). "Why Capable Students Fail in 9th Grade: The Author's District-Level Study Identifies the Barriers before Sparking New Support Measures." *School Administrator 73*(7), 24–27.

Losen, D. J., & Martinez, T. E. (2013). "Out of School and off Track: The Overuse of Suspension in American Middle and High Schools." The Civil Rights Project at UCLA, The Center for Civil Rights Remedies.

Minkos, M. L., & Gelbar, N. W. (2021). "Considerations for Educators in Supporting Student Learning in the Midst of COVID-19." *Psychology in the Schools 58*(2), 416–26. https://doi.org/10.1002/pits.22454.

U.S. Department of Education Office for Civil Rights (2014). "Civil Rights Data Collection. Data Snapshot: School Discipline." Issue Brief No. 1. https://eric.ed.gov/?id=ED577231.

U.S. Government Accountability Office. (2018). *Discipline Disparities for Black Students, Boys, and Students with Disabilities Report*. https://www.gao.gov/assets/700/690828.pdf.

Yang, C., Bear, G. G., & May, H. (2018). "Multilevel Associations between School-Wide Emotional Learning Approach and Student Engagement across Elementary, Middle, and High Schools." *School Psychology Review 47*(1), 45–61. https://doi.org/10.17105/SPR-2017–0003.V47-1.

Chapter 5

A Practicing Middle School Principal's Approaches in Creating and Delivering a Culture for Social-Emotional Learning

Pete Dobmeier

On Sunday, March 15, 2020, in the middle of a birthday party for my sister-in-law, I was called over to the television and learned from a press conference that there would be no school the next day. While snow days are not uncommon in our region (even as we approach spring), it was sunny outside and there were no flurries in the forecast. There was not a power outage or a water main break. Schools across the county and state (and soon the nation) would be closed due to concerns regarding the spread of the Coronavirus. As a middle school principal, it all seemed very abstract to me. As I exchanged text messages with colleagues and waited for communication from our central office regarding next steps, the majority of us came to the conclusion that, at most, we would be out of school for a week or a few weeks.

Of course, we now know that the return to normalcy would not span weeks, but years. During this time, school would look very different. As educators, and as people living through COVID-19, we would struggle to wrap our arms around an adversary that seemingly changed shape and wriggled free each time we thought we had it in our grasp. There was no playbook or roadmap to follow, and we all regularly experienced moments of disorientation.

What follows is a discussion of how one middle school found its way during the pandemic. It reflects our work to navigate a school community through constant change by tying ourselves to a few "north stars" that guided us on the pathway to building a culture focused on social-emotional learning and connection. What we learned changed us as a school and as individuals.

REORIENTING OUR THINKING

The middle school was part of a suburban school district with a history of strong community support and engaged families and students, and it regularly achieved a high ranking in local publications for the academic achievement of our students. This was a district that prided itself on character education and the development of the whole child.

In the years preceding the pandemic, as a district and as a building, the district and school had begun to explore key elements of social-emotional learning (SEL) and vehicles for infusing SEL practices (mindfulness, direct instruction in SEL competencies, restorative practices, and community circles) into its schools. A significant portion of teachers, counselors, and administrators who were so inclined attended professional development sessions in these areas and were sporadically implementing these practices in their schools and classrooms. Regardless of the level of staff members' engagement in SEL practices, there was common agreement that these ideas were "good for kids," but there was not universal commitment to implementing them across the board as part of daily practice. There did not seem to be a true sense of urgency, as many within the school and district leaned heavily on its record of academic success as the primary indicator that they were successfully achieving all parts of its educational mission. This changed when COVID became part of everyone's lives.

In the weeks and months following the school shutdown on March 16, 2020, these ideas related to the importance of social-emotional learning and building connection quickly moved from being abstract philosophical concepts or "add-ons" to concretely essential to the survival of our school community. As COVID took hold and we surrendered the safe, controlled settings of our classrooms to laptops and virtual learning in varied home environments, we quickly recognized that we needed to orient ourselves and our students around some core human principles before any academic learning could occur. Along the way, as our staff learned to take better care of our students, we realized that we were taking better care of each other as well.

North Star #1—Moving from Transaction to Interaction

In the weeks following the initial school shutdown, our district and school implemented a plan that relied on virtual, asynchronous learning for our students. Teachers posted materials online that students could access through their devices, and students could submit work electronically to their teachers. Teachers, students, and parents corresponded via email to pose and answer questions or provide assistance. In a time when all of us (students, families, and staff) were struggling with the reality of being physically separated from one another, this initial way of doing school felt very transactional. We recognized that we needed to take intentional steps toward moving from transaction, or conducting business, to interaction, something more reciprocal and sustaining.

We held regular virtual meetings with our faculty and staff to discuss how things were progressing, listened to feedback, built community and positivity, and continually considered better ways to reach our students and families. All expressed difficulty connecting with and engaging students academically, and all felt something was missing. We recognized that we needed to work together to bring interaction back into the picture.

Our first step involved giving teachers permission to elevate the importance of the nonacademic work they did with students. In our regular meetings, we continually emphasized that grades and output were not as essential as building and sustaining relationships with students and families. With all that our students and families were experiencing, we knew that they would more likely remember how they were treated and supported than the content they were expected to learn at the time. We adopted the following approaches:

- **Personalizing communication:** We encouraged teachers to work with our school counselors to make phone calls to families rather than send emails.
- **Individual supports and office hours:** All teachers established virtual office hours where students could participate in one-on-one meetings to ask questions or get help with their classes. Very quickly, all of us recognized that many students were more interested in talking with their teachers, introducing their pets, and seeing their friends than getting actual academic help. As a result, we kept these office hours and also built in homeroom experiences where students could simply interact with one another and their teachers.
- **Maintaining connection, visibility, and a sense of humor:** We used video announcements as a way to keep families and students connected and informed. Staff members and students submitted videos to share updates on their lives during the shutdown—everything from students conducting home science experiments to a staff member attempting to squirrel-proof his birdfeeder and sharing the entertaining results.

  Each week, I invited students to submit their best jokes. Every Friday, I would publish a video message from my house or my backyard to give updates, reinforce a key theme, and present the winning jokes of the week. Each video ended with the message, "We hope you are well. We love you, and we can't wait to see you soon."

- **Bringing school to home:** A number of faculty members took communication a step further and made prearranged home visits to meet with students through a screen door or talk outside. This was a transformative experience for both the students and the faculty who visited them. It had such an impact that we adopted this approach as a way to recognize our eighth-grade students who would be moving on to high school with no opportunity for formal recognition. With the help of our PTSA, a team of teachers, counselors, and administrators had class shirts and bags produced for our eighth graders and delivered them to families in-person to recognize them for their time at our middle school.

As the year came to a close, we looked for opportunities to bring our families back onto campus in a way that allowed us to connect one more time in person. Through the work of our dedicated faculty, we were able to host a reverse car parade for all of our families and students. They were encouraged to decorate their cars and parade through the campus as our faculty and staff turned out to cheer them on. The joy of reconnecting with our students again did as much for us as it did for our students and families.

In our final faculty meeting of the year, we were still facing uncertainty regarding how the next school year would look. We attempted to draft plans for multiple scenarios: a full return to school, a fully virtual program, some form of a hybrid program. Whatever the model was, we had seen the benefits of the improvised opportunities for interaction we had imbedded in the prior months, and knew we would need to systematize a way to maintain this regardless of the learning model. We also knew that, more than ever, we would need to attend more directly to our students' social-emotional needs in the coming school year.

North Star #2—Building a Homegrown SEL Program

As the school year came to a close in June of 2020 and we reflected on the range of need we observed in our students during the school closure, we recognized that it was our responsibility to provide a guaranteed, viable SEL experience for all of our students. A group of teachers, counselors, a social worker, and building leaders formulated a team to make this a reality during the summer of 2020. The team established criteria for what this homegrown program would look like.

- **It would need to be research-based.** We identified the work of the Collaborative for Academic, Social, and Emotional Learning (CASEL) as a resource that clearly articulated the social-emotional competencies we hoped to build in our students. These included self-awareness, self-management, social awareness, relationship skills, and responsible decision-making.

- **It would need to be suited for any learning model.** Because there was no clear picture of how school would look in the fall of 2020, we had to develop a program that would function in a fully in-person, fully remote, or hybrid structure.
- **It would need to incorporate authentic interaction.** During the shutdown in the spring of 2020, we had witnessed how the intentional pursuit of interaction had positively affected both our students and staff. We knew that this would need to be a component of an effective SEL program at our school. We saw the value of preexisting SEL programs, but recognized the need for something that felt more authentic and interactive and that resonated with our existing culture.
- **It would need to be executed by staff members, regardless of their level of training and expertise in SEL.** While we were able to train all of our faculty in facilitating community circles at the conclusion of the 2020 school year, there was a broad range in the level of additional training and practice individual faculty members had in SEL competencies and SEL instruction. We would need to create programming that allowed the teacher to be a participant in the learning with students, not the "content specialist" role that many had been accustomed to playing.

With these criteria in mind, the group met virtually multiple times during the summer of 2020. We facilitated meetings of the whole group to set goals and create a common structure for how we would deliver the program to reflect each CASEL competency. The team also broke into smaller groups, with each group focused on generating materials for one competency. What resulted was a series of multi-day experiences, or modules, for students centered around each SEL competency. Each module contained common elements:

- **Community circle activities:** Students were provided with daily opportunities to check in and rate how they were feeling. They then responded to a series of questions or prompts using the community circle structure. Each of the prompts tied to the competency that was the focus of the day (e.g., self-awareness or relationship skills), and provided a way for students to reflect on their level of understanding of the competency, tying it to their personal experiences. Because all faculty had been trained in community circles previously, they were able to begin facilitating these experiences with little preparation and were able to participate in the discussions just as the students did. In a number of cases, students had grown familiar enough with the format that they began facilitating the circle discussions themselves.

- **The use of story:** Each module featured film clips, videos, or short stories that demonstrated the competency. In some cases, these were examples of people demonstrating the skill and finding success as a result. In other cases, these were examples of people failing to put the skill into the action with negative, and often comical, consequences. The goal was to have students connect each SEL competency to a familiar story. Again, the faculty member's role was to watch the video with the students, pose some questions that the team had developed, and simply be a participant in the discussion.
- **Self-evaluation and goal setting tools for students:** Over the course of each module, students were provided with multiple opportunities to assess and discuss their level of development in relation to each competency. Once participating in these reflections, students were afforded the opportunity to set personal goals related to their strengths and weaknesses in each area.

Upon developing the content and resources for our program, we also recognized that there would need to be some structural changes to ensure it was successful. We made plans to extend the length of our homeroom period and worked to reassign staff to cut the size of our homerooms in half (from an average of twenty-five students to an average of twelve or thirteen students). This way, every student and teacher in the building would have dedicated time and opportunity to focus on interaction and social-emotional learning.

The start of the 2020–2021 school year was rocky, as our district learning model shifted multiple times in August and September, with us eventually landing on a Hyflex Hybrid Model. In this model, some students opted to remain fully virtual, but most students attended school in person two days a week and tuned in for synchronous virtual instruction two days a week. On Wednesdays, all students were scheduled for virtual homeroom period, participated in asynchronous virtual learning activities for each of their classes, and had the option of attending virtual office hours or extra academic support sessions with teachers.

There were points during the year where the district had to go fully remote due to local infection rates. No matter the learning model, we were able to provide students with an SEL experience that worked in person or virtually, and the extended homeroom periods on Wednesdays provided an opportunity for additional SEL time, as well as time for less structured interaction, as teachers used the Wednesday homeroom periods to play interactive games and do community-building activities with students.

A few months into the school year, when we saw that some students were in need of more connection and attention, we added individual conferencing to homeroom periods. Teachers regularly cycled through their homeroom students to meet one-on-one to simply ask how students were doing and what they needed. This gave students the opportunity to share feelings or ask questions that they may not have been comfortable bringing forward in the community circle setting.

When the learning model shifted again to full-time in-person attendance in the spring of 2021, with our smaller homeroom structure and clearly developed SEL resources, we were able to continue this work with our full-time students and the fraction of students who had remained fully virtual.

In our regular meetings with our faculty to discuss how they and our students were progressing, teachers shared that they felt that the program had truly helped our students navigate their unique situations during the year and that their homerooms were becoming small, tightly-knit communities. Teachers also shared that they noticed their students treated them differently, with more kindness and compassion than usual. It was clear that the teachers' willingness to be part of the discussions, show vulnerability, and learn alongside the students had humanized them in the student's eyes. The unintended consequence of working to improve the lives of our students was that this work did just as much for our faculty.

Having had the opportunity to collaborate with colleagues outside of their grade levels and content areas, the faculty members that participated in the meaningful work of building our SEL program during the summer of 2020 had also formed new bonds. They were elevated in the eyes of their colleagues as leaders and resources in achieving our goals related to interaction and social-emotional learning.

A couple of months into the 2021–2022 school year, a group of students approached one of our school counselors about starting a student SEL club named for our therapy dog, Cosmo. Students began their own meaningful work of building a variety of resources for their classmates, including an interactive SEL landing page featuring our therapy dog, videos, and a weekly newsletter article with SEL-related advice from Cosmo.

North Star #3—Unifying the Entire School Community through Meaningful Work

As was the case in communities across the nation during the pandemic, our school community was divided at times over what was best for our students. With the stops and starts of in-person, fully remote, and hybrid learning, the appreciation many had shown during the initial pause in the spring of 2020 was giving way to impatience and frustration. There was a need to bring positivity, unity, and a sense of perspective and purpose back into the community.

Over the course of the 2020–2021 school year, several committees emerged across the district to help us navigate all aspects of the pandemic. One committee, comprised mainly of assistant principals, district administrators, and student leaders, was tasked with finding creative way of engaging and unifying our students and community. The group landed on the idea of a service project that would include all thirteen schools in our district. The focus would be on partnering with a larger organization to involve all parts of our community in meaningful work that would grant the wishes of six children with serious medical needs in our community.

Representatives from all thirteen schools met regularly to plan the project, and our assistant principal took the lead in our building, meeting regularly with students and staff. Both the district committee and our building committee relied heavily on the input of student leaders to design the activities, fundraising campaigns, and experiences that would be part of the project. The group established criteria for the campaign:

- **Participation and accessibility for all students and families:** Every student and family needed to have the opportunity to support or be part of the fundraising campaign, even if it did not involve contributing funds.
- **Engagement of the broader community:** The goal would be not only to include families in the district, but the larger community, local businesses and organizations.
- **Collaboration with existing district groups and student leadership:** Each building hosted clubs and organizations that would play a role in contributing ideas and executing aspects of the campaign, including Wellness committees, a Superintendent's Inter-High Council, Student Government groups, and the PTSA.
- **An instructional component focused on core themes and social-emotional learning:** We recognized that there would be great value in framing this project as a learning experience. The timing worked perfectly, as we saw an opportunity to link this service project with key elements of the SEL program we had developed and put into place at the beginning of the school year.

Over the course of several months, students generated a hash tag, slogan, and logo for the campaign. We were able to open an online store with merchandise featuring the student-generated slogan and logo. A teacher in our building who had recently published a children's book donated all of the proceeds from her book sales to the campaign. Local businesses and restaurants hosted community events and donated proceeds to the campaign. Schools facilitated socially distanced events for families including virtual trivia nights, drive-in movies, and community walks.

Each school building also produced a video to highlight a core theme of the program to be shared throughout the district. These themes included teamwork, compassion, service, perseverance, diversity/social awareness, kindness, mindfulness, and making connections. At our building, we were able to incorporate these videos into our SEL homeroom experiences to make a concrete connection between the SEL competencies and the value of this service project.

One element of the campaign involved the sale of stars for a nominal amount of money to staff, students, families, and local businesses that could be placed in their front yards, in front of schools, or storefronts. This endeavor raised funds for a good cause, but more importantly, provided a visual reminder throughout the community that we were united and doing meaningful work centered on something that was purely good. It was what all of us needed at that time. The campaign was a success, raising over $110,000 for our six children with serious illnesses. Just as valuable, it provided a peak moment that taught our students and community about the value of empathy and the collective power we have to make positive change.

FINAL THOUGHTS

The pandemic shined a light on some truths that have always been present in our hearts as educators. With the frenzied pace of our daily pre-pandemic work, our focus on fulfilling requirements and meeting mandates, it had become too easy for these truths to lie dormant within each of us. The abrupt, disruptive, and disorienting change in our schools served as a call for us to reevaluate our priorities in education, and it is my hope that this leads to a sustained awakening in the way we move forward. Here is what we learned and carried with us on the path forward:

- **Attending to our students' social-emotional needs and the pursuit of genuine interaction in our schools cannot be left to chance.** By and large, our system of public education, especially at the middle and high school levels, is set up for efficiency through transaction. The pandemic forced us to recognize that we play a much more important role than that of experts who sort and categorize students based on their productivity and compliance. With the challenges that we saw so many of our students facing in their home environments and the isolation we all experienced, it has never been more apparent that schools must work to build supportive and intentional structures centered on engaging and developing good humans, not just good students.

- **Making schools more humane places benefits everyone.** Multiple times throughout the pandemic, we saw evidence of extra humanity in action. It began with us as building leaders shifting our focus from *how much work* our teachers were doing to *how they were doing*, and continued with teachers learning to give grace and making the same shift with students. It involved being more intentional about creating a structure and system where it was OK to invest time in simply seeing if we were all OK.

  It involved the willingness of adults to model vulnerability and learn side-by-side with students, and it led to the adults being even more esteemed in the eyes of their students. It helped all of us find meaning and feel connection. While the pandemic confused us, pushed us to our limits, and forced us into physical separation, it also taught us about the important work that must be done to preserve community. I hope that is a lesson we in education never forget.

KEY PRAGMATIC LEADERSHIP TAKEAWAYS

The development and implementation of a middle-level SEL program in the midst of the pandemic taught us leadership principles that can help any school or organization navigate change at any time. They include:

- Determine your vision and connect it to a moral purpose.
- Assess and understand the talent in the room, and put it to use.
- Engage the community, including the people you serve. Their ideas might be better than yours.
- Listen before doing, but don't wait too long to begin doing.
- Remove barriers to implementation by allowing some to be learners until they can be teachers.
- Be prepared to reevaluate and change existing structures.
- Give people the opportunity to share and celebrate what they have accomplished.

A POSTSCRIPT: A PATH SHIFTED

Just as the pandemic altered the trajectory of this middle school and district, it altered the trajectory of the principal working there. There was always a need for schools at all levels to unapologetically and intentionally elevate the importance of social-emotional learning—the pandemic simply exposed this.

In experiencing this firsthand, I recognized that, as an educational leader, I needed to unapologetically and intentionally lead with relationships, interaction over transaction, and social-emotional learning at the center, and that the best place to do this would be at the ground level, with elementary students and teachers. As a result, I am now the principal of an elementary school where we begin each day with SEL experiences for students, and I teach SEL lessons with our school counselor and classroom teachers on a regular basis. Here, social-emotional learning is not an "add-on." It is what we do every day.

While many of us in education can feel overwhelmed by initiatives, curricular shifts, and the harried pace of life within a school, SEL is something that we as educators, can no longer acknowledge with a brief head nod and a dismissive, "I already do that." Our students and communities are counting on us.

REFERENCES

Collaborative for Academic, Social, and Emotional Learning (CASEL). (2022). *Fundamentals of SEL.* CASEL. https://casel.org/.

Fullan, M. (2001). *Leading in a Culture of Change*. San Francisco, CA: Jossey-Bass.

Heath, C., & Heath, D. (2017). *The Power of Moments.* New York: Simon & Schuster.

Maxwell, J. C. (2022). *The 21 Irrefutable Laws of Leadership*. Nashville, TN: Harper Collins Leadership.

Chapter 6

Intentionally Shattering Silos

Fostering Collaboration and Belonging to Support Well-Being in Schools

Monica J. VanHusen, Daniel Reichard, and Julie Zook

In the bustling corridors of K–12 educational organizations, a pervasive challenge looms large—organizational silos. These silos, whether physical or not, act as formidable barriers, obstructing the vital flow of collaboration and connectivity among the diverse roles within the educational landscape. In this intricate web of learning and development, knowledge often remains confined, withheld from those who need it most for the success of their roles. This problem extends beyond the mere structures of bricks and mortar; it delves into the very essence of how educational institutions function.

These silo structures can significantly shape perceptions related to safety, well-being, and belongingness, ultimately influencing the learning environment and its effectiveness (Maslow, 1943). However, in the post-Covid era of the twenty-first century, school building and district leaders must develop an intentional focus on dismantling traditional silos in order to enhance multiple learning environments that reflect a more wholistic "high-touch" interdisciplinary approach based on the educational interests and needs of the "whole student."

Congdon, Flynn, and Redman (2014) aptly explore the purpose of collaboration, emphasizing the need for spaces that accommodate both individual focus and collective gatherings. Task complexity, often synonymous with cognitive load, task scale, or time constraints, necessitates flexibility in the use of physical spaces (Congdon, Flynn, & Redman, 2014). Yet, even when physical silos are broken down there can still remain silos within departments and schools. Woolner, Thomas, and Tiplady (2018) reinforce the idea that changes in the physical environment serve as a catalyst for broader transformation, but real change is sustained and institutionalized only through the dedicated efforts of leadership within the school setting.

Leadership, in its multifaceted form, plays a pivotal role in breaking down these silos. Principals, teachers, and central office departments all share the responsibility of fostering collaboration and connectivity among various roles, thus nurturing well-being within the organization. Many organizational theorists emphasize the importance of culture and mindset changes over structural alterations.

Senge (2006), for instance, elaborates on the five disciplines of a learning organization, which are systems thinking, personal mastery, mental models, shared vision, and team learning. All of which is needed to be present for an educational institution to thrive and be a place that can blossom through the ebb and flow of educational policy and change. Fullan (2008), in his work *The Six Secrets of Change*, places the onus on leaders to initiate and sustain change, underscoring the critical role they play in creating conditions conducive to change. Focusing on the physical spaces of an organization where silos can occur is important, but not the only factor of why silos occur.

As Rosalynn Carter once said, “A leader takes people where they want to go. A great leader takes people where they don’t want to go, but ought to be.” In the context of education, a great leader is one who weaves a comprehensive web of support, knowledge, vision, and information, bridging the gaps that silos create, alleviating stress, and nurturing a culture of social-emotional well-being, both within physical spaces and the digital realm.

This chapter explores how leaders within an educational organization combat the building of silos and engage in managing collaboration and belongingness to help promote educator well-being. It also provides actionable steps that leaders can take to initiate change and break down these silos, promoting collaboration and fostering a shared sense of purpose. Throughout this exploration, we emphasize the importance of trust in building relationships, nurturing well-being, and ultimately transforming the educational landscape for the better.

SILO-HERO MENTALITY

Looking into educational organizations, we are confronted with the concealed partitions known as “silos,” and their far-reaching effects on educators and students. Silos within organizations are a common occurrence stemming from factors like organizational structure, differing cultures and priorities, internal competition, a lack of trust, and technological barriers (Ashkanasy, Ayoko, & Jehn, 2014). One such factor is known as the silo-hero model.

As stated by Molek, de Jager, and Pucelj (2023), organizational cultures that reward heroic behavior, and prioritize individual performance over collaboration and teamwork can hinder positive organizational growth and healthy team identity. This can lead to leadership making it a norm to foster compartmentalization and a silo-hero mentality. Different departments or groups within an organization become excessively fixated on their individual objectives, withholding valuable information and knowledge from their peers in the same institution (Molek, de Jager, & Pucelj, 2023).

While this silo-hero mentality may have worked for past organizations, within a post-COVID-19 workplace the silo-hero model mentality can hinder organizational performance. Silos do not nurture a growth mindset. Highly resistant to change, silos block easy access to the information they hold, thwarting positive change and progress across K–12 schools and districts (Owens, 2017). The adverse effects, such as reduced efficiency, poor decision-making, communication problems, diminished innovation, and low morale among employees can negatively impact student learning by hindering a well-rounded education and limiting teacher collaboration.

In addition to the factors contributing to the existence of silos in educational organizations, it's essential to acknowledge the unique challenges that educational institutions face. The nature of education often involves a multitude of stakeholders, each with their own distinct goals and priorities. Despite all attempts to integrate stakeholder needs into the organization's goals, stakeholders get caught up in attempts to satisfy their more parochial needs and in the process form coalitions with others who have similar aspirations (Hoy & Miskel, 2013, p. 247).

Teachers, administrators, students, parents, and even community members all have a vested interest in the educational process. This complex web of relationships can sometimes exacerbate the formation of silos, as various groups may inadvertently work in isolation, each pursuing their specific objectives. Moreover, the top-down hierarchies and regulatory frameworks common in education can further entrench siloed thinking. These factors underscore the need for educational leaders to actively address and dismantle silos, promoting a culture of collaboration and belongingness for the benefit of both educators and students.

TEACHERS INTENTIONALLY CULTIVATING A CULTURE OF BELONGING

From the minute an educator steps foot in a new learning space, their mind is flooded with questions about what others will think of them as a human and teacher and whether or not there is a place for them in the school ecosystem. This need for belonging and the feeling and acknowledgment that others believe in their capacity to be successful is something shared by students entering their classrooms at the start of the academic year (Ryan & Deci, 2017).

One of the challenges posed by silos in education is the need to cultivate a culture of belonging. Much can be learned from the physical, psychological, and emotional safety teachers and administrators intentionally and relentlessly work to develop over the course of an academic year for the students they serve. How can we extend these practices and intentions to ensure that all teachers feel a profound sense of belonging within the educational community? To address this question, we offer you the opportunity to step into the remarkable story of a teacher who left an indelible mark on one of the authors of this chapter.

Mr. Nesta, the subject of our narrative, embodies the essential actions and behaviors required to cultivate a deep sense of belonging between teachers and their students. As you delve into his story, we challenge you, the reader, to discover the actionable elements that are instrumental in creating a nurturing environment of belonging in education leading to breaking down silos in education.

Dan's Story of Belonging in High School

At school, Dan was the most timid and shy student who walked the halls of a high school in rural Pennsylvania. He lacked a lot of confidence, struggling to understand what he was reading and learning how to skillfully form sounds contributed to this lack of confidence. It wasn't until his chorus teacher began working with Dan that everything changed for Dan in his educational journey. Mr. Fran Nesta was his chorus teacher from seventh until twelfth grade. Mr. Nesta believed in the positive transformative power that relationships can hold in education. He worked to always ask Dan about how he was doing, was interested in his hobbies outside of school, and always spent that extra minute talking to Dan when he probably had other work to finish. He made his hundreds of students feel this same way. He made them feel they belonged in the classroom space of his school. Mr. Nesta encouraged Dan to try out for the school musical, The Music Man. *Dan was given a minor role as a townsperson. The moment that mattered happened a couple of nights before the show. The entire cast was engaged in the "gym" of River City in the middle of a giant*

> *brawl. Mr. Nesta was looking for someone to stand up and yell at the top of their lungs, "STOP!" He looked at Dan and said, "Dan, I need you to stand up on that chair and put an end to this brawl." In a crowd of eighty of his peers, Dan tried a couple of times and then after a little bit of caring positive looks and verbal encouragement from his teacher, he got up and screamed, "STOP!" and the cast cheered.*
>
> *That single moment changed Dan's life. It only happened because Mr. Nesta believed in Dan. He intentionally created the conditions, over time, for this event to take place. He made Dan feel that he belonged and that he could accomplish actions in front of others.*
>
> *It was in that moment that Dan realized every last interaction we have, every high five, hug, or handshake, every note of encouragement, each conversation we have before or after class, every second chance we grant, our attendance in the stands at a game, as well as our concerns when something doesn't quite seem right matters to others, especially students in our care.*
>
> *All of those things matter because they're investments over time, adding up to a sense of belonging, self-belief, and the sense that we're part of something bigger than ourselves.*

Mr. Nesta's approach and creation of a culture of belonging inspired Dan to become a teacher. Upon graduation from Keystone Junior-Senior High School in 2008, Dan obtained his bachelor's degree in K–6 Elementary Education and began his own education leadership career serving as a third- and fifth-grade teacher for nine years. He devoted each moment of his time in the classroom to ensure his students had their "stand on the chair moment" to unleash the confidence to be their full self. Dan's efforts in the classroom led him to be recognized for his innovative teaching techniques and creation of a strong classroom community leading to high student achievement at the local, state, and national levels. Dan now works to cultivate the next generation of teachers for a large school division in Virginia. He is regularly called upon to speak at the local, state, and national levels on topics including cultivating beginning teacher talent, innovating within the classroom, and building strong classroom communities. Mr. Nesta's intentional strategies and cultivation of belonging led to the success Dan experiences today.

Mr. Nesta's approach to empowering his students holds a crucial lesson for leaders aiming to break down silos in educational institutions. He understood that fostering a sense of belonging and collaboration required empowering individuals within the collective. This empowerment was a deliberate process, encompassing several elements that connect directly to breaking down silos. He maintained a clear vision of his classroom and helped focus his students every day on the task at hand. When leaders bring new educators on board each year, it is paramount that the vision and mission are provided with such "real-classroom-world" actionable examples more than just statements placed on a poster on the wall.

For the thousands of students who had Mr. Nesta as their junior/senior high school chorus teacher, each student knew they were working to become the best versions of themselves in his class through music. Yes, Mr. Nesta's students were singing and learning how to harmonize and make beautiful pieces of music come to life, but he modeled, provided feedback, and constantly invested in the building of confidence and the creation of a sense of family and team via his personal interactions with his students.

Mr. Nesta intentionally harnessed the strengths of each of his hundreds of students each year to help the chorus achieve its mission and help each person become the human they dreamed of being. He was a master of pulling a small group aside, talking to a student after class, or pulling a student from study hall to ensure each of his students knew, understood, and could explain how they fit into the bigger picture of the chorus. He ensured that all of his individual students were all moving along the path toward the larger communal goal. This is due to the fact that Mr. Nesta internalized his educational mission in such an interpersonal manner that his work with students reflected the students' current realities and facilitated the accomplishment of their personal visions via achieving individual small goals that provided impetus for future accomplishments (Fullan, 2007). When everyone comprehends the overarching goals and their role within the institution, it becomes easier to unite diverse departments and stakeholders, thus, breaking down silos in educational institutions.

Mr. Nesta knew he couldn't do it alone. He methodically and intentionally empowered his students one by one. This required ensuring they knew and understood the vision/mission, could see where they fit into the greater whole of his class, watched his daily modeling, and received his messages of belief over time. His students became the humans he knew they could be due to this unflappable belief in the capacity of his students. Leaders have the same great power. To ensure all educators feel seen, heard, loved, and empowered in their school community in order to effectively break down silos and create "authentic learning communities" for all.

SCHOOL LEADERS BREAKING DOWN SILOS VIA FIVE PRINCIPLES OF INTENTIONAL LEADERSHIP

Intentional Leadership principles serve as a crucial framework for K–12 school leaders who aim to break down silos and foster collaboration, connection, communication, and clarity among their staff members. By aligning their leadership practices with the tenets of Intentional Leadership, school leaders can create an environment that not only reduces uncertainty but also prioritizes the emotional well-being of staff during periods of change. In the context of school leadership, the principles below are particularly effective in ensuring that all members of the school community come together regularly to work cohesively, reduce organizational barriers, and enhance staff morale and well-being.

Julie's Story of Intentionally Building Leadership to Promote Belonging for Faculty

Julie was a second-year principal, working in a middle school made up of 750 students and approximately ninety staff members, including sixty classroom teachers. The school's instructional program was taught in a seven-period-per-day schedule. Students attended all classes, every day, for approximately fifty minutes per class. During the fall of 2002, discussions began around the idea of moving to a schedule where students attended four classes per day with each class lasting approximately ninety minutes. Students would have science one semester and social studies the other. The research showed that this was a more effective academic schedule for middle school students.

It was clear to Julie, early on, that she would have to get the majority of her staff on board with this change. Staff were not shy about sharing their concerns and worries about this new schedule. Some of the concerns she heard were: "How do I teach for ninety minutes? How will the kids handle a ninety-minute block of time? We can't teach the whole science curriculum in one semester. What about student behaviors? I have to see my students every day. Every other day won't work as they will forget the material I am teaching." Julie began to think strategically and move forward intentionally to ensure that silos were not created during this significant organizational change based on contemporary research. Julie took the time to listen to the concerns and began to think through what she would do to address these concerns. The first decision was that the 2002–2003 school year would be spent planning for the new schedule. The staff members were provided the needed time to learn, process, and prepare for the new schedule. Julie identified a team of staff members who would visit three to four schools that were already teaching in a similar block schedule. The team of teachers was strategically chosen, and included some teachers who were excited about the change and others who were skeptical. She recalls specifically including her art teacher who was a strong, effective, and well-loved teacher, but one who could not see how this new schedule would work for his program. After all the visits were made, Julie and the team members discussed and processed what was learned and the data they gathered was shared with the entire school staff.

Julie also created time to meet with teachers who wanted to talk about the details and process their concerns with her. She listened, reassured, reminded them of their strengths and abilities and talked with them about the challenges that change can bring to us as humans. The following are some of the intentional practices that were implemented:

- *open and transparent communication with staff;*
- *opportunities for staff to process and ask questions;*
- *creating a cross-curricular/cross-grade-level team;*
- *schedule time for staff to process and discuss;*
- *provide time to visit schools that had implemented a similar schedule;*
- *a full year to plan and prepare for the new schedule.*

Julie worked hard to create a staff that was ready and excited for the new instructional schedule. She paid attention to their emotional needs and kept watch on the stress level of her teachers. She ensured that teachers were provided the time and space to discuss the changes and participate in some of the decision-making. By identifying a team of teachers to visit schools and work together to share information with the staff, she was breaking down barriers by bringing staff from different grade levels and subject areas together to work as a team around this inevitable change that was coming to the school.

Julie's intentional leadership experience, as reviewed above, served her middle school well at that time and through the subsequent years in terms of providing a more appropriate and effective instructional focus on addressing the needs of middle school students during their personal and physical periods of individual growth and development. Julie worked to refine the leadership characteristics and practices that she found supported both students and staff members. She continued in her leadership journey serving as a middle and elementary school leader for over twenty years. She received training as a leadership coach and currently works as a mentor and coach to numerous school leaders in Virginia.

In reflecting on the successes of her administrative career at both the school building and district levels, Julie contends that most of her professional successes as an educational leader related to her application of the five key principles of intentional leadership in her strategic plans and daily operations as articulated below:

- *Understanding the Needs of the Faculty:* Intentional leaders prioritize building relationships and trust with their staff members. By understanding the individual and collective needs of the faculty, they can minimize resistance and ensure that the emotional and mental well-being of staff is taken into account during any change process (Spiro, 2018). Also listening to what isn't being said—being sensitive not only to what is said regarding the change initiative but also to nonverbal cues from the audience to assess members' levels of buy-in or distrust (Kaufman, 2023). This aligns with the core tenet of Intentional Leadership, which is to be sensitive to the needs and concerns of the team.

- *Creating a Common Sense of Purpose:* Intentional leaders actively work to create a common sense of purpose and culture within the organization. By ensuring that all staff members understand the common goals and actively participate in building a culture of collaboration, leaders can break down silos and reduce stress among staff. Intentional leaders lead by example and foster a shared vision.
- *Providing Opportunities for Collaboration and Communication:* Intentional leaders emphasize ongoing communication and collaboration. This practice aligns with breaking down silos, as regular communication and encouraging staff to share concerns can enhance their well-being. Being clear, consistent, and transparent in communication also reinforces an emotionally supportive environment advocated by intentional leadership (Galbraith, 2018). Consistent and transparent communication establishes a well-defined pathway, eliminating the need for strenuous efforts to seek answers or generate unnecessary discourse. This, in turn, cultivates a positive work environment where staff members can concentrate on their primary tasks of teaching and learning, leading to increased job satisfaction.
- *Evaluating and Readjusting:* Regular check-ins and evaluations represent a vital aspect of Intentional Leadership. Leaders must continually evaluate the advancement of changes and gauge the extent of staff alignment with these changes. Moreover, they need to possess the capacity to nurture and oversee educators to sustain and enhance their engagement throughout the process (Fullan & Kirtman, 2019). By embedding these evaluation and reflection opportunities, leaders ensure that they continuously support the well-being of staff through the change process and maintain a sense of connection and belonging.
- *Implementing Proactive Practices:* Intentional leaders are proactive in aligning every interaction and action with their goals and vision for a collaborative and supportive school environment. As Fullan states in *Leading in a Culture of Change*, change can be understood and led, but it cannot be controlled (Fullan, 2007, p. 36). They check in regularly with staff, provide opportunities for collaboration, communicate consistently, and celebrate successes. Leadership actions are what energize people to pursue a desired goal (Fullan, 2007). These practices not only support well-being but also reinforce the principles of Intentional Leadership.

The above authentic and quite personal reflections of both Dan, as an evolving high school student but unsure of his learning space, and Julie, as a relatively new but emerging school administrator, illustrate the long-term meaningful impact of educational intentionality. The authors of this chapter encourage school leaders to generate enthusiasm for more educators to replicate such meaningful intentionality in their respective efforts to improve social-emotional learning by breaking down existing institutional silos and fostering more collaboration and a greater sense of personal belonging for all stakeholders.

It should be noted that Maslow was probably not the first educational psychologist of the last century to admonish the silo effect of schooling and its restrictive impact upon students (Maslow, 1943); and probably Danielson, a famed education researcher of this century, won't be the last to rebuke twenty-first century school silos (Danielson, 2002) as identified below:

> In many schools, teachers work almost in complete isolation: they prepare for their own classes on their own, develop their own tests. Such teachers work almost as independent contractors: they are hired to do a job and they do it, but not as members of a team. This isolation is detrimental to students, as the teachers cannot be aware of the approaches and strategies that others have found successful, and might even be working at cross purposes without even knowing it (Danielson, 2002, p. 62).

Dufour, the contemporary seminal advocate of developing "Professional Learning Communities" (PLCs), supports the above negative perspectives of both Maslow and Danielson regarding educational silos as he asserts that, "even though most educators know better," they still do not practice in a collaboration culture, "despite compelling evidence that working collaboratively represents best practice, teachers in many schools continue to work in isolation" (Dufour, 2004). Thus, it's time that educational leaders recognize the inefficiency of the silo structures of schooling in America and intentionally work to breakdown those silos and encourage collaboration among their faculty and staff to improve social-emotional teaching and learning for all students.

The authors of this chapter contend that the present emphasis on social-emotional learning provides a significant and unique opportunity for intentional educational leaders to break down the existing silos in their respective schools since social-emotional learning programs, projects, and activities are generally multi-aged and inter-disciplinary in nature, thus, not grade-level or subject specific. This enables intentional education leaders to facilitate broad-based whole-child educational thinking among their faculty, parents, and students. Intentional leaders must begin fostering reflective analyses about the professional social-emotional learning practices currently employed in their school buildings. They must encourage authentic collaboration to improve the frequency and quality of those "best-practices" of social-emotional learning in order to foster a school-wide sense of belonging.

A pragmatic approach that intentional school leaders may consider employing is one that uses a focused professional learning community (PLC) tasked with improving the quantity and quality of student-centered learning based on teacher professional reflections of current practices compared to desired instructional practices. The key concepts and procedural elements of such an intentionally focused Social-Emotional Learning–Professional Learning Community based on contemporary research are enumerated below.

SOCIAL-EMOTIONAL LEARNING–PROFESSIONAL LEARNING COMMUNITY (SEL-PLC)

A Professional Learning Community (PLC) focused on improving social-emotional learning in all school teaching and learning settings needs to be based on meaningful personal and professional reflections of key stakeholders including: administrators, teachers, support staff, parents, students, and community members. All stakeholders need to reflect about their instructional practices in terms of programs, projects, and activities that they are currently employing in social-emotional teaching-learning situations and think about their desired practices in those settings. This type of discrepancy reflective experience provides all SEL-PLC participants with the opportunity to reflect on what works for them in certain situations and what they would like to improve upon so that it works better for more students.

Dufour, the quintessential promoter of professional learning communities, contends that an effective PLC should have a key instructional improvement focus so that their members are not simply analyzing and fixing "window dressing" type issues but are intensively involved in pragmatically solving issues of professional practice that matter most to students, like social-emotional learning (Dufour et al., 2008). Consequently, at the present time, due to the aftermath of COVID-19, there is a definite urgent need and acute professional responsibility to facilitate collaborative stakeholder reflections about current instructional approaches including strategies, techniques, and activities associated with social-emotional teaching and learning. Intentional instructional leaders at the building and school district levels need to coordinate a more comprehensive and effective focus on social-emotional learning (SEL) based on reflections of desired and actual professional practices in their respective local contexts.

Consequently, there is a need to employ research-based strategic planning and practical models that may be used by intentional leaders employing SEL-PLCs to facilitate professional reflections about current social-emotional educational practices and assess desired levels of implementing even more quality social-emotional learning programs, projects, and activities in their respective teaching-learning settings. Accordingly, there exist numerous educational strategies, techniques, and models designed to assist intentional leaders on focusing their contextual PLCs on instructional discrepancies and planning to narrow the gap between desired instructional practices and current realities vis-à-vis social-emotional learning for all.

A conceptual discrepancy model that has been researched and analyzed in several case studies to help school leaders and practicing teachers identify the professional discrepancies that exist between individual desired teaching-learning practices and current instructional realities within diverse contexts is detailed in studies conducted by teams of researchers associated with the *Desired and Current Use of Constructivist Activities and Techniques Research Project* (Polka & VanHusen, 2014; Polka et al., 2016; VanHusen & Polka, 2023).

The survey instrument and procedural guide recommended in those studies and others to assist in analyzing and incorporating the results of individual professional discrepancy data into pragmatic strategic and tactical approaches to facilitate the transition of school faculties to more student-centered instruction has been reported in several different school settings (Polka, 2010; Peace et al., 2017; Eller et al., 2019; Hersi & Bal, 2021). This type of instructional discrepancy analysis has the capacity to accelerate the shattering of contextual silos and promote comprehensive planning for both short-term and long-term instructional improvement since it enables PLC members to share their instructional desires and practical expertise regarding instructional practices regardless of subject or grade-level parameters in a collaborative forum with a focus on meeting student social-emotional learning (SEL) needs.

The authors of this chapter provide figure 6.1, which summarizes the key intentional moves that leaders can and should employ to actively break down existing real or perceived silos within their respective school cultures and effectively coordinate focused social-emotional learning improvements via SEL-PLCs or similar strategic people-oriented change models.

FINAL THOUGHTS

In the ever-evolving landscape of K–12 education, the challenge of organizational silos casts a long shadow. These barriers, whether physical or conceptual, hinder the essential flow of collaboration and connectivity among

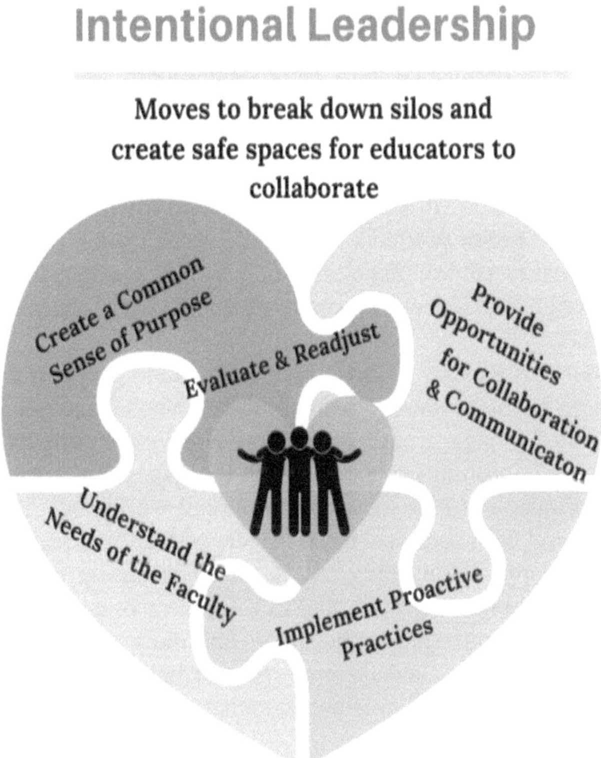

Figure 6.1. Intentional leadership moves to break down silos and create safe spaces for educators to collaborate on student social-emotional learning.

the diverse roles within the educational ecosystem. Silos restrict the sharing of knowledge, vital for the success of educational institutions, and impact crucial aspects like safety, well-being, and a sense of belongingness. The influence of silos extends to the learning environment, profoundly affecting its effectiveness (Maslow, 1943). Breaking down these educational silos is not just about reshaping physical structures; it delves into the core of how educational organizations function and, subsequently, what teachers teach and students learn. The principles of Intentional Leadership offer a compelling framework for educational leaders seeking to dismantle these silos and foster collaboration, communication, and emotional well-being.

As illustrated in this chapter, fostering a culture of belonging is paramount in this endeavor. Educators, just like students, yearn for acknowledgment and a sense of value within the school learning community. Leaders can learn from the deliberate actions of teachers like Mr. Nesta, who created environments where belonging and collaboration thrive, as well as from Principal

Julie who effectuated organizational changes by focusing on the human needs of the faculty implementing the changes. These environmental improvements didn't just happen by chance; they were intentionally crafted over time by leaders who cared for and cared with the people of their human organization. John Ruskin, a nineteenth-century English philosopher, epitomizes the significance of intentional leadership in schools today in a quote: "Quality is never an accident; . . . it is always the result of intelligent efforts and the will to create a superior product." Ruskin believed leaders must take action to create the quality environments they believe that teachers and students in their care deserve and expect, especially related to social-emotional learning at present time.

Great leaders, as Rosalynn Carter aptly said, "take people not only where they want to go but also where they ought to be." Such leaders are the significant architects of change, weaving a comprehensive web of support, knowledge, vision, and information that bridges the gaps silos create, alleviates stress, and nurtures a culture of social-emotional well-being. Through trust, intentionality, and collaboration, these leaders transform educational institutions and the people within them for the better, ensuring that all members of the school, as a human growth and development organization, feel seen, heard, loved, and empowered in their roles and daily activities. They intentionally break down silos, and foster a sense of belonging and purpose that ultimately benefits both educators and students.

KEY PRAGMATIC LEADERSHIP TAKEAWAYS

- *Understanding silos:* Educational leaders must acknowledge the existence and impact of silos within K–12 educational organizations. These silos act as barriers to collaboration, knowledge sharing, and overall well-being, affecting the learning environment and student success.
- *Leaders as change agents:* Education leaders play a crucial role in breaking down silos and fostering a culture of collaboration and belonging. They are instrumental in transforming the educational landscape, aligning their actions with a vision of improved well-being for all stakeholders.
- *Cultivating belonging and well-being:* Educational leaders must recognize that they have the ability to increase or decrease staff well-being. Educational institutions are continually adjusting and changing. Leaders shouldn't forget the needs of all stakeholders as they navigate these changes.
- *Silo-hero mentality:* Leaders should be aware of the detrimental effects of the Silo-Hero mentality. Environments where silos exist tend to

support individual growth and recognition. In school settings, where the focus is on supporting the growth of all teachers and students, coming together as one team is critical.

- *Five principles of intentional leadership:* When leaders lead with a clear intention, school environments become places where change is understood and embraced. These five intentional practices are: (1) understanding the needs of faculty, (2) creating a common sense of purpose, (3) providing opportunities for collaboration and communication, (4) evaluating and readjusting, and (5) implementing proactive practices.

REFERENCES

Ashkanasy, N., Ayoko, O., & Jehn, K. (2014). "Understanding the Physical Environment of Work and Employee Behavior: An Affective Events Perspective." *Journal of Organizational Behavior 35*(8), 1169–84. https://doi-org.ezproxy.niagara.edu/10.1002/job.1973.

Congdon, C., Flynn, D., & Redman, M. (2014). "Balancing We and Me: The Best Collaborative Spaces Also Support Solitude." *Harvard Business Review*. https://hbr.org/2014/10/balancing-we-and-me-the-best-collaborative-spaces-also-support- solitude.

Danielson, C. (2002). *Enhancing Student Achievement: A Framework for School Improvement.* Alexandria, VA: Association for Supervision and Curriculum Development.

Dufour, R. (2004). "What Is a 'Professional Learning Community'?" *Educational Leadership 61*(8), 6–11.

Dufour, R., Eaker, R., & Dufour, R. (2008). *Revisiting Professional Learning Communities at Work: New Insights for Improving Schools.* Bloomington, IN: Solution Tree Press.

Eller, A., Polka, W., & Mete, R. (2019). Small-Town and Rural Idaho Elementary Teachers' Desired Versus Current Use of Differentiated Instructional Practices. *Educational Research: Theory and Practice 30*(2), 61–74.

Fullan, M. (2007). *Leading in a Culture of Change. San Francisco, CA: Wiley & Sons.*

———. (2008). *The Six Secrets of Change.* San Francisco: Jossey-Bass.

Galbraith, M. (2018, October 5). "Don't Just Tell Employees Organizational Changes Are Coming Explain Why." *Harvard Business Review.* https://hbr.org/2018/10/dont-just-tell-employees-organizational-changes-are-coming-explain-why.

Hersi, A., & Bal, I. (2021). Planning for Differentiation: Understanding Maryland Teachers' Desired and Actual Use of Differentiated Instruction." *Education Planning 28*(1), 55–71.

Hoy, W., & Miskel C. (2013). *Educational Administration Theory, Research and Practice* (9th ed). New York: McGraw Hill.

Maslow, A. (1943). "A Theory Of Human Motivation." *Psychological Review 50*(4), 370–96. https://doi.org/10.1037/h0054346.

Molek, N., de Jager, J. E., & Pucelj, M. (2023). "Hero Culture and Silo Mentality: A Systematic Literature Review." *Journal of Universal Excellence (JUE)/Revija Za Univerzalno Odličnost (RUO) 12*(1), 1–17. https://doiorg.ezproxy.niagara.edu/10.37886/ruo.2023.001.

Owens, A. (2017). "Tearing Down the Silos in K–12 Curricula." (2017). National Institute for STEM Education, January 24. https://nise.institute/resources/news/2017_01_24_stemscopes_tearing_down_silos_k12_ascd.pdf.

Peace, T., Polka, W., & Mete, R. (2017). "Assessing and Promoting Student-Centered Teaching and Learning Practices Using a Quantitative Educational Planning Tool: Results of 2016 Indiana Case Study." *Educational Planning 24*(2), 21–37.

Polka, W. (2010). "The Art and Science of Constructivist Supervision: Transforming Schools by Applying Needs-Based Research." *Journal for the Practical Application of Constructivist Theory in Education 5*(1), 1–28.

Polka, W., & VanHusen, M. (2014). "Applying Teacher Reflection Strategies to Promote Greater Differentiation of Instruction: A Practical Research Model and Procedural Guide." In E. Pultorak (Ed.). *Reflectivity and Cultivating Student Learning: Critical Elements for Enhancing a Global Community of Learners and Educators*, 111–35. Lanham, MD: Rowman & Littlefield Education Publications.

Polka, W., VanHusen, M., Young, W., & Minervino, K. (2016). "Facilitating Greater Instructional Differentiation via Research-Based Teacher Reflections and Site-Based Procedural Guidelines." *Educational Research: Theory & Practice 28*(1), 37–52.

Ryan, R. M., & Deci, E. L. (2017). *Self-E Theory: Basic Psychological Needs in Motivation, Development, and Wellness.* New York: Guilford Press.

Senge, P. (2006). *The Fifth Discipline: The Art and Practice of the Learning Organization*. New York: Broadway Business.

Spiro, J. (2018). *Leading Change Handbook*. New York: The Wallace Foundation. https://www.wallacefoundation.org/knowledge-center/Documents/leading-change-handbook.pdf.

VanHusen, M., & Polka, W. (2023). "Instructional Leadership: The Spark to Lead Change." In W. Polka, J. McKenna, & M. VanHusen (Eds.), *Coping with Educational Crises: Approaches from School Leaders Who Did It!* Lanham, MD: Rowman & Littlefield Education Publications.

Woolner, P., Thomas, U., & Tiplady, L. (2018). "Structural Change from Physical Foundations: The Role of the Environment in Enacting School Change." *Journal of Educational Change 19*, 223–42. https://doi.org/10.1007/s10833-018-9317-4.

Chapter 7

Providing Community Care Services to Children during Crises and Beyond

Olasumbo O. Adelakun

Life isn't about waiting for the storm to pass. It's about learning how to dance in the rain.

—Vivian Greene

This chapter highlights experiences of educators in a before-and-after-school program in Ontario, Canada, leading up to, during the COVID-19 shelter-in-place crisis, and beyond. The COVID-19 pandemic became a reality and life changer for Ontarians and our global village in March 2020. It is safe to say that this pandemic affected people across the globe one way or another and it has revealed as Maya Angelou asserts, that in the grand scheme of things, "*we are more alike than we are different.*"

No amount, or level of education or life experiences prepared anyone for all that came to them during the two years of active crisis situations related to COVID-19. The role of an educator for example, is to help improve the life experiences of others by creating environments that accommodate the needs of curious minds and promote a high level of critical thinking. Yet, none of the important skills and experiences educators bring and utilize in the classroom, could have prepared them for a pandemic such as this one, which has forced rapid change and adaptation.

The COVID 19 pandemic, an unseen adversary, disrupted lives across all countries and communities and negatively affected global economic growth. As it continued to spread, national economies and businesses were left counting the costs, and many governments struggled with lockdown measures to tackle the spread of the virus.

* * *

Its impact on schools, including before- and after-school childcare services, was profound as contact and closeness between children and staff were avoided, leaving many afraid to even leave their homes. As updates about the rising infection numbers were provided on the news, fear and anxiety levels were heightened and simple physical and social interactions that people once took for granted were cautiously reconsidered.

In the beginning, according to Statistics Canada, almost 3 million Canadians were out of work and 2.5 million more were working reduced hours because of restrictions imposed by public health officials, who forced many businesses including childcare facilities to close. But the only childcare centers and services that were allowed to open were those providing services for essential workers (Bogart & Lee, 2020).

Like many other establishments, regular licensed childcare centers were closed indefinitely in March 2020, a move that experts referred to as a crisis, the first of its kind. Six months into the crisis and the question of how the world could move forward was still being asked: How do people actually get infected? Was it by being in crowded places, close proximity, poor ventilation, or the ability of the virus to survive on different surfaces thereby increasing its spread? The answers to these questions would be the key to moving forward safely and successfully.

However, until a year into the pandemic, not even the best minds had a good understanding of the etiology, mode of spread of the virus, who the most vulnerable groups were or even all the ways in which it could spread. As the world watched in horror and the number of infected people spiked, most could only make educated guesses about what would happen next, or how the spread could be effectively controlled.

In childcare settings, the theory was that children could catch coronavirus but only develop mild symptoms, with few deaths in comparison to other age groups. The added risk with children however was that they could spread germs quickly, aiding proliferation of the virus in classrooms and playgrounds. With no data or research available at the time, parents of school children in Ontario were under intense pressure.

Families suddenly found themselves cooped up together in their homes with nowhere to go, making it extremely difficult for them to strike a healthy balance between their work lives and family lives. To make matters worse, their children did not have the much-needed outlets that families have become reliant on such as school, extra-curricular activities and friends with whom to play.

This led to "family burnout" in a lot of cases, with many parents overwhelmed, experiencing exhaustion and frustration, which sometimes resulted in emotional distancing from their children (Coyne, 2020). The experiences of educators, many of whom are parents themselves, were not so different from those expressed by parents of before- and after-school program participants.

Obviously, the relationships and bonds that were formed between educators, the children, and their families were disrupted and reshaped when COVID-19 hit. Communication was reduced to emails from educators to families to check on their well-being, short video recordings, and the sharing of recipes and activities online.

Milton Community Resource Centre (MCRC), a small not-for-profit organization in Ontario, Canada, which provides services to children and families of Milton and the surrounding communities, is a forward thinking and pro-active childcare organization that operates significant before- and after-school programs for elementary students. The organization was consistent in ensuring its employees and the communities it servcs were coping under the unprecedented crisis circumstances.

Organizational leaders took it upon themselves to ensure daily communications were sent to staff, encouraging them to check in on the families of the children in their classes, and also to ensure that staff were aware of the effects the pandemic could have on individual mental health and well-being. Managers of the Milton Community Resource Centre (MCRC) strongly encouraged staff to speak up and seek help, consistently shared self-help practices, and continuously provided external sources of help to staff.

BEFORE- AND AFTER-SCHOOL PROGRAMS IN ONTARIO

The role of before- and after-school community-based programs is to support social-emotional learning and whole-child development by utilizing programs that implement evidence-based models that promote the development of social-emotional skills. These programs provide a safe and structured environment for the children of working parents where there is demand for it. In Ontario, Canada, school boards are required, by regulations, to ensure that before- and after-school programs are provided for every elementary school, serving students from kindergarten to grade 6.

The programs must be available on every instructional school day as they are known to keep children from engaging in risky behaviors by turning aimless hours after school into productive learning time. These programs also give parents peace of mind to enable them to focus on their jobs without the pressures of rushing home from work or the guilt of neglecting their children.

THE REGGIO EMILIA APPROACH TO EARLY CHILD EDUCATION AT MCRC

The cure of boredom is curiosity; there is no cure for curiosity.

—Dorothy Parker

In most Ontario before- and after-school community programs, children that initially attend such programs range in age from four to six and are classified as either Junior Kindergarten or Senior Kindergarten students. In addition, school age children ages six to eleven in elementary school grades one grade to six also make up a significant portion of the community centers' population. At MCRC, the program is very interactive and hands-on as it is based on the Reggio Emilia approach, which utilizes a student-centered and constructivist self-guided curriculum. With this approach, children are taught how to use "symbolic languages" such as painting, sculpting, and drama in everyday life and "one hundred languages" (many different ways) to express their understanding.

This learning philosophy views children as independent, creative, curious beings and believes in the rights and opinions of the individual child. It also views parents as participants in their child's learning process and views school as a safe place. The educator is viewed as a child's partner and one who recognizes many learning possibilities, listens, inquires, observes, documents and reflects upon a child's experiences (Coquitlam Childcare Center, 2017).

Community and group work are crucial to this approach in early childhood education.

The educator's role in this environment is to observe the children, record what they know, what they are curious about, and what challenges them. These observations are used to identify the children's strengths, help them expand their academic and social potentials, and determine the next steps to support further learning.

Many types of learning are based on interrelationships; however. with Reggio Emilia there is a closer interaction between the children, their families, and the teachers. This means the children are known to gain more and perform best when they are part of a "learning community" not when working independently, hence the importance of working in small groups to encourage interaction with the world around them.

The formal classroom setting, therefore, plays a pivotal role in this mode of learning and is seen as a space that enhances these experiences. However, as the whole world was navigating through a new normal in teaching and learning promulgated by the pandemic, which was suddenly thrust upon all educators, new conversations occurred related to operations of the childcare community.

Conversations in childcare settings began to center around the mental well-being of children and educators as it related to prolonged isolation and stress caused by COVID-19. The social distance aspect has been the most confusing for the children who found themselves cut off from their peers and were forced into isolation indoors with their families. These were challenging times all around, and the commonality between the experiences of the children, their families, and educators was multifaceted, and creed or socioeconomic status were not really mitigating factors.

Many people are still feeling the loss of someone or something; for many, it was their livelihood as well as their daily behaviors and practices. The uncertainty of the crisis made it very difficult to handle for most adults, and children are still worried about losing their parents because they've heard that adults are at higher risk of contracting the disease than they are.

PROGRAM PARTICIPANTS, THEIR FAMILIES, AND THE LOCKDOWN

However, a very powerful and important principle of the Reggio Emilio approach is to create an environment where the classroom serves as a "living organism" in which real-life interactions and relationships are shared among the children, their families, and the educators. Therefore, it was difficult to explain the lockdowns to children whose very core is the desire to become more socially adept and whose social development is more dependent on peer groups than family.

Children were labeled "super-spreaders" to justify the need to keep them home from school and help flatten the curve for COVID-19, and some parents reported higher levels of stress, which was and still is a big concern, because prolonged stress can become very toxic and harmful. Stress is said to also affect brain growth and development, which can ultimately lead to problems with learning and create negative behaviors in children (Hegarty, 2020).

On the other hand, in the absence of substantive data and scientific consensus, it is still difficult to determine how the virus affected children and how this crisis impacted them emotionally and psychologically. It is obvious, however, that an indefinite lockdown could have long-term effects on children and was not a sustainable option for childcare centers. Researchers have shown that when children have positive relationships with their peers, stable routines that encourage healthy behaviors, and social and emotional skills development, they are less likely to experience toxic stress, increase their natural resilience, and withstand adversity as they grow.

CHILD-CARE EDUCATORS FACED THE CRISIS AND ANXIOUSLY ADAPTED

> POTHOLES: *Things in life we hit that invariably nudge us off our path. This could be trauma, abuse, unemployment, neglect or untreated mental health problems which can remain unresolved or untreated, not dealt with. If we hit enough potholes on our journey in life without the resources or the help to navigate around them or pull us out, we risk falling through the cracks.*
>
> —Christian Picciolini

On February 12, 2020, Milton Community Resource Centre's Human Resources department received a memo from Dr. Hamidah Meghani, Medical Officer of Health for the Halton Region in Ontario to members of staff. Dr. Megani stated that there were no reported cases in this region and the virus had allegedly originated from China, where the situation was still unfolding.

In addition, according to the memo, travelers from China to Canada, particularly from Hubei Province and Mainland China were instructed to self-quarantine at home for fourteen days from the day they left China and were provided with emergency numbers to contact the Health Department with any questions. Others were given recommendations as to how best to prevent the spread of the virus. Even though day-to-day work continued, anxiety levels among educators rose very quickly.

March 11, 2020, saw the release of more updates from the Medical Officer of Health (MOH), stating that the risk to the Milton community was very low. The organization also issued a statement at the same time, informing staff that the World Health Organization (WHO) had announced that this could be a global pandemic. They requested that staff traveling out of Canada needed to identify their travel plans and dates to Human Resources (HR). At this point the levels of discomfort among some staff became apparent, and there was uncertainty as to what to do, especially with everyone working in such close proximity.

Also, parents had a lot of questions that the staff could not answer, children were clearly anxious, and educators with young families and elderly relatives at home were worried about inadvertently infecting their loved ones if exposed at work. The most disturbing piece of information was that there could be asymptomatic carriers within the school community. There was talk among the children about where the disease originated from and how it spreads. Unfortunately, a lot of misinformation was circling causing many assumptions about the actual dangers of the disease to be made.

The next day, March 12, HR confirmed through a memo from the regional health office that the MOH had confirmed the first case in Halton, Ontario, a woman who had just arrived from Hawaii. This was a game changer.

On March 16, the Chief Medical Officer of Health, Dr. David Williams, directed all daycare centers to close with the intention of reopening in April. This was actually a relief; welcome news to staff members and families who had been hoping for school closures to reduce interactions and the risk of exposure and transmissions. Subsequently, the centers stayed closed with no guarantees that they would be ready to re-open by September 2020.

Self-Care during the Pandemic

The pandemic has certainly taken a toll on educators, and this cannot be overlooked or underestimated. As described by Picciolini it has indeed been a "*pothole*." The biggest concern for many were the uncertainties and lack of information. Being on the frontlines with high exposure to COVID-19 and the possibility of infecting a family member were serious concerns. This is because, historically, as an educator working exclusively with children, staff members are susceptible to ailments that children have and often have to take time off work because of annual bouts of the flu or coughs and colds, which almost always occurred within the first three weeks of school in September.

Thankfully, the MCRC a forward-thinking organization, ensured that daily self-help information went out to staff members to ensure optimal mental health and well-being. One such worksheet containing several coping strategies is the "Mental First Aid, COVID-19 Self-Care and Resilience Plan" developed by the Mental Health Commission of Canada.

Some of these strategies suggested to staff are:

- Volunteering for a meaningful cause
- Making a gratitude list
- Practicing yoga
- Reading a good book
- Writing in a journal
- Dance
- Watching movies
- Acupuncture
- Gardening

- Game night with friends or family
- Getting creative—painting, drawing
- Trying a new hobby

TIME TO REFLECT, REPOSITION, AND RESET CHILD CARE

Sadly, many people around the world lost their lives due to the COVID-19 crisis, and for many others, the decisions of their governments to close schools impacted their income drastically. However, in every situation, there are lessons to be learned. In the process of self-care, this period can serve as a time to reflect, reposition, and reset.

Reflect: Looking at past experiences thoroughly, trying to determine if up until now, one's time has been spent productively. Ensuring that people are not just pushing through, or constantly moving in order to keep up, but realizing they must STOP, step off the treadmill and reflect on the things that are working for them and those that are not.

Reposition: What lessons have they learned from this pandemic? Apart from the fact that it has shown, unequivocally, that *no one* is truly in control of anything. How do they go forward with a new approach equipped with this knowledge, to make their dreams a reality?

Reset: What should their new mindset be and what steps must they take to reset? Many are faced with a golden opportunity now through no choice of their own, but nevertheless a blessing. So, they can hit the reset button by starting a new chapter and making improvements in daily life.

The personal experiences of some families to date through this crisis have been mostly positive. It has been an opportunity to bond, exercise daily, eat healthier, and sleep much better. This is reminiscent of a family that once had a pet gerbil that would spin on its wheel for long periods of time. The pet store owners where the gerbil had been purchased had warned the family that it needed the wheel to fulfil its daily exercise requirements. After a couple of months, it was let out of its cage by the children. They felt sad that it was trapped and "Baby," as they called him, spent the rest of his days roaming free through their home! This freedom enabled him to wander from the first floor to the top floor and at times he would not be seen for a couple of days, but he would always make his way back to his cage to eat.

The pandemic highlights the value of the kind of freedom "Baby" had. When government lockdowns, forced restrictions to movement, social distancing, and masking are considered, the following question comes to mind: If before- and after-school programs cannot operate the way they used to, how would children, families and staff cope?

In reality, people have adapted, and schools are creating an atmosphere in which children are comfortable enough to enjoy programs and are benefitting from being in much smaller groups. This has allowed for increased participation and better communication. The key is flexibility, because at the end of the day, children tend to be a lot more resilient than we give them credit for.

GOING FORWARD: POST CRISIS THOUGHTS

This too shall pass.

—Rumi

On Friday June 12, 2020, the Premier and Minister of Education suddenly announced that childcare centers including before and after school programs in Ontario could open, with restrictions. They were only given three days' notice, leaving organization Directors scratching their heads and scrambling. The news has been described as surprising, exciting, and worrisome at the same time. Questions about how centers can adapt spaces and programs, what to say to parents, how to ensure every child gets a spot are just a few of the questions that organizations were anxious to have the government answer (Hindman, 2020).

Education community centers were concerned about how to keep staff and children safe and how to source and provide personal protective equipment since there was still a scarcity, two very real concerns. Also, the guidelines for opening recommended that toys be kept clean and not shared by children, sensory bins removed from classes and physical distances maintained. Other recommendations were to reduce educator to child ratios of one to fifteen, to a total of ten people per group (including educators) as well as limiting parent access to facilities during drop off or pick up of their children.

These recommendations were difficult to implement for a myriad of reasons, and during crisis times like these it is doubtful that stakeholders representing educators were at the decision-making table. Their input and participation in decision-making was crucial because they would be able to paint a more realistic picture of how things actually work in childcare facilities. But, of course, they were not at the decision-making tables.

Prior to the COVID-19 pandemic, educator to school age child ratio was one to fifteen as mandated by Ministry of Education's Schedule 1 (2018) to ensure that program participants are not left unattended at any time or left to roam the hallways by themselves. Educators keep time-stamped records of parent drop offs and pick-ups, whilst maintaining a head count of program participants. To restrict parents from entering facilities meant that in order to maintain ratios and for the safety of the participants, educators had to bring a group of children with them to the entrance every time a parent arrived to drop off or pick up their child.

The alternative to these operational procedures was to increase the number of educators per classroom in order to maintain ratios, and ensure that there was always an additional educator available to pick program participants up when they arrive or drop them off at the entrance when their parents pick them up.

Today, paranoia and fear amongst educators is rampant. Even though many agree that going back into the classroom is beneficial to all, they are still on edge. There are very limited numbers of students in afterschool program now compounded by staff shortages. Educators are burned out and with concerns about the possible virus mutations and variants, are simply not willing, for such low wages to risk working in this environment.

New Guidelines

As the Ontario economy continues to open up, the Ministry of Education, in February 2022 provided childcare services with new operational policies to enhance health and safety measures and make expectations clear within these facilities. The policies are designed to be shared with families to ensure that they are also aware of these expectations.

Some of these key requirements and MCRC's policies are:

- Programs operate at reduced capacity.
- At MCRC, parents are provided with the entrance door code now, they are allowed in the building but not in the classrooms.
- Child-care staff and providers must be trained on health, safety and operational measures in alignment with local public health unit's directions.
- School boards provide safety recommendations for child care operators to enter and exit their centers which are located within school premises. This will enable them to prepare these spaces for programs and meet the ministry's operational guidelines.
- Program providers encouraged to collaborate with child and youth mental health agencies to support strong connections and make the best use of mental health resources and supports across the integrated system of care.
- As from Monday March 28, 2022, masks will no longer be required.

So Where Are We Now?

With COVID-19, we've made it to the life raft. Dry land is far away

—Marc Lipsitch and Yonatan Grad

Lipsitch and Yonatan's quote applies very much to the situation in the world today! Even though the new COVID-19 vaccines, like the life raft described above, are saving lives, they are, however, not long-term viable options or cures. They are designed to prevent adverse reactions in people upon exposure to the virus, as multiple variants have since emerged and continue to emerge. "Dry land" therefore, which signifies the end of the pandemic, is nowhere in sight and to date scientists cannot tell whether the currently available vaccines will protect people against the mutating viruses.

The after-school system in Ontario has undoubtedly changed for good. The significant education disruptions resulting from the COVID-19 pandemic brought about mass school closures and remote learning leading to a mandatory closure of before and after-school programs. For educators in these programs, it has meant no communication or interactions with children or their families. While schools were on remote learning for the remainder of the first impacted school year, in-person learning was made available only to students who could not be accommodated through remote learning because of their special needs.

On June 2, 2021, when Ontario's premier Doug Ford announced that schools would not be returning to in-class learning until the fall, he based his decision on the fact that his consultations with numerous health experts did not give him the complete certainty and "consensus" he wanted, and he was not willing to take chances with the health of Ontario's children. Children being away from school for so long had not been anticipated, the prediction was that elementary schools would opt for smaller cohorts and outdoor learning where possible but, after a third wave hit Ontario, in-person instruction in schools was shut down again.

Looking back just a few months, predictions about hybrid learning were accurate because, starting in September 2021, Ontario school boards began implementing different modes of delivery in teaching and learning, giving students the option of learning in person or remotely and offering opportunities for students to switch learning models in October and January if parents or guardians requested it. This hybrid model of learning and teaching is now the new normal.

In a move to lower children's risk of infection and return to some form of normalcy, Health Canada in March 2022 approved the use of the pediatric Pfizer vaccine for children aged five to eleven and the regular Pfizer vaccine for individuals aged twelve and older. It was determined that these vaccines would help build up a child's immunity, reduce the risk of getting and spreading the virus and make symptoms milder in the event that a child has been infected.

Having come this far, some of the crucial lessons learned are that education cannot work with a "one-size-fits-all" approach, flexibility is essential in dealings with students, and technology will become a normal tool for teaching and learning. As educators and leaders who many families look to for answers, we have seen that the pandemic has taught patience, empathy, compassion, and the need to support one another.

It has also further revealed inequities in society because some segments of the population have been neglected in education and the shortcomings of traditional education were exacerbated during the crisis. Knowing this now, it is imperative that affordable, flexible, and practical online educational systems be put in place to help students succeed and also to help create a level playing field for them.

Staying safe and healthy is the priority for everyone going forward and the hybrid model will encourage student engagement and the building of a community of learners. The challenge, however, will always be physical distance and inability to build close relationships between children, their families, and educators.

FINAL THOUGHTS

Knowing that things can never go back to the way they were, childcare providers are now having to adapt to new policies and operating procedures which are based solely on recommendations by public health departments and the government.

Educators must pause, take a step back, and reset because they cannot give what they don't have in terms of energy and caring time. Therefore, all school leaders need to recognize the importance for teachers, especially those who teach very young children, to basically get through each day and continue to provide students and their families with what they need most—"high-touch" caring and personal security, because families rely on them to set the tone and lead the way.

Experts have already established that each lost day of school results in fewer children reaching the expected grades in reading and math, and short periods of time out of education can have a lasting impact on children's learning. Therefore, missed opportunities for learning will likely result in children forgetting what they have learned. The reality is that it is difficult to determine at this time what the long-term impacts of this pandemic crisis will be on education. The general consensus is that the impact could be a lifelong effect on cognitive abilities.

In retrospect, the biggest concern post-COVID was not just the impact of the pandemic on education but it's impact on children's health and safety when in school and after-school programs. One of the positive things that has evolved from this is the need to explore different modes of delivery in teaching and learning. For before- and after-school programs, smaller cohorts are a win-win because they have proven to enable students to learn faster, perform better, and participate more. Children also received more individualized attention from their educators. For those that employ the Reggio Emilia pedagogical approach, the impact of the pandemic on education was slightly softened because the approach is tailored toward experiential learning through play-based and hands-on education, as opposed to a prescribed curriculum. As staying at home became a daily way of life for families and educators, the before- and after-school program educators continued developing ideas and initiatives to enable this "learning community" to stay together, play together, and make school together.

Moving forward, similar approaches that encourage smaller cohorts and learning outdoors in nature may be the norm. Nature serves as outdoor classrooms which inspire children to explore and investigate, therefore, schools may consider reducing winter classes and incorporating summer classes if outdoor learning becomes part of the new normal.

Humans are creatures of habit. The preferable impact on education would have been that years of established formats and systems would not undergo such an incredible and very rapid overhaul. However, change is inevitable and as we continue to evolve, so does everything around us. Having witnessed two years of the impact of the pandemic on the education system, the mindset definitely changes.

Educators, government, and the ministry of education officials will have to continuously return to the drawing board as often as is necessary to address the exigencies of crises and ensure communities that wherever the next crisis takes us, the interest, safety, and well-being of children will remain a priority. This most recent crisis has shown the world that what was once thought possible as a response to crises may not be possible in the future. It is important to note that the same solutions may not work for all, therefore, living in the moment with what we know, crossing bridges as we get to them, being less rigid, more fluid, and watching how things unfold in the future and reacting accordingly is probably the best and safest approach going forward.

SOCIAL-EMOTIONAL NEEDS OF CHILDREN POST COVID-19

In her book *The Deepest Well: Healing the Long-Term Effects of Childhood Adversity*, Dr. Nadine Burke Harris (2018), a pediatrician and founder of San Francisco's Centre for Youth Wellness, states that childhood trauma is a catalyst for poor health outcomes later in life. The traumatic stress as a result of the overwhelming and frightening experiences many children went through is affecting their ability to cope today; two years after the World Health Organization declared that the global COVID-19 emergency has ended.

In Canada, however, as we approach the respiratory virus season, senior public health officials are advocating for the return to the use of masks and social distancing. Many children who may have lost relatives to COVID-19 or seen relatives get seriously ill are starting to hear frightening news from the media again. Educators who work with young children on a daily basis in schools and after-school programs are also experiencing stressors, different levels of worry and confusion that children can pick up on. Many are dealing with mental health problems induced by these experiences.

The general consensus is that depending on funding, many children who are still coping with the residual negative consequences of COVID-19 may benefit from the expansion of high-quality programs including academic, behavioral, and social-emotional ones. After-school programs are known for providing academic support and opportunities for children to engage in healthy relationships with peers and adults, much of which was lost during the pandemic.

Educators are now making it a priority to ensure that in addition to homework help, sports, arts, and crafts, children are learning social-emotional skills such as self-awareness, self-management, empathy, social awareness, and decision-making. Educators are modeling these behaviors and providing classroom activities to teach these skills, engage in discussions, and reflect on emotions, actions, and experiences. These steps are integrated into a framework designed to create the time and space for children to share their concerns, celebrate each other, and connect.

The prolonged learning environment that before- and after-school programs provide makes them a great place for children to practice social-emotional skills that they may use in their daily lives, at school, and at home. Incorporating social-emotional learning can have a lasting and positive impact on a child's overall development and it remains to be seen in the long term the benefits of this new approach to before- and after-school care.

KEY PRAGMATIC LEADERSHIP TAKEAWAYS

- *All educational leaders need to comprehensively understand and diligently implement child-centered learning programs such as the Reggio Emilia pedagogical approach, tailored toward experiential learning through play-based and hands-on education, as opposed to a prescribed curriculum.* This type of constructivist curriculum design enables children to explore their environment in creative and non-prescribed manners and enables educators to truly serve as "guides on the side" as opposed to "dispensers" of knowledge as well as involving parents in instructional experiences with their children.
- *Educational leaders need to consider "greening" the school learning environment to include more nature in their curriculum and more of a wholistic ecosystem of learning.* The outdoor community environment needs to be utilized more as a key "architectural" aspect of schooling. Students, at all ages, need to explore their community environment and use it as their primary "learning laboratory" and parents need to be encouraged to participate in all school activities to further enhance the "community" learning experience for all. So that if the "brick and mortar" buildings associated with traditional "schooling" are closed due to a crisis, learning may be reinforced throughout the community and enhanced by the child's "first and foremost teachers"—their parents.
- *Staffing ratios need to be reduced to more appropriate levels to foster more individualized and differentiated instruction for students at all grade levels.* This recent pandemic crisis illustrated the value of limiting student-teacher ratios to a degree where more personalized learning could be addressed and more "high-touch" caring could occur to address the social-emotional needs of students and their families.
- *School leaders need to recognize the inherent necessity and value of employing community assistance programs to help parents care for their families, especially during crisis situations.* The experiences of the Milton Community Resource Centre (MCRC) described above should be used as a reference in terms of the approaches employed by the managers of that community-based learning organization to provide valuable personal care information for students and their families on a regular basis. Schools should be viewed as "lighthouses of hope" in their community and should be recognized as dispensers of information services as well as safety products to help families promote healthy and safe lifestyles at any time but especially during crisis situations.
- *School leaders at all levels of the instructional continuum need to be vigilant regarding the mental health and stress factors related to their*

faculty and staff. The stress and burnout of professional educators and care-givers was exacerbated by the recent unanticipated global pandemic, but it also reflected that if caregivers and educators are expected to "go the extra mile" to nurture others in crisis settings, there will be a personal toll on them. It must be recognized that an individual's "high-touch" caring tank is only so full, and it has to be "refilled" and "recharged" on a regular basis so that they may continue providing the caring attention that students and their families need and expect of them. Social-emotional health and wellness is not for students and families only; it is an imperative concern for those who provide services to students and their families.

REFERENCES

Bogart, N., & Lee, V. (2020). "Childcare Restrictions Preventing Some from Going Back to Work As Economy Reopens." CTV News, May 18. https://www.ctvnews.ca/health/coronavirus/child-care-restrictions-preventing-some-from-going-back-to-work-as-economy-reopens-1.4944380.

Coquitlam Childcare Center—Group Daycare. (2017). Reggio Emilia Approach, November 14. https://parklandplayers.com/reggio-emilia-approach/.

Coyne, Lisa W. (2021). "Fighting Family Burnout during the COVID-19 Crisis." McLean Hospital, February 18. https://www.mcleanhospital.org/news/fighting-family-burnout-during-covid-19-crisis.

Harris, N. B. (2018). The Deepest Well Summary and Study Guide. SuperSummary. https://www.supersummary.com/the-deepest-well/summary.

Hegarty, E., & Hofman, L. (2020). "5 Ways That Afterschool Buffers Toxic Stress." Afterschool Alliance, May 29. https://www.afterschoolalliance.org/afterschoolSnack/5-ways-that-afterschool-buffers-toxic-stress_05-29-2020.cfm.

Hindman, C. (2021). "The Ontario Daycare Reopening Plan Is a Hot Mess." *Today's Parent*, May 3. https://www.todaysparent.com/blogs/trending/the-ontario-daycare-reopening-plan-is-a-hot-mess.

Mental Health Commission of Canada. (2020). *Mental Health First Aid COVID-19 Self-Care and Resilience Guide*. https://files.constantcontact.com/6d1562b4101/9cda0d7d-dbb5-4aee-a965-77f867ec9b6b.pdf.

Ministry of Education. (2018). "Operating a Licensed Child Care Program." https://www.ontario.ca/page/operating-licensed-child-care-program.

———. (2020). COVID-19: "Health and Safety measures for Child Care." https://www.ontario.ca/page/covid-19-reopening-child-care-centres.

———. (2022). "Operational Guidance: Pre-Program Considerations." https://www.ontario.ca/document/covid-19-operational-guidance-child-care/operational-guidance-pre-program-considerations.

Chapter 8

Improving Socio-Emotional Experiences for Special Education Students

A Persistent Balancing Conundrum between Fidelity to Regulations and Meeting Student Needs

Lisa Condino

The author of this chapter has been a special education teacher for over twenty-five years, serving students with various types of disabilities. She is currently employed as a sixth- and seventh-grade consultant teacher providing instruction and support for students with learning disabilities, both in and out of the general education setting. The school district in which she is employed is a small rural farming district in New York State with a K–12 student population of slightly over one thousand students. Of those students, 184 (16%) receive special education services (New York State Education Department [NYSED], 2019).

THE PANDEMIC SAGA BEGINS

On March 2, 2020, the school district superintendent sent a letter to all families in the district providing information on the 2019 Novel Coronavirus (COVID-19) that had apparently originated from Wuhan, Hubei Province, China. The superintendent of schools explained what the virus was, how it spreads, how to best prevent being infected, and how this school district was planning to deal with it at the local level. There was no indication or way of knowing that this new strain of virus would soon have such a profound effect on a global level.

What began as rumors, claiming that school districts across the nation would most likely close their doors due to this new strain of virus, suddenly became a stark reality. The rapid spread of this virus, causing illnesses ranging from the common cold to more problematic diseases such as severe acute respiratory syndrome (SARS-CoV), quickly turned into what we now know as the Coronavirus Pandemic (World Health Organization [WHO], 2020). COVID-19 has had devastating effects on people around the world socially, professionally, organizationally, and educationally.

The COVID-19 health crisis has significantly impacted educational systems worldwide. Schools, colleges, and universities were forced to close their doors in an attempt to contain the spread of the virus. Educators became faced with the question of how to provide review, instruction, and assessments to students who came from diverse socioeconomic backgrounds. They had to devise a way to get various resources to students and make sure that individuals received different levels of support at home. Most educators had to learn and utilize less-familiar methods of instruction and collaborate via videoconferencing, due to social distancing requirements.

Administrators were tasked with prioritizing services to students, creating plans to provide those services, and implementing those services in the most effective way possible. Parents were suddenly having to homeschool their children, despite having their own jobs to worry about. Children's social lives, including schooling, became restricted to the use of social media, texting, and emailing.

INITIAL CRISIS IMPACT ON SPECIAL EDUCATION STUDENTS

Students with disabilities were especially vulnerable during this time of crisis. They were at a high risk for experiencing the negative effects that educators knew would most likely occur due to the sudden changes in their educational services, programs, and daily lives. Staying in compliance with special education legislation was difficult and confusing, especially since there were no specific provisions made in state or federal laws for what to do in the case of a global crisis.

Administrators, teachers, parents, and advocates of students with disabilities had to refer to state and federal online dispatches for guidance on how to proceed with the implementation of special education programs for students with special needs.

On March 12, 2020, the U.S. Department of Education (USDOE) released a fact sheet outlining sections of the Individuals with Disabilities Education Act (IDEA) and Americans with Disabilities Act (ADA) that pertained to the education of students with disabilities during a time of crisis (Gavin, 2020). This question-answer sheet stated that although IDEA and ADA do not specifically address situations in which schools are closed for an extended periods of time due to a viral outbreak, sections of these federal laws do contain provisions to be used for exceptional circumstances, such as this national crisis.

The main directive in the memo from the USDOE stated that school leaders must ensure that students with disabilities have equal access to the same opportunities as their general education peers, including the provision of free and appropriate public education (FAPE), and ensure that each student with a disability is provided the special education and related services identified in the student's IEP or 504 accommodation plan (USDOE, 2020).

New York State also provided frequent updates on what was expected in regard to providing students with disabilities with instructional services. On March 13, 2020, one of the first guidance documents sent out to schools regarding the provisions of education for students with disabilities was issued from the New York State Education Department (NYSED).

This document recommended that school districts begin designing plans to meet the requirements set forth IDEA, and also refer to federal guidance from the USDOE.

New York State listed provisions and considerations that school districts should be following as they created their contingency plans. Schools that were continuing to provide instruction to the general education student population must ensure that students with disabilities have equal access to the same educational opportunities. The State also directed school district leaders to create protocols for clear and effective communication between administration and staff and with the parents and guardians of students who have "Individualized Education Plans" (IEPs). This would assist in assuring that the needs of individuals with disabilities are being met to the greatest extent possible.

School leaders were required to ensure that each student with a disability be provided the special education services identified in the student's IEP wherever possible. This could include receiving special education and related services at an alternate location, online, via telephone calls, and "other curriculum-based instructional activities" (Office of Special Education [OSE], 2020).

On Friday, March 13, 2020, Niagara County issued a state of emergency, and the Niagara County Health Department recommended all schools (PreK–12) close for students, effective Monday, March 16 and until further notice. The school district superintendent directed all staff to report to work on Monday, March 16 to receive further instruction and updated information. All extracurricular and school activities for students were canceled.

The atmosphere in the meeting was somber and everyone in the room sat anxiously waiting, with pens, notepads, and hand-held devices prepared to take notes on what the administration had decided would be the next steps regarding this emergency crisis. The superintendent made the priorities clear: food, medicine, communication, and academics. Forty-five percent of the school district's student population are from low socioeconomic families. Therefore, providing food services to the students was vital to the health and safety of the students and their families. Breakfast and lunch were to be provided to district students on Mondays, Wednesdays, and Fridays via buses stationed at three areas around the district. School staff were asked to volunteer to hand out these meals.

The families of students taking medication either at home or in school were contacted by school nurses. The district had to make sure that the students had enough of the medication that they needed at home. If not, they were asked to come pick up the medication or the school would figure out a way to get the medication to those families unable to find transportation to the school.

The school superintendent stated that the leadership of the Administrators' Association, Teachers' Union, and Civil Services Union would be meeting at 10:00 a.m. daily for briefing about the current crisis and debriefing about improving the school district's responses to it. Nightly updates would be going out to all staff beginning that night. Teachers were told that parents would be contacted via Blackboard Connect and that if anyone had questions or concerns, they should consult with the superintendent directly.

PROVIDING APPROPRIATE INSTRUCTION

The sudden shut-down of schools threw all educators into a frenzy. How were we going to get all students what they needed with little to no interruption in their educational and psychological services? The first three factors that were addressed directly impacted students with special needs, as many of these children are from low socioeconomic households, take medications related to their disability daily, and have families/guardians who are difficult to communicate with on a regular basis for various reasons. The final and most difficult task, however, was providing appropriate instruction to students, especially the students with IEPs.

Teachers were directed to prepare both electronic and paper copies of assignments from their subject area that covered five weeks of schoolwork. Electronic work was to be assigned using Google Classroom for those students who had access to a computer and the internet. Hard copies of assignments for each class were to be made into packets for students without access to the internet.

Homeroom teachers were instructed to contact each student's parents/guardians to ask if they had access to the internet. For the time-being, however, teachers had to move quickly to create fifty packets of work to minimize the time that students went without exposure to academics.

Special education teachers had to review and modify the work they assigned to their respective students, not only in the core subject of English, mathematics, social studies, and science, but also in the other subjects that their students were taking at that time, such as technology, family and consumer sciences, and health. All assignments had to be modified according to each special education student's IEP. In addition, if the student was classified as a student who needed instruction in Languages Other Than English (LOTE), it was the teacher's responsibility to provide or facilitate such instruction as required for each student.

Every grade level worked together furiously to create work packets, all of which had to be finished before the end of the day. As stressful and rushed as these focused educators all were, it was amazing to watch how everyone came together and helped one another during this unprecedented time of crisis. The intensive cooperative spirit was like nothing previously experienced by most educators.

Many of the teachers worked well past the required workday hours, and the packets were made and ready to be sent out the following day. Parents were instructed to pick up their child's packet between 11:00 a.m. and 2:00 p.m. either Tuesday, March 17 or Wednesday, March 18. The principals of each building would hand them through the door to each parent. Packets were mailed out to the parents of students unable to pick up the packets of work.

The district's Special Education Department was also in the midst of conducting end-of-the-year meetings for Committees on Special Education (CSEs) and Annual Review. CSE meetings are held to review and discuss each student's progress for the past year and to make plans for the upcoming school year. At an annual review meeting, the team reviews the student's progress toward the existing goals on the IEP and determines whether or not he/she is being successful in the current placement.

The director of Special Education canceled both types of meetings until March 30. At that time, CSEs and annual review (AR) meetings were rescheduled and held virtually. This meant that all members of the Committee, including the parent/guardian of the student, the special education teacher, a general education teacher, the school psychologist, the CSE chairperson, and any other related service provider had to know how to use or learn how to use Google Hangouts, which was the method of video communication chosen by the school district leaders. Parents who did not have access to the internet were asked to be present via phone.

New York State school districts had also been informed that when students returned to school, they would be required to review the delivery of special education and related services to students eligible for special education services during the time schools were closed. They would also be looking at cases in which there were no services rendered to students with disabilities. The Committee on Special Education would then make an individualized determination on whether and to what extent compensatory services might be needed, consistent with applicable requirements, including making up for any skills that may have been lost (OSE, 2020).

The State also suggested that CSEs consider including distance learning plans on students' IEPs going forward. This would specify what instruction would take place online and what services would be provided should a similar situation occur in the future (OSE, 2020).

On March 27, 2020, the Office of Special Education (OSE) sent out another memo stating the provisions of services that were to be provided to students with disabilities during the COVID-19 crisis. Focusing on student and educator well-being, the OSE directed that students with disabilities be provided with a free appropriate public education (FAPE) consistent with protecting the students' health and safety and the health and safety of those who provide those services. To do this, the NYSED gave school districts flexibility in determining the methods in which they provide FAPE to the extent that federal and state laws allow (OSE, 2020).

The need for continued communication in a manner that was comprehensible to everyone in the community, including those individuals whose first language is not English, was also addressed more specifically in this memo. All school districts were advised to establish mechanisms for communicating regularly with staff, students, families, and impacted communities in the language or mode of communication they best understand, regarding the provision of services to students with disabilities, to meet the requirements of IDEA (OSE, 2020).

REGULATORY AMENDMENTS DUE TO COVID-19 CRISIS

On April 16, 2020, the State Education Department announced regulatory amendments that were made for the provision of special education programs and services and due process procedures due to the novel coronavirus (COVID-19) outbreak. Both the USDOE and the NYSED emphasized that all schools were to follow special education legislation at both the federal and state levels during the time that the schools are closed. Services are mandated, but the method in which these services are delivered is not specified. Special education teachers created work packets containing assignments that were designed specifically for each student according to the individualized needs stated in their IEPs.

Special education teachers creatively modified online programs and worksheets that were assigned to students by general education teachers. Special education teachers also prepared for attendance at Annual Review and Reevaluation meetings via video-conferencing and continued to develop and fill out required paperwork. Their responsibility of providing special education students with a quality education based on IEPs and special education legislation became more complicated than ever and definitely illustrated their focused learning concerns and personal caring attitudes toward their students.

However, parents of students with special needs were watching their children regress. Many students were not being provided with the one-on-one services that they regularly received, such as occupational and physical therapy and speech and language services, due to social distancing rules. Also, not all parents had access to the assistive technology that is normally utilized to accommodate children's physical, cognitive, and sensory deficits.

Parents did not all have the basic resources that were needed for learning in this crisis situation, such as computers, iPads, or internet service, to participate in distance learning. This resulted in parents of students with special needs having an added amount of anxiety and frustration to deal with at home (Hill, 2020).

EDUCATION IN THE TIME OF COVID: NEW SCHOOL YEAR BEGINS

The first day of school for the 2020–2021 school year was very similar to the first day of teaching for any newly hired educator. Nobody knew what to expect. Not only were teachers going to have a whole new group of unfamiliar students, but they had to adjust and adapt to an entirely new way of teaching and learning. Teachers and administrators had to make the students coming into the building for in-person learning as comfortable, calm, and normal-feeling as possible. And that is exactly what the administration and teachers did in this rural school district by maintaining a "high-touch" personal approach and establishing a "friendly and welcoming" school climate that emphasized the "fun" of being back together in school.

The superintendent of schools and the reopening committee had met during the summer to make the final detailed plans on how to successfully bring students back to school as safely as possible. The reentry needs of elementary and secondary students were discussed separately in their respective buildings as the different ages of the children impacted the decisions made. It was agreed that the elementary students would attend school all five days of the week.

The children whose parents opted to keep them home during the 2020–2021 school year were to participate in online learning settings and log onto Google Classroom at the times dictated by their teachers. Students who were attending in person were seated at desks that were placed six feet apart and surrounded by plexiglass. They were to wear their masks at all times during the school day.

The secondary students would be divided into three cohorts: Cohort A, which consisted of students whose last names began with the letters A through M; Cohort B, which consisted of students whose last names began with the letters N through Z; and Cohort C, which included the students who would attend all classes virtually throughout the school year. On Mondays and Tuesdays, Cohort A students attended school in person while Cohort B students were expected to log onto Google Classroom for each of their classes during their designated scheduled time periods.

Wednesdays were considered virtual days, which meant that there was no in-person learning on those days. All students were to log onto their homeroom for attendance, and then the various subject area teachers would post an assignment to their Google Classroom for the day. Students were responsible for checking each of their classes to read the teacher's message and what the teacher had posted for the Wednesday assignment; in other words, Wednesday become asynchronous learning days for all students.

Those assignments were due either the following day or when indicated in the teacher's message. Students in Cohort B attended school in-person on Thursdays and Fridays while Cohort A students logged on to each classroom at the appropriate time via Google Classroom.

The first week of school was chaotic. Before the students left their homes, a COVID questionnaire on Google Docs had to be completed and submitted to the school, stating that they did not have any signs or symptoms of COVID-19, nor had they been exposed to anyone known to have the virus.

Face masks had to be worn from the time the children stepped onto the bus until they were dropped off again in the afternoon. Students had to carry all personal belongings, materials, school supplies, and laptops in their backpacks throughout the day, as lockers were not able to be used because of COVID restrictions.

In addition, students were taught the routine of using the hand sanitizer located near the doorway to every class upon entering and leaving the room. They also had to watch a video that explained what COVID-19 was, how it was spread, and what they were expected to do to prevent the spread of the virus.

MODIFYING ASSESSMENTS AND RECORDS

The usually simple task of taking attendance was a process in itself. There were students both in the classroom and online every day of the week except Wednesday. The students who were virtual had to log onto their homeroom and each of their Google Classrooms at the scheduled times. Teachers had to mark the students online either "remote present," "remote absent excused," "remote absent unexcused," or "remote tardy." Students who were supposed to be in the classroom physically were then either marked present or absent. This task alone took up valuable teaching time throughout the day.

For special education teachers, however, there were additional issues that had to be addressed. Solutions and decisions had to be made quickly to ensure that students with IEPs and 504 Accommodation Plans received the appropriate services to which they were entitled. First, the special education teachers had to keep a log of the names of the students receiving special education services for all classes and what was taught in each of the classes throughout the day.

This log also included any of the supplementary and related services, accommodations, modifications, and forms of assistive technology that were used during the lesson each day. This mandatory documentation took more time away from assisting the students as it had to be done every period every day.

The second issue that had to be addressed was how testing accommodations and modifications were going to be provided to students. While it was easier to administer assessments to the students who attended school in person, special education teachers had to come up with a way to give tests and quizzes to students who had accommodations such as tests read, tests administered in a separate location, or extended time. This meant creating another Google Classroom made specifically for reading tests.

Students who were attending in person were taken to a separate classroom and logged onto the Google Classroom with the students who were remote. The students who had "tests read" on their IEPs would then take the test as it was read to them. There were also times when the students who were remote learners on the day of an assessment were told that they would be given the test on the next day that they were present in person. Flexibility was a must to manage unforeseen and emerging situations throughout the year.

Progress monitoring was the third most difficult issue that had to be figured out by special educators. Special education teachers had to take into consideration the social-emotional state of each student and how he/she was adapting to the hybrid learning schedule or learning entirely from home. General and special education teachers had to collaborate more specifically on what measures would be used to monitor student retention of skills learned and comprehension of new skills being taught.

There were fewer assessments and assignments during this school year, and those that were given were often graded on a curve to give students a fair advantage. The passing grade for the school was eventually lowered from 70 percent to 65 percent due to the number of failures that began to emerge a few months into the 2020–2021 school year.

All of this made it very difficult to accurately monitor the progress of students. Regular and open communication between teachers and parents was more important than ever this school year to discuss student difficulties and strengths.

LIMITED TIME WITH STUDENTS

The most frustrating aspect of the 2020–2021 school year was the limited time that teachers had with the students. Only being able to work with and interact with students in person two days out of the week had a negative impact both academically and socially. All students suffered from the time constraints on available assistance with understanding subject area content, assignments, and projects. This was especially true for students with disabilities. Although they all had one period a day to seek additional support and assistance, it was almost impossible to give the students in the classroom and online the attention and help that they required.

Students also lost social time and opportunities that they would usually have during the school year. Only being in-person two days a week, and teachers trying to utilize every precious second for academics gave them even less time to interact socially. Teachers were also unable to form the usually strong relationships and rapport that they normally do with their students, due to the limited time they had together.

RETURNING TO "NEW" NORMALCY

When students and staff returned to school in September 2021, we were faced with getting used to the norms of the past again while keeping with some of the procedures and new norms of the present. While everyone entering the school buildings still had to wear a mask, teachers were excited and anxious to have all students back for in-person learning again. This held especially true for students in the special education programs. Services and supports that were almost impossible to deliver were now more easily accessible and available. Simply being able to work with students in person every day instead of every other day was the most important significance of having all students return to school.

Now that school was back in session and there was a sense of normalcy, the administration wanted to remind students and their parents/guardians of what would be expected moving forward. This would include many items that were not fully enforced in the 2020–2021 school year due to the pandemic. The school principal visited all of the social studies classrooms within the first weeks of the 2021–2022 school year to go over the student expectations and updated COVID protocol.

A school district–produced memo, *Points of Emphasis*, was mailed to parents/guardians and a copy was given to each student. The topics that were covered were homework completion, mask guidelines, twelfth-period assistance and detention, proper use of social media, the ineligibility list, dress code, code of conduct, and appropriate use of Chromebooks, which all students were now assigned and carried from class to class.

Although the administration reminded students and parents of the school expectations and rules that they were supposed to follow, things were still somewhat lax when it came to both academics and behavior during the first half of the 2021–2022 school year. Teachers were able to use their judgment in certain situations. The homework policy states that if a student does not complete and submit homework, he/she will receive a 0 percent, be assigned twelfth-period detention and complete the missed assignment. Teachers were told to use their discretion when enforcing this rule because of the difficulty some students may be experiencing while attempting to readjust to the school environment.

Extending due dates for assignments was common as students reacclimated to a more structured learning environment. The passing grade of 65 percent remained in place after being lowered from 70 percent during the 2020–2021 school year. Teachers were also more judicious in turning in failing grades for students.

If a student was failing two or more subjects, they would be placed on the ineligibility list. Students on the ineligibility list could not attend extracurricular activities, nor could they participate in sports for a week. Teachers took into consideration the academic and psychological issues that individuals were having that may have been caused from being online learners or from only attending in-person learning two days a week for the 2020–2021 school year.

The 2021–2022 school year began with a mixed-method set of instructional techniques throughout the district. Many teachers continued to utilize the technology that had been forced upon them during the pandemic. Online programs and applications that were unfamiliar before COVID-19 now became components of everyday instruction in many of the classrooms. Instructors chose the technological tools that had proven most effective for learners and integrated them into their lessons, activities, and classroom assignments.

Virtual teaching and learning became nonexistent. Only students with severe medical concerns were allowed to learn via Google Classroom, and a teacher assigned only for online learners was responsible for their education. If students were absent, the assignments that they missed were posted on the Google Classroom so that they could complete work while they were out. Some students took advantage of this opportunity, and others did not. There was no form of consequence for the latter.

One of the most noticeable differences in both the general education and special education populations was the lack of ability to appropriately socialize and interact with one another. Issues with conduct began to arise almost immediately. Parents were calling the school more frequently with complaints of verbal and physical bullying that their children had allegedly endured.

Social media was being used by both parents and students to bash the school as well as one another. Behaviors such as physical assaults that were once unheard of in this small rural school began to be a weekly occurrence. Teachers and administrators were finding themselves spending more time addressing inappropriate student behaviors and having less time to focus on academic instruction.

Many teachers believed that inadequate and inconsistent consequences were being given to students for their misbehaviors. Teachers felt that more severe and consistent punishments should be given for the same inappropriate behaviors. This led to a disconnect between administrative and teaching staff, as teachers felt that they were not being supported by the administration. The administration began to get frustrated with teachers as they received more and more disciplinary reports and teacher complaints. The morale of the faculty was obviously low, and educators at all levels appeared to be exhausted and burned out.

Most educators believed that the 2020–2021 school year would have been the most stressful as we were right in the middle of the pandemic. We were wrong. The stress levels in our rural school district seemed much higher during the 2021–2022 school year. Educators were now trying to assist each child with his or her individual academic and/or psychological needs. Every child was affected differently, and it was our job to identify and address those needs.

Students with special needs were particularly affected by the pandemic. Remote learning was less effective than the in-person and one-on-one instruction that most students with disabilities require to be most successful. There was less structure and support due to students only being in school half of the week, online, or not at all. Hands-on related services such as speech, occupational, and physical therapy were administered remotely, which lessened their effectiveness. Although educators did their absolute best to follow the mandates on each student's IEP, it was impossible to be 100 percent compliant.

The toll that the past two years of the COVID-19 pandemic had on the mental health of teachers, administrators, students, and parents became more apparent than ever during the first few months of the 2021–2022 school year. Many now suffered from depression, anxiety, and other psychological issues. Not only did New York State recognize these effects, but so did the district.

The New York State Department of Education in conjunction with the New York State Department of Mental Health sent out electronic memos with resources that teachers, students, administrators, parents, and community members could utilize for mental health support. Links to toolkits, mental health service providers, crisis hotlines, videos, and books were listed. Some of the money that was received from the state for COVID relief was used to address these issues for both the students and the adults residing in the district.

Due to the obvious need for more intense psychological support for the students, the school district administration created a new school social worker position and hired a full-time social worker. This individual is tasked with addressing the needs of the students in the school and making home visits to the parents and families within the community to assist them with their social-emotional needs. The district administration also purchased a work-life service program for teachers and parents to access. A link was added on our school website for the students, staff, parents, and community members to easily access and utilize.

This service included counseling, financial planning services, support for healthy lifestyle changes, assistance in finding childcare, and many other helpful resources. One more way that the district attempted to address the mental health of the faculty was by providing professional development options to choose from on Superintendent's Conference days. This included activities such as yoga, meditation, motivational speaker presentations, and physical activities. This allowed educators to choose both educational instruction as well as psychological remediation that was much needed by all at this time.

There is no telling what effect the global shutdown of schools and major interruptions of student learning are going to have in the long-run. Students with disabilities will most likely continue to show varying degrees of regression, placing them further behind educationally, socially, and emotionally. Schools are going to require additional resources and funding to mitigate the negative impacts of COVID-19 on the education of students with disabilities.

School administrators, teachers, parents, students, board of education members, and community members are going to have to work together to repair the educational damage that has been caused by this global crisis. By working collaboratively and with positive mindsets, educators can create common goals to help students with special needs recover from this setback and begin moving forward again. Teachers will again be able to provide a quality education for students with disabilities in compliance with state and federal laws and commissioner's regulations.

FINAL THOUGHTS

There were some unexpected positive outcomes that emerged from this global crisis that impacted students with special needs as well as their teachers and parents. Because there was less assistance available, students with special needs were forced to be more independent and self-sufficient. Through hard work and intrinsic motivation to do well and be successful, most students receiving special education services excelled.

Many of these individuals realized how much more they were capable of accomplishing with little to no help. Students who had no interest in school pre-pandemic now had new-found confidence in their abilities and wanted to be in school five days a week.

As chaotic and unusual as the 2020–2021 school year was, all those involved came together and cooperatively made it work. Through all the negativity, confusion, and uncertainty, all levels of this rural educational system had one goal in mind: to provide students with the best education possible and help their families cope through the crisis. In addition, it was truly amazing to see how hard the educators in this school community worked to make sure that this happened.

There were many positive professional benefits that occurred to teachers and administrators as a result of the COVID-19 crisis. Teachers were forced into learning new technologies and different methods of teaching. Google Classroom, Docs, Sheets, Slides, and Forms were now being used across curriculum K–12. Teachers and students had to learn KAMI, a digital classroom tool with which all assignments were completed and turned in online. Teachers, students, and parents had more of an opportunity to collaborate and communicate through the technology that was now being used on a daily basis.

As previously identified, students learned to be more independent and responsible for their own learning. And, most importantly of all, educators became aware of how much is taken for granted and how valuable human and material resources are, so that children are provided with quality educations appropriate to each one's individual needs.

Although there will be some students who require remediation and additional support due to the regression caused by the effects of this crisis, most of the students showed resilience and determination to succeed academically. As the nation returns to somewhat "normal" practices, educators, administrators, parents, students, and the community as a whole need to continue to work together to ensure that our students are provided with the supports and services that they require to either keep progressing or to close the gap that was made or widened due to this terrible pandemic crisis.

The social-emotional damage that has been done must also be addressed. Individuals needing support and assistance in these areas need to be identified and provided with the services that they require. Educators have proven themselves capable of overcoming arguably one of the most devastating events in educational history.

The positive results and the knowledge gained due to the effects of the COVID pandemic crisis must be utilized to strengthen the educational system so that students, with and without disabilities, are provided with high-quality education to ensure academic, social, and psychological success.

KEY PRAGMATIC LEADERSHIP TAKEAWAYS

- *Educational leaders need to comprehensively understand the special programs in their respective schools, and they need to continually gain more information about the special education teachers and their students.* Most educators had to learn and utilize less-familiar methods of instruction and collaborate via videoconferencing, due to social distancing requirements related to the global COVID-19 pandemic. However, school leaders were tasked with prioritizing services to students, creating plans to provide those services, and implementing those services in the most effective way possible. For those who do not have in-depth knowledge and understanding of the programs, special education services or the special education students, this was difficult and made managing the crisis even more demanding.
- *Fidelity to state and federal guidelines related to students with disabilities needs to be adhered to, even in crisis situations.* School building and special education supervisors who are responsible for oversight regarding the development, implementation, and evaluation of special education programs and services to all students must maintain their legal and ethical fidelity to those programs and students. This recent crisis modified some of the regulations, but there were still mandates that needed

to be followed and programs and services to be provided, assessed, and reported to state and federal agencies.

- *Parents of children with special needs expect that their children will receive their approved services during the school day, whether there is a crisis or not.* School leaders need to be sure to appropriately communicate with parents whose children are receiving services in terms of when and how those services will be delivered and assessed.
- *Children with special needs may need more personal nurturing during a crisis situation due to the social-emotional changes that they are experiencing.* School leaders need to assure that special education teachers are well prepared and provided with the necessary resources to care for their students during times of significant emotional stress.
- *Special needs children need to have their learning materials, resources (technology), and personnel (service providers) readily available during periods when they may not be in school for their instruction and services.* School leaders need to be knowledgeable about their special education students and their special needs and provide the necessary supports in a timely and efficient manner.
- *School leaders are expressly reminded to be sure to include their special education students in any and all extra-curricular or unique events.* Students with disabilities have the right to be included in all school activities in which they can participate and should be welcomed at the events, as should their parents, to celebrate with their peers.

REFERENCES

Gavin, J. (2020). "Are Special Education Services Required in the Time of COVID-19?" The American Bar Association, March 31. https://www.americanbar.org/groups/litigation/committees/childrens-rights/articles/2020/are-special-education-services-required-in-the-time-of-covid19/.

Lee, A. (2020). "Every Student Succeeds Act (ESSA): What You Need to Know." Understood. https://www.understood.org/en/school-learning/your-childs-rights/basics-about-childs-rights/every-student-succeeds-act-essa-what-you-need-to-know.

Office of Special Education. (2020). "Emergency Regulations for the Provision of Special Education Programs and Services and Due Process Procedures in Response to the Novel Coronavirus (COVID-19) Outbreak in New York State." New York State Education Department. http://www.p12.nysed.gov/specialed/publications/2020-memos/special-education-emergency-regulations-covid-19-response-april-2020.pdf.

Office of Special Education. (2020). "Provisions of Services to Students with Disabilities during Statewide School Closures Due to Novel Coronavirus

(COVID-19) Outbreak in New York State." New York State Education Department, March 27. https://stateaid.nysed.gov/corona%20virus/nysed-covid-19-provision-of-services-to-swd-during-statewide-school-closure-3-27-20.pdf.

Office of State Assessment. (2020). "New York State Alternate Assessment." New York State Department of Education, March 16. http://www.p12.nysed.gov/assessment/ nysaa/.

United States Department of Education. (2020). "Questions and Answers on Providing Services to Children with Disabilities during the Coronavirus Disease 2019 Outbreak." https://www.isbe.net/Documents/qa-covid-19-03-12-2020.pdf.

World Health Organization. (2020). "Coronavirus Disease." https://www.who.int/health-topics/coronavirus#tab=tab_1.

Chapter 9

Applications of Multi-tiered Systems of Support to Promote Social, Behavioral, and Academic Success for Students with Attention-Deficit/ Hyperactivity Disorder

Jennifer Sikov, Carolina Ramirez, Sophia Frontale, Alix Printup, Melanie Rengel-Isea, Emily Sutton, and Gregory A. Fabiano

Approximately 10–12 percent of children in the general education population exhibit the symptoms and associated school-based impairments related to attention-deficit/hyperactivity disorder (ADHD) (American Psychiatric Association, 2022; Fabiano et al., 2013; Froehlich et al., 2007). ADHD significantly impacts academic, social, and behavioral functioning in home, peer, and educational settings (Barbaresi et al., 2007; Biederman, 2004; Harrison et al., 2012; Lahey et al., 2016; Mannuzza & Klein, 2000; Power et al., 2017; Semrud-Clikeman, 2012). In educational settings, youth with ADHD are disproportionately likely to earn poor grades and standardized test scores, be assigned to remedial/special education classes, be rated by teachers as underperforming, and to drop out of school (Arnold et al., 2020; DuPaul & Langberg, 2015; Kent et al., 2011). Largely exacerbated by chronic school behavior, academic failure, and discipline problems from elementary through high school, young adults with ADHD have significantly lower post-high school educational attainment, poor employment outcomes and financial outcomes (Altszuler et al., 2016, Kuriyan et al., 2013), increased substance use and criminal activity (Barkley, Murphy, & Fischer, 2008), and educational/vocational failure (Kent et al., 2011).

CASE STUDY: SAMUEL'S STORY

The impact of ADHD on school performance can be illustrated through a hypothetical case study of Samuel. Samuel is a seven-year-old boy currently enrolled in the first grade, who has been diagnosed with ADHD combined type. At school, Samuel's behavior has been a source of concern for his teachers and school staff. He talks excessively to classmates during instruction, disrupting the classroom. Additionally, Samuel frequently stands up during class, distracting the other students and interrupting the class. He misplaces his homework assignments and classroom materials. Moreover, Samuel's social interactions are strained due to his impatience when waiting his turn and needing to be in charge, hindering his ability to engage in activities that demand patience, such as board games or group activities.

At home, Samuel's parents have identified additional areas of concern. While completing homework assignments, he struggles to remain seated and focused, leading to poor homework completion and lower academic performance. During bedtime, he is restless, causing drowsiness and fatigue during the day, which has led to increased irritability. Morning routines present challenges as Samuel frequently forgets essential steps, resulting in tardiness for school and leaving behind necessary materials such as homework assignments. As a result, Samuel arrives late to class and therefore misses the opportunity to interact positively with his teachers and peers in unstructured situations, while also missing orienting instructions and daily routine overviews provided by the teacher at the beginning of the day.

The behaviors described above are characteristic of many children with ADHD. Schools currently use problem-solving frameworks to plan and implement intervention. Integrating a problem-solving framework to outline intervention strategies and supports, multi-tiered system of supports (MTSS) in school settings are one way to ensure appropriate interventions are implemented (Fuchs & Fuchs, 2006). MTSS models implement behavioral interventions within the general education setting, aimed to both help schools efficiently and effectively address complex student problems across academic, social, and behavioral sectors (Sugai et al., 2016), as well as provide students with ADHD the support they need without waiting for a special education classification (Vujnovic et al., 2013). To date, there has been work toward developing MTSS for academic concerns (Ikeda et al., 1996; Kovaleski, Tucker, & Stevens, 1996; Telzrow, McNamara, & Hollinger, 2000), yet there has been relatively less exploration into how evidence-based interventions for youth with ADHD can be applied within an MTSS model. As outlined below, interventions for ADHD in school settings are optimally addressed within an MTSS framework, as this approach is consistent with best practice recommendations (DuPaul & Stoner, 2004). The past three decades have unsuccessfully tried to shoehorn children with ADHD into a model of school intervention (e.g., traditional special education placement or Section 504 Accommodation Plans after long periods of inefficiently and ineffectively addressed behavioral failure; Fabiano et al., 2023) that simply does not work.

OVERVIEW OF MULTI-TIERED SYSTEMS OF SUPPORT (MTSS) FOR ADHD

MTSS are school-wide, multi-level instructional and behavioral systems aimed to address academic, behavioral, and socioemotional challenges (Jimerson, Burns, & VanDerHeyden, 2016; Singh et al., 2019; Weist et al., 2018) through three increasingly intensive tiers of intervention and support. Critical to the MTSS model is the consistent monitoring of students' response to the interventions and establishing criteria for transitioning between intensity and differentiation for tiers of support (Forman et al., 2013; Gresham, 2005; McIntosh & Goodman, 2016). Tier 1 represents the general education curriculum and classroom management system, and is provided to all students regardless of individual risks and needs (August, Gewirtz, & Realmuto, 2010; Horner, Sugai, & Anderson, 2010). Tier 1 often includes classroom-wide support systems (e.g., reading skills) and behavioral health curricula, small group socio-emotional skills training, and comprehensive parent and child skills training (August et al., 2001; Pfiffner et al., 2014). Purportedly, Tier 1 programming meets the needs of most students (~80%) and for the ~20 percent of students who do not respond adequately to Tier 1, Tier 2 supports are added. Tier 2 consists of more targeted support programs designed to provide a student with additional opportunities to practice skills matched specifically to his/her skill deficit and acute concerns (Vaughn, 2003). For academics, this level of support typically includes supplemental small-group instruction and skill building, such as Coping Power (see Lochman & Wells, 2002), Social Skills Training (see Eiraldi, Mautone, & Power, 2012), brief behaviorally focused interventions (e.g., check in/check out system; Hawken & Horner, 2003), or individualized interventions that can be conducted in the general education classroom (e.g., behavioral contracts; daily report cards). Tier 3 includes intensive and systematic interventions, intended for a small percentage of students (~5%) who are unresponsive to programming at Tiers 1 and 2 (Crone, Hawken, & Horner, 2010). Tier 3 interventions represent the most intensive level of support and occur individually or in a small-group setting. Tier 3 often includes a comprehensive evaluation and intensive services to identify students with a specific disability, high-risk, and/or those meeting eligibility criteria for special education programming (Fuchs & Fuchs, 2007; Lewis et al., 2017). Overall, MTSS represents a needs-driven, equity-based approach to ensuring that all children receive the supports they need to be successful and is adapted to incorporate students' risk status and ongoing response to an intervention (August, Piehler, & Miller, 2018).

At this time, there is no definitive, well-disseminated, elementary school based MTSS program for children with ADHD (see Fabiano et al., 2023 for additional discussion). A first step in establishing an MTSS within schools for ADHD is the identification of best practice interventions that can be used across tiers of support. There are several summative resources that document evidence-based treatments for ADHD. When the three meta-analyses that focused on school-based outcomes across designs and measures were considered together (DuPaul & Eckert, 1997; DuPaul et al., 2019; Fabiano et al., 2009), positive behavior supports clearly are evidence-based. Fabiano et al. (2015) reported that they clearly supported the use of classroom contingency management strategies for intervening to treat ADHD in classroom settings. These results were updated, replicated, and extended by Fabiano et al. (2021), which also supported the use of classroom contingency management as a key component of effective intervention for ADHD.

COMPONENTS OF MTSS WITH ADHD POPULATIONS

Tier 1

Among school age populations with ADHD, multiple supports should be provided to problem solving teams to facilitate the effective integration of MTSS relating to academic skills and socio-emotional learning. This will include training of the problem-solving team to read and understand behavioral and academic graphs and interpret data with regard to norms. This will also include training for teachers in the school on Tier 1 classroom routines and management strategies (e.g., frequent and labeled praise, effective commands, use of classroom rules and structure with systematic consequences for positive and negative behaviors) (Fabiano et al., 2018; Pelham et al., 2005; Reddy, Fabiano, & Dudek, 2013). Classroom management strategies should be oriented toward positive reinforcement and consequences to enable a positive school climate and social-emotional learning.

Aspects of school-wide positive behavioral interventions and supports can include: (1) clear academic and behavioral expectations (e.g., daily lesson plans, rules for engaging others), (2) affirmative and constructive feedback (e.g., clear rubrics, focus on one skill), and (3) reinforcement of appropriate behavior (Wills et al., 2019). As exclusionary discipline practices are often utilized within limited resource settings and disproportionately to marginalized students (Ritter & Anderson, 2018), they should be minimized to avoid exacerbating school disengagement (Skiba, Arredondo, & Williams, 2014). Classroom-wide behavioral interventions (e.g., Good Behavior Game) have been shown to increase desirable behavior in children with ADHD (Barrish, Saunders, & Wolf, 1969; Embry, 2002). Social-emotional learning (SEL) interventions focused on schoolwide approaches to helping students identify, communicate, and regulate their emotional responses are also pivotal in Tier 1 supports. With an emphasis on being mindful, respect for others, and positive thinking, SEL interventions can augment student's self-awareness, self-management, social awareness, relationship skills, and responsible decision-making (Acosta et al., 2019; Gol-Guven, 2017; Snyder et al., 2012) and as such serve as a framework for universal social/emotional/behavioral support and expectations.

Tier 2

For children assigned to the problem-solving team who are identified as at-risk for ADHD because they exceed criterion on the screening tools or evidence in-class impairment, multiple targeted interventions can be employed, such as (a) daily report cards; (b) brief behaviorally focused interventions (e.g., check in/check out; (c) training interventions (e.g., social skills, organizational skills).

a. The daily report card (DRC) can be used to monitor and target both academic (e.g., productivity, accuracy) and behavioral (e.g., reducing disruptive and increasing adaptive behavior) needs on a daily basis (Eiraldi, Mautone, & Power, 2012; Pyle & Fabiano, 2017; Vannest et al., 2010; Volpe & Fabiano, 2013). School-based problem-solving teams and parents will collaboratively decide on targeted behavior, positive behavior goals based on screening data from Tier 1, and daily/weekly goals for obtaining a reward at home. Behaviors will be monitored by the teachers, and adjustments will be made to the DRC as needed. The DRC will also target the academic enabling behaviors typically impaired in children with ADHD including work completion and accuracy, organization/preparation for class, neatness of work, academic engagement, and on-task behavior.
b. Brief behavioral interventions can target specific behaviors such as academic engagement (e.g., on task attending, task completion),

social-emotional learning, and self-regulation. Such interventions have been shown to improve task engagement, work completion, and response accuracy (Ducharme & Shecter, 2011; Vogelgesang et al., 2016). For example, check-in/check-out (Miller et al., 2015) involves daily "check-ins" with an adult at the beginning and end of the school day to meet behavioral and academic goals. It can be implemented through daily morning check-ins and afternoon check-outs with a mentor; daily report cards from a teacher to parents regarding academic and behavioral performance; frequent teacher monitoring and feedback; and school-parent communication strategies (Kearney & Graczyk, 2020; Maynard et al., 2013).

c. Social skills training, emotional regulation techniques, and targeted organizational interventions such as the Challenging Horizons Program have the potential to enhance social problem-solving, emotional management, and both verbal and nonverbal communication within an organization. These interventions can be effectively administered through small-group instruction (Evans et al., 2011; Fabiano et al., 2014; Mikami, Jia, & Na, 2014; Storebø et al., 2019). Given that youths with ADHD often encounter difficulties in forming relationships and difficulties with social adjustment (Semrud-Clikeman, 2012), incorporating these targeted socio-emotional and organizational interventions can serve as a beneficial approach in providing Tier 2 support.

Tier 3

For children who do not respond sufficiently to Tier 1 and 2 programs, and continue to have impaired ratings on the screeners, they will be referred to a Tier 3 intervention that will include function-based approach interventions. The teacher will meet with one of the problem-solving team consultants to identify remaining target behaviors and develop a treatment plan for an enhanced Behavioral Intervention Plan (BIP). A specific BIP-E will be operationalized to facilitate implementation and integrity/fidelity monitoring, and the target behaviors and any additional information (e.g., school rewards; Premack contingencies) will be listed on the DRC. A function-based approach as this is (1) Consistent with the approach of most child study teams within the school problem-solving model; (2) it promotes the use of intervention aligned with function; and (3) it is feasible for use in general education settings.

One example of Tier 3 interventions may be utilized for students who require alternative educational supports that involve combining academic settings and in-person instruction with family, food, housing, physical and mental health, and other social services via school-community partnerships (Warren,

2008) or school-supported family resource centers. This may include after-school/extended school (e.g., extended classes, medical and mental health services, after-care, tutoring), community-based learning centers, specialized schools, and summer programs (Fabiano et al., 2014; Kearney, 2008). This process can also draw typically difficult-to-reach students and families to educational and behavioral health services (Diamond & Freudenberg, 2016).

MULTICULTURAL CONSIDERATIONS IN AN MTSS FOR ADHD

The burden of ADHD can be particularly devastating for racial and ethnic minority children who already face high rates of educational underachievement, overrepresentation in the criminal justice system, and low economic mobility (NAACP, n.d.; National Center for Educational Statistics, n.d.; Reeves, 2001). They may experience disproportionate under-diagnosis and under-treatment, poor linkage to school services, and decreased utilization of subspeciality care compared to non-minority patients, contributing to poorer clinical outcomes (Basch, 2011; Bauermeister et al., 2003; Bird et al., 2008; Bussing, Schoenberg, & Perwien, 1998; Mehta, Lee, & Ylitalo, 2013; Morgan et al., 2013a, 2013b; Pastor & Reuben, 2005; Price et al., 2013; Zima et al., 2010). In working with racial and ethnic minority students and families, it is vital for schools and problem-solving teams to incorporate a culturally informed understanding and meaning of symptoms, experiences with discrimination and unique stressors, and cultural values and beliefs in the MTSS model. This is also crucial when working with parents, whereby the perception of ADHD stigmatization, parental fear of stigma, and avoidance of labels may engender minority parents to be especially sensitive about publicly disclosing their child's ADHD diagnosis or deter them from being open to school-based services (Bailey, Jaquez-Gutierrez, & Madhoo et al., 2014; Dempster, Wildman, & Keating, 2012).

Sociocultural factors can also contribute to disparities in family educational and mental health service utilization, such as (a) cultural differences in caregivers' etiological beliefs of ADHD, (b) lack of available culturally congruent and linguistically appropriate services, (c) challenges around quality of communication and collaboration with professionals, and (d) potential concerns about the impact of educational services and mental health care on family's immigration status (Alvarado & Modesto-Lowe, 2017). Furthermore, a potentially significant barrier to diagnosis and treatment is that of the overall perception and attitudes to mental health and treatment held by minoritized populations. There is a history of discrimination and stigmatization among minoritized populations (Alvarado & Modesto-Lowe, 2017, p. 173; Dong et al., 2020). Thus, there may be a mistrust of health services in the wake of well-known historical exploitations of their bodies, minds, and health such as was done to African Americans during the Tuskegee experiment—although one should acknowledge that this is but one of a multitude of atrocities committed toward minoritized populations (Alvarado & Modesto-Lowe, 2017, p. 173). This mistrust of overall health services and by extension mental health services in schools, exacerbates the already prominent negative stigma associated with mental health and/or labels that parents fear will negatively impact their children or adolescents (Alvarado & Modesto-Lowe, 2017, p. 173; Dong et al., 2020; Smith, Rodríguez, & Bernal, 2011).

The Guidelines for Providers of Psychological Services to Ethnic, Linguistic, and Culturally Diverse Populations unequivocally state that culture and language impact psychological services (Smith, Rodríguez, & Bernal, 2011, p. 166). Sociocultural factors (e.g., cultural beliefs, religion values, expectations) are likely to influence caregiver problem recognition and management, including knowledge of ADHD, attitudes about psychopathology, and treatment decision-making (Coker et al., 2009; Reardon & Galindo, 2003; Toppelberg et al., 2013). Furthermore, families may experience communication barriers, lack of extended family support, societal discrimination, and change in social status (Measham et al., 2014), contributing to difficulties advocating for their children's needs in school (Halgunseth, Ispa, & Rudy, 2006). Therefore, it is necessary to practice a culturally responsive approach to working with families of children with ADHD within MTSS, highlighting the role mental health professionals can play in ensuring positive outcomes for all students. Specifically, cultural adaptation of evidence-based interventions within each tier can serve to decrease disparities of mental health utilization by improving relations and communication with families and increasing treatment acceptability and caregiver engagement by reducing the emphasis on labeling (Bal, 2018).

Universal screening of academics and behavior in Tier 1 requires the collaboration of parents, school workers, and mental health specialists to determine culturally relevant positive behavioral standards that acknowledge any gaps that may exist between school and home behavior expectations for students (e.g., making eye contact when an adult speaks), as well as highlight culturally responsive strategies that must be considered that are relevant to both the child's culture at home and school. Tier 1 whole-classroom management programs can be adapted to the students' cultural backgrounds after consultation and input from caregivers. This may be done by conducting interviews and focus groups with teachers, caregivers, and principals on the strengths, barriers, acceptability, and fidelity of the intervention, along with gathering their perceptions of the effectiveness of various consequences (e.g., large- or small-group contingencies, response cost, positive reinforcement, and ignoring undesirable behavior) based on cultural relevance.

Tier 2 interventions can be delivered in consideration of family's specific sociocultural needs. School based problem-solving teams can consider culturally congruent compromises within planned intervention approaches and empower parents to be open to new parenting approaches. Additionally, school environments can provide certain resources not available at home, such as extended computer access, unstructured time with peers, school supplies, individual time or lunch with a teacher or counselor, public recognition of accomplishments, extra time at a specialized class (e.g., music, art), and preferential seat assignments (Balu & Ehrlich, 2018). For families with financial, food, or housing insecurity that could disrupt learning and school attendance, schools can work with caregivers to set realistic behavioral and attendance goals, address transportation barriers (e.g., carpool, bus, school transportation), develop problem-solving strategies, and provide access to necessary external resources (Finning et al., 2020).

Previous literature has shown that mental health services and treatments targeted to specific cultural contexts are several times more effective than those services and treatments that are non-culturally targeted (Smith, Rodríguez, & Bernal, 2011; Fallon et al., 2012). In the case of ADHD, minoritized populations have been shown to prefer behavioral interventions such as the MTSS to assist their children and adolescents in the treatment of this disorder (Dong et al., 2020). The MTSS and its implementers need to develop a cultural awareness and sensitivity to potential cultural differences between them and the families they aim to assist (Dong et al., 2020). This requires the necessary cultural adaptations of interventions such as the MTSS, which is crucial to providing adequate and effective assistance to these families (Dong et al., 2020). A culturally adapted MTSS can break down some of the barriers that minoritized populations face in accessing and utilizing mental health services in addition to increasing treatment effectiveness and acceptability for these children and adolescents (Dong et al., 2020). Some of these adaptations include psychoeducation on school policies and supports, and increased parental communication with school personnel to help ensure that minoritized populations and diverse perspectives are represented in the development and implementation of ADHD interventions (Dong et al., 2020). In conclusion, minoritized populations face a multitude of barriers to the diagnosis and treatment of ADHD. Yet the inclusion of culturally relevant interventions such as the culturally adapted MTSS can help to break down some of these barriers and increase the effectiveness of these treatments.

Developmental Considerations

Age and development also create a challenge for implementation of MTSS in schools. Middle and older adolescents have greater social, emotional, and behavioral motivation from their peers than adults (Romer, Reyna, & Satterthwaite, 2017), and schools typically shift from adult-provided supports in elementary and middle school to independent and peer-driven supports (Flannery & McGrath Kato, 2017). With increased independence and peer influence, this shift can be leveraged by involving students throughout the tiered intervention planning and implementation processes (Flannery & McGrath Kato, 2017). Furthermore, as older adolescents near the end of their education, they face increased pressures to demonstrate college and career readiness skills (e.g., academic engagement, academic mindsets, learning processes, critical thinking, social skills, and transition knowledge) (Morningstar et al., 2017), and interventions and school supports should be adapted accordingly.

Multidisciplinary Team to Support MTSS

A multi-disciplinary team approach is commonly considered an essential component for managing ADHD in students and this process involves professionals from various disciplines to work collectively in the diagnosis, assessment, and treatment of ADHD in students. For instance, school psychologists play a key role in assisting students with ADHD in the school setting. They can conduct psychological assessments that can highlight the key strengths and challenges of the child. They work closely with parents and teachers as a primary reference of knowledge (Miller, 2013) to educate them on what ADHD is and the different strategies that should be implemented to help the child succeed both at home and at school (Danciu, 2011). School psychologists also collaborate with parents and teachers to develop IEPs and 504 plans that cater to the child's needs in the classroom. Importantly, even prior to these more formal school supports, they can work with the general education teacher through the MTSS to provide evidence-informed positive behavior support strategies at Tiers 1–3. Other members that could be important in the process and involvement of the multidisciplinary team are clinical and educational psychologists, psychiatrists, pediatricians, speech therapists, and other professionals to work alongside the student's parents and educators. Therefore, being a part of this multidisciplinary team comes with the responsibility of communicating effectively among team members to gain a clear understanding of the student's needs, strengths, challenges, and treatment goals. With this being said, the multidisciplinary team should develop an individualized treatment plan tailored to the specific needs of each student with ADHD to implement the appropriate evidence-based interventions and psychoeducation to learn effective strategies for managing symptoms.

CASE STUDY, REVISITED

The tier system described above will now be used in the context of Samuel's case. In Tier 1, Samuel's teacher (and school psychologist) should schedule a meeting with his parents to discuss the behavior concerns at hand. Some of the things that would be discussed include prepping Samuel's bookbag ahead of time to address him forgetting packing his bookbag in his nightly routine. Sleep routines should also be addressed in this meeting, with the teacher (or school psychologist) inquiring about Samuel's sleep schedule (e.g., does he nap after school? What other factors could be preventing him from going to sleep earlier?). Lastly, school personnel should address ways that parents can help him get to school on time, whether that may be leaving ten minutes earlier, and making sure that his clothes are picked out and that lunch is packed the night before school. The classroom Tier 1 supports could include more frequent praise and positive attention for rule-following and academic productivity and an emphasis on the educator providing clear and direct behavioral requests to promote compliance the first time a request is issued.

If Tier 1 is not successful in getting Samuel's behavior issues back on track, the plan should move to Tier 2. In this tier, a daily report card will be implemented. For example, the goals for the week as reflected on his DRC would start off with Samuel remaining seated during instruction time with six or fewer reminders, completing/returning homework four out of five days a week, and successfully waiting his turn in line with four or fewer reminders. These daily report card items address Samuel's teacher's concerns of frequently interrupting others, having difficulty waiting his turn, and disrupting the class by being out of his assigned seat or area. His rewards for meeting goals could be five minutes of screen time per day for each goal achieved.

If Samuel needs a more intensive intervention at Tier 3, his behavior plan should move to a functional behavior assessment (FBA). ADHD testing and an IEP plan should also be considered. The FBA would focus on addressing Samuel's problematic behavior of standing up and walking around the classroom during inappropriate times. Antecedents and consequences of behavior were identified by a school psychologist as teacher instruction to work on an assignment quietly (antecedent), followed by the problematic behavior, resulting in delay of the independent work time on the assignment (consequence). The function of the behavior for Samuel was avoidance, while the desired behavior is to work independently without interruptions. A plan would then be put into place to introduce an alternative behavior of receiving a five-minute break to stand up after working quietly for ten minutes. This also serves his maintaining consequence of delay of independent work time. After this alternative behavior plan was successful, the new behavior would slowly be introduced–Samuel would be allowed to work quietly (but being allowed to stand) and then receiving a reward after work is completed.

FINAL THOUGHTS

The future of MTSS should grow to include ADHD-specific and evidence-based treatments in order to address the growing prevalence of ADHD impairments in schools. This includes developing a more accurate measurement of the prevalence of ADHD to illustrate the necessity of providing an overarching MTSS to the entire school (Fabiano & Pyle, 2019). Prior to implementation, researchers should seek to address how children with ADHD interact with the structure of MTSS. Such as, what does it look like for a child with ADHD to move across tiers? How long would they have to display the correct behavior? Future work also should address the process of implementing interventions within an MTSS. For example, a current question relates to how many tiers an optimal framework includes or what possible maintenance features should be included (Fabiano & Pyle, 2019). These answers have the potential to create a strongly structured MTSS with more guidance to those administering it. School leaders should seek to evaluate both the teaching and learning of methods to implement the MTSS. For example, resource allocation procedures, addressing how administrators approach what tiers should receive more resources as each tier varies in intensity is a question of practical importance (Fabiano & Evans, 2019). Strengthening the MTSS would also include evaluating and altering assessment approaches, progress monitoring, measurements, recruitment, and retainment (Fabiano & Pyle, 2019). For example, assessing the effectiveness of MTSS-related professional development training (Eagle et al., 2015) should be conducted. Another way to improve upon the model's approach would be research group dynamics related to effective and sustained intervention, since most of the MTSS is team-based and collaborative (Eagle et al., 2015).

KEY PRAGMATIC LEADERSHIP TAKEAWAYS

- MTSS is a framework of interventions of increasing intensity that provides support to students with challenging behaviors, when they need it, largely within general education settings.

- The initial tier reflects classroom-wide positive behavior supports, the second tier implements targeted supports for students identified as at-risk, and the third tier is reserved for intensive, protracted interventions for students where such support is indicated.
- MTSS avoids much of the labeling and "waiting to fail" that is implicit in other school approaches to providing support (e.g., referral for special education), and therefore may be more inclusive of the broad array of students within a school.
- School leaders can oversee an effective MTSS plan by ensuring that the implementers are using the approaches as prescribed with fidelity.

REFERENCES

Acosta, J., Chinman, M., Ebener, P., Malone, P. S., Phillips, A., & Wilks, A. (2019). "Evaluation of a Whole-School Change Intervention: Findings from a Two-Year Cluster-Randomized Trial of the Restorative Practices Intervention." *Journal of Youth and Adolescence 48*(5), 876–90. https://doi.org/10.1007/s10964-019-01013-2.

Altszuler, A. R., Page, T. F., Gnagy, E. M., Coxe, S., Arrieta, A., Molina, B. S., & Pelham Jr, W. E. (2016). "Financial Dependence of Young Adults with Childhood ADHD." *Journal of Abnormal Child Psychology 44*(6), 1217–29.

Alvarado, C., & Modesto-Lowe, V. (2017). "Improving Treatment in Minority Children with Attention Deficit/Hyperactivity Disorder." *Clinical Pediatrics 56*(2), 171–76. https://doi.org/10.1177/0009922816645517.

American Psychiatric Association. (2022). *Diagnostic and Statistical Manual of Mental Disorders, Fifth Edition.* Washington, DC: American Psychiatric Association.

Arnold, L. E., Hodgkins, P., Kahle, J., Madhoo, M., & Kewley, G. (2020). "Long-Term Outcomes of ADHD: Academic Achievement and Performance." *Journal of Attention Disorders 24*(1), 73–85. https://doi.org/10.1177/1087054714566076.

August, G. J., Gewirtz, A., & Realmuto, G. M. (2010). "Moving the Field of Prevention from Science to Service: Integrating Evidence-Based Preventive Interventions into Community Practice through Adapted and Adaptive Models." *Applied and Preventive Psychology 14*(1), 72–85. https://doi.org/10.1016/j.appsy.2008.11.001.

August, G. J., Piehler, T. F., & Miller, F. G. (2018). "Getting 'SMART' about Implementing Multi-Tiered Systems of Support to Promote School Mental Health." *Journal of School Psychology 66*, 85–96. https://doi.org/10.1016/j.jsp.2017.10.001.

August, G. J., Realmuto, G. M., Winters, K. C., & Hektner, J. M. (2001). "Prevention Of Adolescent Drug Abuse: Targeting High-Risk Children with a Multifaceted Intervention Model—The Early Risers 'Skills for Success' Program."

Applied and Preventive Psychology 10(2), 135–154. https://doi.org/10.1017/S0962-1849(02)01005–3.

Bailey, R. K., Jaquez-Gutierrez, M. C., & Madhoo, M. (2014). "Sociocultural Issues in African American and Hispanic Minorities Seeking Care for Attention-Deficit/Hyperactivity Disorder." *The Primary Care Companion for CNS Disorders 16*(4). https://doi.org/10.4088/PCC.14r01627.

Bal, A. (2018). "Culturally Responsive Positive Behavioral Interventions and Supports: A Process–Oriented Framework for Systemic Transformation." *Review of Education, Pedagogy, and Cultural Studies 40*(2), 144–74. https://doi.org/10.1080/10714413.2017.1417579.

Balu, R., & Ehrlich, S. B. (2018). "Making Sense out of Incentives: A Framework for Considering the Design, Use, and Implementation of Incentives to Improve Attendance." *Journal of Education for Students Placed at Risk (JESPAR) 23*(1–2), 93–106. https://doi.org/10.1080/10824669.2018.1438898.

Barbaresi, W. J., Katusic, S. K., Colligan, R. C., Weaver, A. L., & Jacobsen, S. J. (2007). "Long-Term School Outcomes for Children with Attention-Deficit/Hyperactivity Disorder: A Population-Based Perspective." *Journal of Developmental and Behavioral Pediatrics: JDBP 28*(4), 265–73. https://doi.org/10.1097/DBP.0b013e31811ff87d.

Barkley, R. A., Murphy, K. R., & Fischer, M. (2008). *ADHD in Adults: What the Science Tells Us*. New York: Guilford.

Barrish, H. H., Saunders, M., & Wolf, M. M. (1969). "Good Behavior Game: Effects of Individual Contingencies for Group Consequences on Disruptive Behavior in a Classroom1." *Journal of Applied Behavior Analysis 2*(2), 119–24. https://doi.org/10.1901/jaba.1969.2-119.

Basch, C. E. (2011). "Inattention and Hyperactivity and the Achievement Gap among Urban Minority Youth." *The Journal of School Health 81*(10), 641–49. https://doi.org/10.1111/j.1746–1561.2011.00639.x.

Bauermeister, J. J., Canino, G., Bravo, M., Ramírez, R., Jensen, P. S., Chavez, L., Martínez-Taboas, A., Ribera, J., Alegría, M., & García, P. (2003). "Stimulant and Psychosocial Treatment of ADHD in Latino/Hispanic Children." *Journal of the American Academy of Child and Adolescent Psychiatry 42*(7), 851–55. https://doi.org/10.1097/01.CHI.0000046864.56865.30.

Biederman, J. (2004). "Impact of Comorbidity in Adults with Attention-Deficit/Hyperactivity Disorder." *The Journal of Clinical Psychiatry 65*, Suppl 3, 3–7.

Bird, H. R., Shrout, P. E., Duarte, C. S., Shen, S., Bauermeister, J. J., & Canino, G. (2008). "Longitudinal Mental Health Service and Medication Use for ADHD among Puerto Rican Youth in Two Contexts." *Journal of the American Academy of Child and Adolescent Psychiatry 47*(8), 879–89. https://doi.org/10.1097/CHI.0b013e318179963c.

Bussing, R., Schoenberg, N. E., & Perwien, A. R. (1998). "Knowledge and Information about ADHD: Evidence of Cultural Differences among African-American and White Parents." *Social Science & Medicine (1982) 46*(7), 919–28. https://doi.org/10.1016/s0277-9536(97)00219–0.

Coker, T. R., Elliott, M. N., Kataoka, S., Schwebel, D. C., Mrug, S., Grunbaum, J. A., Cuccaro, P., Peskin, M. F., & Schuster, M. A. (2009). "Racial/Ethnic Disparities in the Mental Health Care Utilization of Fifth Grade Children." *Academic Pediatrics 9*(2), 89–96. https://doi.org/10.1016/j.acap.2008.11.007.

Crone, D. A., Hawken, L. S., & Horner, R. H. (2010). *Responding to Problem Behavior in Schools, Second Edition: The Behavior Education Program*. New York: Guilford Press.

Danciu, E. L. (2011). "Multidisciplinary Approach of the Attention Deficit Hyperactivity Disorder (ADHD) between Hope and Reality." *Procedia—Social and Behavioral Sciences 15*, 2967–71. https://doi.org/10.1016/j.sbspro.2011.04.224.

Dempster, R., Wildman, B., & Keating, A. (2012). "The Role of Stigma in Parental Help-Seeking for Child Behavior Problems." *Journal of Clinical Child and Adolescent Psychology: The Official Journal for the Society of Clinical Child and Adolescent Psychology, American Psychological Association, Division 53* 42. https://doi.org/10.1080/15374416.2012.700504.

Diamond, C., & Freudenberg, N. (2016). "Community Schools: A Public Health Opportunity to Reverse Urban Cycles of Disadvantage." *Journal of Urban Health: Bulletin of the New York Academy of Medicine 93*(6), 923–39. https://doi.org/10.1007/s11524-016-0082-5.

Dong, Q., Garcia, B., Pham, A. V., & Cumming, M. (2020). "Culturally Responsive Approaches for Addressing ADHD within Multi-tiered Systems of Support." *Current Psychiatry Reports 22*(6), 27. https://doi.org/10.1007/s11920-020-01154-3.

Ducharme, J. M., & Shecter, C. (2011). "Bridging the Gap between Clinical and Classroom Intervention: Keystone Approaches for Students with Challenging Behavior." *School Psychology Review 40*(2), 257–74. https://doi.org/10.1080/02796015.2011.12087716.

DuPaul, G. J., Chronis-Tuscano, A., Danielson, M. L., & Visser, S. N. (2019). "Predictors of Receipt of School Services in a National Sample of Youth with ADHD." *Journal of Attention Disorders 23*(11), 1303–19. https://doi.org/10.1177/1087054718816169.

DuPaul, G. J., & Eckert, T. L. (1997). "The Effects of School-Based Interventions for Attention Deficit Hyperactivity Disorder: A Meta-Analysis." *School Psychology Review 26*(1), 5–27.

DuPaul, G. J., Eckert, T. L., & Vilardo, B. (2012). "The Effects of School-Based Interventions for Attention Deficit Hyperactivity Disorder: A Meta-Analysis 1996–2010." *School Psychology Review 41*(4), 387–412. http://naspjournals.org/loi/spsr.

DuPaul, G. J., & Langberg, J. M. (2015). "Educational Impairments in Children with ADHD." In *Attention-Deficit Hyperactivity Disorder: A Handbook for Diagnosis and Treatment*, fourth edition, 169–90. New York: Guilford Press.

DuPaul, G. J., & Stoner, G. (2014). *ADHD in the Schools: Assessment and Intervention*. New York: Guilford Press.

Eagle, J. W., Dowd-Eagle, S. E., Snyder, A., & Holtzman, E. G. (2015). "Implementing a Multi-Tiered System of Support (MTSS): Collaboration between School

Psychologists and Administrators to Promote Systems-Level Change." *Journal of Educational and Psychological Consultation 25*(2–3), 160–77.

Eiraldi, R. B., Mautone, J. A., & Power, T. J. (2012). "Strategies for Implementing Evidence-Based Psychosocial Interventions for Children with Attention-Deficit/Hyperactivity Disorder." *Child and Adolescent Psychiatric Clinics of North America 21*(1), 145–59. https://doi.org/10.1016/j.chc.2011.08.012.

Embry, D. D. (2002). "The Good Behavior Game: A Best Practice Candidate as a Universal Behavioral Vaccine." *Clinical Child and Family Psychology Review 5*, 273–97.

Evans, S. W., Schultz, B. K., Demars, C. E., & Davis, H. (2011). "Effectiveness of the Challenging Horizons After-School Program for Young Adolescents with ADHD." *Behavior Therapy 42*(3), 462–74. https://doi.org/10.1016/j.beth.2010.11.008.

Fabiano, G. A., & Evans, S. W. (2019). "Introduction to the Special Issue of *School Mental Health* on Best Practices in Effective Multi-tiered Intervention Frameworks." *School Mental Health 11*, 1–3. https://doi.org/10.1007/s12310-018-9283-2.

Fabiano, G. A., Lupas, K., Merrill, B. M., Schatz, N. K., Piscitello, J., Robertson, E. L., & Pelham, W. E. (2024). "Reconceptualizing the Approach to Supporting Students with Attention-Deficit/Hyperactivity Disorder in School Settings." *Journal of School Psychology 104*, 101309.

Fabiano, G. A., Pelham, W. E., Coles, E. K., Gnagy, E. M., Chronis, A. M., & O'Connor, B. C. (2009). "A Meta-analysis of Behavioral Treatments for Attention-Deficit/Hyperactivity Disorder." *Clinical Psychology Review 29*, 129–40.

Fabiano, G. A., Pelham, W. E., Majumdar, A., Evans, S. W., Manos, M., Caserta, D., Girio-Herrera, E. L., Pisecco, S., Hannah, J. N., & Carter, R. (2013). "Elementary and Middle School Teacher Perceptions of Attention-Deficit/Hyperactivity Disorder Incidence." *Child and Youth Care Forum 42*, 87–99.

Fabiano, G. A., & Pyle, K. (2019). "Best Practices in School Mental Health for Attention-Deficit/Hyperactivity Disorder: A Framework for Intervention." *School Mental Health 11*, 72–91.

Fabiano, G. A., Reddy, L. A., & Dudek, C. (2018). "Teacher Coaching Supported by Formative Assessment for Improving Classroom Practices." *School Psychology Quarterly 33*, 293–304.

Fabiano, G. A., Schatz, N. K., Aloe, A. M., Chacko, A., & Chronis-Tuscano, A. M. (2015). "A Review of Meta-Analyses of Psychosocial Treatment for Attention-Deficit/Hyperactivity Disorder: Systematic Synthesis and Interpretation." *Clinical Child and Family Psychology Review 18*, 77–97.

Fabiano, G. A., Schatz, N. K., Aloe, A. M., Pelham Jr., W. E., Smyth, A. C., Zhao, X., Merrill, B. M., Macphee, F., Ramos, M., Hong, N., Altszuler, A., Ward, L., Rodgers, D. B., Liu, Z., Ersen, R. K., & Coxe, S. (2021). "Comprehensive Meta-analysis of Attention-Deficit/Hyperactivity Disorder Psychosocial Treatments Investigated within Between Group Studies." *Review of Educational Research 91*, 718–60. https://doi.org/10.3102/00346543211025092.

Fabiano, G. A., Schatz, N. K., & Pelham, W. E. (2014). "Summer Treatment Programs for Youth with ADHD." *Child and Adolescent Psychiatric Clinics of North America 23*(4), 757–73. https://doi.org/10.1016/j.chc.2014.05.012.

Fallon, L. M., O'Keeffe, B. V., & Sugai, G. (2012). "Consideration of Culture and Context in School-Wide Positive Behavior Support: A Review of Current Literature." *Journal of Positive Behavior Interventions 14*(4), 209–19. https://doi.org/10.1177/1098300712442242.

Finning, K., Waite, P., Harvey, K., Moore, D., Davis, B., & Ford, T. (2020). "Secondary School Practitioners' Beliefs about Risk Factors for School Attendance Problems: A Qualitative Study." *Emotional and Behavioural Difficulties: The Journal of the Association of Workers for Children with Emotional and Behavioural Difficulties 25*(1), 15–28. https://doi.org/10.1080/13632752.2019.1647684.

Flannery, K. B., & McGrath Kato, M. (2017). "Implementation of SWPBIS in High School: Why Is It Different?" *Preventing School Failure: Alternative Education for Children and Youth 61*(1), 69–79. https://doi.org/10.1080/1045988X.2016.1196644.

Forman, S. G., Shapiro, E. S., Codding, R. S., Gonzales, J. E., Reddy, L. A., Rosenfield, S. A., Sanetti, L. M. H., & Stoiber, K. C. (2013). "Implementation Science and School Psychology." *School Psychology Quarterly: The Official Journal of the Division of School Psychology, American Psychological Association 28*(2), 77–100. https://doi.org/10.1037/spq0000019.

Froehlich, T. E., Lanphear, B. P., Epstein, J. N., Barbaresi, W. J., Katusic, S. K., & Kahn, R. S. (2007). "Prevalence, Recognition, and Treatment of Attention-Deficit/Hyperactivity Disorder in a National Sample of US Children." *Archives of Pediatrics & Adolescent Medicine 161*(9), 857–64.

Fuchs, D., & Fuchs, L. S. (2006). "Introduction to Response to Intervention: What, Why, and How Valid Is It?" *Reading Research Quarterly 41*(1), 93–99.

Fuchs, L. S., & Fuchs, D. (2007). "A Model for Implementing Responsiveness to Intervention." *TEACHING Exceptional Children 39*(5), 14–20. https://doi.org/10.1177/004005990703900503.

Gol-Guven, M. (2017). "The Effectiveness of the Lions Quest Program: Skills for Growing on School Climate, Students' Behaviors, Perceptions of school, and Conflict Resolution Skills." *European Early Childhood Education Research Journal 25*(4), 575–94. https://doi.org/10.1080/1350293X.2016.1182311.

Gresham, F. M. (2005). "Response to Intervention: An Alternative Means of Identifying Students as Emotionally Disturbed." *Education and Treatment of Children 28*(4), 328–44.

Halgunseth, L. C., Ispa, J. M., & Rudy, D. (2006). "Parental Control in Latino Families: An Integrated Review of the Literature." *Child Development 77*(5), 1282–97. https://doi.org/10.1111/j.1467 8624.2006.00934.x.

Harrison, J. R., Vannest, K., Davis, J., & Reynolds, C. (2012). "Common Problem Behaviors Of Children and Adolescents in General Education Classrooms in the United States." *Journal of Emotional and Behavioral Disorders 20*(1), 55 64. https://doi.org/10.1177/1063426611421157.

Horner, R. H., Sugai, G., & Anderson, C. M. (2010). "Examining the Evidence Base for School-Wide Positive Behavior Support." *Focus on Exceptional Children 42*(8), Article 8. https://doi.org/10.17161/foec.v42i8.6906.

Ikeda, M. J., Tilly, W. D., Stumme, J., Volmer, L., & Allison, R. (1996). "Agency-Wide Implementation of Problem Solving Consultation: Foundations, Current Implementation, and Future Directions." *School Psychology Quarterly 11*, 228–43, doi:10.1037/h0088931.

Jimerson, S. R., Burns, M. K., & VanDerHeyden, A. M. (2016). "From Response to Intervention to Multi-Tiered Systems of Support: Advances in the Science and Practice of Assessment and Intervention." In S. R. Jimerson, M. K. Burns, & A. M. VanDerHeyden (Eds.), *Handbook of Response to Intervention: The Science and Practice of Multi-Tiered Systems of Support*, 1–6. New York: Springer US. https://doi.org/10.1007/978-1-4899-7568-3_1.

Kearney, C. (2008). *Helping School Refusing Children and Their Parents: A Guide for School-based Professionals*. New York: Oxford University Press, USA.

Kearney, C. A., & Graczyk, P. A. (2020). "A Multidimensional, Multi-tiered System of Supports Model to Promote School Attendance and Address School Absenteeism." *Clinical Child and Family Psychology Review 23*(3), 316–37. https://doi.org/10.1007/s10567-020-00317-1.

Kent, K. M., Pelham, W. E., Jr, Molina, B. S., Sibley, M. H., Waschbusch, D. A., Yu, J., Gnagy, E. M., Biswas, A., Babinski, D. E., & Karch, K. M. (2011). "The Academic Experience of Male High School Students with ADHD." *Journal of Abnormal Child Psychology 39*(3), 451–62.

Kovaleski, J. F., Tucker, J. A., & Stevens, L. J. (1996). "Bridging Special and Regular Education: The Pennsylvania Initiative." *Educational Leadership 53*, 44–47.

Kuriyan, A. B., Pelham, W. E., Molina, B. S. G., Waschbusch, D. A., Gnagy, E. M., Sibley, M. H., . . . & Kent, K. M. (2013). "Young Adult Educational and Vocational Outcomes of Children Diagnosed with ADHD." *Journal of Abnormal Child Psychology 41*, 27–41.

Lahey, B. B., Lee, S. S., Sibley, M. H., Applegate, B., Molina, B. S. G., & Pelham, W. E. (2016). "Predictors of Adolescent Outcomes among 4–6-Year-Old Children with Attention-Deficit/Hyperactivity Disorder." *Journal of Abnormal Psychology 125*(2), 168–81. https://doi.org/10.1037/abn0000086.

Lewis, T. J., McIntosh, K., Simonsen, B., Mitchell, B. S., & Hatton, H. L. (2017). "Schoolwide Systems of Positive Behavior Support: Implications for Students at Risk and with Emotional/Behavioral Disorders." *AERA Open 3*(2). https://doi.org/10.1177/2332858417711428.

Lochman, J. E., & Wells, K. C. (2002). "The Coping Power Program at the Middle-School Transition: Universal and Indicated Prevention Effects." *Psychology of Addictive Behaviors: Journal of the Society of Psychologists in Addictive Behaviors 16*(4S), S40–54. https://doi.org/10.1037/0893–164x.16.4s.s40.

Mannuzza, S., & Klein, R. G. (2000). "Long-Term Prognosis in Attention-Deficit/Hyperactivity Disorder." *Child and Adolescent Psychiatric Clinics of North America* 9(3), 711–26.

Maynard, B. R., McCrea, K. T., Pigott, T. D., & Kelly, M. S. (2013). "Indicated Truancy Interventions for Chronic Truant Students: A Campbell Systematic Review." *Research on Social Work Practice 23*(1), 5–21. https://doi.org/10.1177/1049731512457207.

Measham, T., Heidenreich-Dutray, F., Rousseau, C., & Nadeau, L. (2014). "Cultural Consultation in Child Psychiatry." In L. J. Kirmayer, J. Guzder, & C. Rousseau (Eds.), *Cultural Consultation: Encountering the Other in Mental Health Care*, 71–87. New York: Springer. https://doi.org/10.1007/978-1-4614-7615-3_4.

Mehta, N. K., Lee, H., & Ylitalo, K. R. (2013). "Child Health in the United States: Recent Trends in Racial/Ethnic Disparities." *Social Science & Medicine (1982) 95*, 6–15. https://doi.org/10.1016/j.socscimed.2012.09.011.

McIntosh, K., & Goodman, S. (2016). *Integrated Multi-Tiered Systems of Support: Blending RTI and PBIS*. New York: Guilford Press.

Mikami, A. Y., Jia, M., & Na, J. J. (2014). "Social Skills Training." *Child and Adolescent Psychiatric Clinics of North America 23*(4), 775–88. https://doi.org/10.1016/j.chc.2014.05.007.

Miller, L. M., Dufrene, B. A., Sterling, H. E., Olmi, D. J., & Bachmayer, E. (2015). "The Effects of Check-In/Check-Out on Problem Behavior and Academic Engagement in Elementary School Students." *Journal of Positive Behavior Interventions 17*(1), 28–38. https://doi.org/10.1177/1098300713517141.

Miller, C. (2013). "School-Based Assessment of Attention Deficit Hyperactivity Disorder: Development of A Resource Guide for School Psychologists" (Order No. 3560127). Available from ProQuest Dissertations & Theses A&I; ProQuest Dissertations & Theses Global. (1355751929). https://www.proquest.com/dissertations-theses/school-based-assessment-attention-deficit/docview/1355751929/se-2.

Morgan, P. L., Staff, J., Hillemeier, M. M., Farkas, G., & Maczuga, S. (2013a). "Racial and Ethnic Disparities in ADHD Diagnosis from Kindergarten to Eighth Grade." *Pediatrics 132*(1), 85–93. https://doi.org/10.1542/peds.2012–2390.

Morgan, P. L., Staff, J., Hillemeier, M. M., Farkas, G., & Maczuga, S. (2013b). "Racial and Ethnic Disparities in ADHD Diagnosis from Kindergarten to Eighth Grade." *Pediatrics* 132(1), 85–93. https://doi.org/10.1542/peds.2012–2390.

Morningstar, M. E., Lombardi, A., Fowler, C. H., & Test, D. W. (2017). "A College and Career Readiness Framework for Secondary Students with Disabilities." *Career Development and Transition for Exceptional Individuals 40*(2), 79–91. https://doi.org/10.1177/2165143415589926.

NAACP. (n.d.). "NAACP Criminal Justice Fact Sheet." Retrieved July 31, 2017, from http://www.naacp.org/criminal-justice-fact-sheet/.

National Center for Educational Statistics. n.d. "Status and Trends in the Education of Racial and Ethnic Minorities." https://nces.ed.gov/pubs2010/2010015/.

Owens, J. S., Holdaway, A. S., Zoromski, A. K., Evans, S. W., Himawan, L. K., Girio-Herrera, E., & Murphy, C. E. (2012). "Incremental Benefits of a Daily Report Card Intervention Over Time for Youth with Disruptive Behavior." *Behavior Therapy 43*(4), 848–61. https://doi.org/10.1016/j.beth.2012.02.002.

Pastor, P. N., & Reuben, C. A. (2005). "Racial and Ethnic Differences in ADHD and LD in Young School-Age Children: Parental Reports in the National Health Interview Survey." *Public Health Reports (Washington, D.C.: 1974) 120*(4), 383–92. https://doi.org/10.1177/003335490512000405.

Pelham, W. E., Massetti, G. M., Wilson, T., Kipp, H., Myers, D., Standley, B.B.N., Billheimer, S., & Waschbusch, D. A. (2005). "Implementation of a Comprehensive Schoolwide Behavioral Intervention: The ABC Program." *Journal of Attention Disorders 9*, 248–60.

Pfiffner, L. J., Hinshaw, S. P., Owens, E., Zalecki, C., Kaiser, N. M., Villodas, M., & McBurnett, K. (2014). "A Two-site Randomized Clinical Trial of Integrated Psychosocial Treatment for ADHD-Inattentive Type." *Journal of Consulting and Clinical Psychology* 82(6), 1115. https://doi.org/10.1037/a0036887.

Power, T. J., Watkins, M. W., Anastopoulos, A. D., Reid, R., Lambert, M. C., & DuPaul, G. J. (2017). "Multi-informant Assessment of ADHD Symptom-Related Impairments among Children and Adolescents." *Journal of Clinical Child and Adolescent Psychology: The Official Journal for the Society of Clinical Child and Adolescent Psychology 46*(5), 661–74. https://doi.org/10.1080/15374416.2015.1079781.

Price, J. H., Khubchandani, J., McKinney, M., & Braun, R. (2013). "Racial/Ethnic Disparities in Chronic Diseases of Youths and Access to Health Care in the United States." *BioMed Research International.* https://doi.org/10.1155/2013/787616.

Pyle, K., & Fabiano, G. A. (2017). "A Meta-analysis of Single-Subject Design Studies Utilizing the Daily Report Card Intervention for Students with ADHD." *Exceptional Children 83*, 378–95.

Reardon, S., & Galindo, C. (2003). *Hispanic Children and the Initial Transition to Schooling: Evidence from the Early Childhood Longitudinal Study.* Presentation to the National Academies/National Research Council, Panel on Hispanics in the United States.

Reddy, L. A., Fabiano, G. A., & Dudek, C. (2013). "Instructional and Behavior Management Practices Implemented by Elementary General Education Teachers." *Journal of School Psychology 51*(6), 683–700.

Reeves, R. V. (2001, November 30). "The Other American Dream: Social Mobility, Race and Opportunity." Brookings. https://www.brookings.edu/blog/social-mobility-memos/2013/08/28/the-other-american-dream-social-mobility-race-and-opportunity/.

Ritter, G. W., & Anderson, K. P. (2018). "Examining Disparities in Student Discipline: Mapping Inequities from Infractions to Consequences." *Peabody Journal of Education 93*(2), 161–73. https://doi.org/10.1080/0161956X.2018.1435038.

Romer, D., Reyna, V. F., & Satterthwaite, T. D. (2017). "Beyond Stereotypes of Adolescent Risk Taking: Placing the Adolescent Brain in Developmental Context." *Developmental Cognitive Neuroscience 27*, 19–34. https://doi.org/10.1016/j.dcn.2017.07.007.

Semrud-Clikeman, M. (2012). The Role of Inattention on Academics, Fluid Reasoning, and Visual-Spatial Functioning in Two Subtypes of ADHD. *Applied*

Neuropsychology. Child 1(1), 18–29. https://doi.org/10.1080/21622965.2012.665766.

Singh, N. N., Lancioni, G. E., Karazsia, B. T., Myers, R. E., Hwang, Y.-S., & Anālayo, B. (2019). "Effects of Mindfulness-Based Positive Behavior Support (MBPBS) Training Are Equally Beneficial for Mothers and Their Children with Autism Spectrum Disorder or with Intellectual Disabilities." *Frontiers in Psychology 10*, 385. https://doi.org/10.3389/fpsyg.2019.00385.

Skiba, R. J., Arredondo, M. I., & Williams, N. T. (2014). More Than a Metaphor: The Contribution of Exclusionary Discipline to a School-to-Prison Pipeline. *Equity & Excellence in Education 47*(4), 546–64. https://doi.org/10.1080/10665684.2014.958965.

Smith, T. B., Rodríguez, M. D., & Bernal, G. (2011). "Culture." *Journal of Clinical Psychology 67*(2), 166–75. https://doi.org/10.1002/jclp.20757.

Snyder, F. J., Vuchinich, S., Acock, A., Washburn, I. J., & Flay, B. R. (2012). "Improving Elementary School Quality through the Use of a Social-Emotional and Character Development Program: A Matched-Pair, Cluster-Randomized, Controlled Trial in Hawai'i." *Journal of School Health 82*(1), 11–20. https://doi.org/10.1111/j.1746–1561.2011.00662.x.

Storebø, O. J., Elmose Andersen, M., Skoog, M., Joost Hansen, S., Simonsen, E., Pedersen, N., Tendal, B., Callesen, H. E., Faltinsen, E., & Gluud, C. (2019). "Social Skills Training for Attention Deficit Hyperactivity Disorder (ADHD) in Children Aged 5 to 18 Years." *The Cochrane Database of Systematic Reviews 6*(6), CD008223. https://doi.org/10.1002/14651858.CD008223.pub3.

Sugai, G., Simonsen, B., Freeman, J., & Salle, T. L. (2016). "Capacity Development and Multi-Tiered Systems of Support: Guiding Principles." *Australasian Journal of Special Education 40*(2), 80–98. https://doi.org/10.1017/jse.2016.11.

Telzrow, C. F., McNamara, K., & Hollinger, C. L. (2000). "Fidelity of Problem-Solving Implementation and Relationship to Student Performance." *School Psychology Review 29*, 443–61.

Toppelberg, C. O., Hollinshead, M. O., Collins, B. A., & Nieto-Castañon, A. (2013). "Cross-Sectional Study of Unmet Mental Health Need in 5- to 7-Year-Old Latino Children in the United States: Do Teachers and Parents Make a Difference in Service Utilization?" *School Mental Health 5*(2), 59–69. https://doi.org/10.1007/s12310-012-9089-6.

Vannest, K. J., Davis, J. L., Davis, C. R., Mason, B. A., & Burke, M. D. (2010). "Effective Intervention for Behavior with a Daily Behavior Report Card: A Meta-analysis." *School Psychology Review 39*, 654–72.

Vaughn, S. (2003, December). "How Many Tiers Are Needed for Response to Intervention to Achieve Acceptable Prevention Outcomes?" Paper presented at the National Research Center on Learning Disabilities Responsiveness-to-Intervention Symposium, Kansas City, MO. http://www.nrcld.org/symposium2003/vaughn/vaughn.pdf.

Vogelgesang, K. L., Bruhn, A. L., Coghill-Behrends, W. L., Kern, A. M., & Troughton, L. C. W. (2016). "A Single-Subject Study of a Technology-Based Self-Monitoring Intervention." *Journal of Behavioral Education 25*(4), 478–97.

Volpe, R. J., & Fabiano, G. A. (2013). *Daily Behavior Report Cards: An Evidence-Based System of Assessment and Intervention*. New York: Guilford Press.

Vujnovic, R. K., Holdaway, A., Owens, J. S., & Fabiano, G. A. (2014). "Response to Intervention for Youth with ADHD: Incorporating an Evidence-Based Intervention within a Multi-tiered Framework." In M. Weist, N. Lever, C. Bradshaw, & J. S. Owens (Eds.), *Handbook of School Mental Health*, second edition, 399–412. New York: Springer.

Warren, M. (2008). Communities and Schools: A New View of Urban Education Reform. *Harvard Educational Review 75*(2), 133–73. https://doi.org/10.17763/haer.75.2.m718151032167438.

Weist, M. D., Eber, L., Horner, R., Splett, J., Putnam, R., Barrett, S., Perales, K., Fairchild, A. J., & Hoover, S. (2018). "Improving Multitiered Systems of Support for Students with 'Internalizing' Emotional/Behavioral Problems." *Journal of Positive Behavior Interventions 20*(3), 172–84. https://doi.org/10.1177/1098300717753832.

Wills, H. P., Caldarella, P., Mason, B. A., Lappin, A., & Anderson, D. H. (2019). "Improving Student Behavior in Middle Schools: Results of a Classroom Management Intervention." *Journal of Positive Behavior Interventions 21*(4), 213–27. https://doi.org/10.1177/1098300719857185.

Zima, B. T., Bussing, R., Tang, L., Zhang, L., Ettner, S., Belin, T. R., & Wells, K. B. (2010). "Quality of Care for Childhood Attention Deficit/Hyperactivity Disorder in a Managed Care Medicaid Program." *Journal of the American Academy of Child and Adolescent Psychiatry 49*(12), 1225–37. https://doi.org/10.1016/j.jaac.2010.08.012.

Chapter 10

Social-Emotional Intelligence

A Guide for Parents and Teachers

Sharon Singh

Social-emotional intelligence (SEI) begins to develop at birth. It can sometimes be referred to as emotional intelligence (EI) and research is even suggesting that it might actually play a more important role than intellectual intelligence (IQ) (Goleman, 1995). This perspective continues to be supported by the current research conducted by Chandrahasa and Bommanavar (2022), Trad et al. (2022), and Alwali and Alwali (2022). Regardless of what you call it, SEI is an important part of development and every individual's overall well-being. Things to consider when looking at SEI can include a child's temperament and attachment style. Parents and teachers also play an important role with this developmental process as they are who a child will have their first interactions with. Let's talk a little more about what social-emotional intelligence is.

WHAT IS SOCIAL-EMOTIONAL INTELLIGENCE?

When trying to understand *social-emotional intelligence* (SEI) it is important to view it from social and emotional aspects in relation to childhood experiences. When considering these two aspects, the social piece relates to building positive, healthy relationships, and the emotional piece relates to the display of and managing emotions. For example, consider what happens when an infant cries and the parent responds. What is the response, positive or negative? The emotion of crying and the response from the parents is an example of the beginning of SEI developing relationships. The more positive the response from the caregiver the better the chances the child has to regulate the emotion of crying. Eventually, with enough positive and consistent responses, the child may stop crying at the sight and/or sound of the caregiver, because they have been consistent with responding to their needs of hunger, tiredness, or a wet diaper. This is also explained at the base of *Maslow's Hierarchy of Needs* as physiological needs, the sense of safety and belongingness that is met during the early human growth and development stage.

Additionally, the parent is required to also communicate with the infant during the response phase. Talking to the infant helps with communication and language development. The communication part is also a way of building a positive and trusting relationship with the child and contributes to the type of attachment style being developed. Social and emotional development influences self-confidence, empathy, and the ability to continue to build positive, healthy relationships, which is why interactions during the early years play such an important role. Piaget's discusses cognitive development through play, but through constant play there are also emotional functions that are developing as well. This occurs with communication and can be seen through their play by the actions and communication styles they mimic (Suizzo, 2000).

Why Is It Important?

It is obvious from early childhood experiences, such as those explained above, that SEI is an important part of child development and personal growth. Since SEI begins at birth, it is the starting point for human interactions, but the type of those interactions is important. Consider the example above when an infant is crying and the parent's response, how is the parent responding? The type of response matters and requires consistency, but to be clear, the responses need to be authentic and of quality each time. Given appropriate, authentic, and quality interactions, a sense of connectedness is created that supports the social and emotional aspect of SEI. Each time the parent or caregiver interacts or responds with the infant this needs to take place, because it is creating the foundation of how all future relationships will be developed.

The development of SEI also contributes to well-being. When looking at well-being, both physical and mental health are included. Parents might think a child has no stress or problems, so they do not need to worry about mental health, but in fact this is not true (Shillington et al., 2023). Similar to how early interactions and communication contribute to the foundation of building relationships, so too does developing well-being or positive mental health also start in the early years. What a child learns in the early years becomes the foundation for all aspects of life. With more and more recognition of mental health. it is important to understand that this begins early and as children grow and develop, the effects of their well-being and mental health begin to show.

Positive, authentic interactions and relationship building need to start in the early years. Without it or if there is extreme inconsistency, then social and emotional development will be affected in a negative way. Social-emotional intelligence when nurtured in the early years helps children with a sense of belonging, their well-being, expression, and engagement. These four pillars have been recognized as essential for learning and success in school and beyond (Ontario Ministry of Education, 2014).

Who Plays a Role?

When considering SEI, there are a few key people who are essential to the development. First are the parents and/or main caregivers. They are the first to communicate and interact with the child starting in infancy. Stimulation is important even in the infancy stage because learning and development has started, even in the pre-natal experiences. It is important for parents to again be consistent with interactions, making them authentic and of quality, as this is a continuous process.

Next are educators, as they will spend a lot of time with children once they enter childcare or school. Providing children opportunities for higher-order thinking (e.g., problem solving and critical thinking) is important and can be implemented with Bloom's Taxonomy (University of Central Florida, 2023). Both parents and educators need to continue nurturing SEI because it is a continuous process. As children learn in a more structured environment at school, parents who may have struggled with self-regulation can also benefit as educators can now bridge the gap between school and home. Parents and educators need to communicate with each other as they can assist one another, especially when SEI challenges arise.

Theorists have examined how SEI plays a role in child development and have explored theories regarding how this happens and the significance of it beginning with parents. Erik Erikson's Psychosocial Development Theory explains how individuals go through various stages and phases of growth and the SEI results based on the experiences during each stage. When infants cry they communicate that they are tired or hungry, and in the subsequent response from the caregiver, the infant is developing trust or mistrust, explained by Erikson as the first stage of development (table 10.1). Again, the type of response, its consistency, and even interactions during this period of growth and development contribute to the trust or mistrust that is developing during this stage. When a stage is not fulfilled, a false sense of mistrust, suspicion, and anxiety may result, which can be a very unhealthy way to begin SEI development.

Another theorist worth mentioning is Urie Bronfenbrenner and his *Ecological Systems Theory* (Evans, 2024). Bronfenbrenner identifies different

Table 10.1. Erickson's Stages of Social-Emotional Development

Approximate Age	*Virtues*	*Psycho Social Crisis*	*Significant Relationship*	*Existential Questions*	*Favorable Outcomes*	*Unfavorable Outcomes*
0–2 years	Hopes	Basic Trust vs. Mistrust	Mother	Can I trust the world?	Faith in environment and future events	Suspicion, fear of future events
2–4 years	Will	Autonomy vs. Shame and Doubt	Parents	Is it okay to be me? Can I control my own behavior?	A sense of self-control and adequacy	Feelings of shame and self-doubt
4–5 years	Purpose	Initiative vs. Guilt	Family	Is it okay for me to do, move, and act? Can I become independent?	Ability to be a "self-starter," to initiate one's own activities	A sense of guilt and inadequacy to be on one's own
5–12 years	Competence	Industry vs. Inferiority	Neighbors, School	Can I make it in the world of people and things? Can I learn the necessary skills to be successful?	Ability to learn how things work, to understand and organize	A sense of inferiority at understanding and organizing

13–19 years	Fidelity	Identity vs. Role Confusion	Peers, Role Model	Who am I? What can I be? What are my interests?	Seeing oneself as a unique and integrated person	Confusion over who and what one really is
20–24 years	Love	Intimacy vs. Isolation	Friends, Partners	Can I love?	Ability to make commitments to others, to love	Inability to form affectionate relationship
25–64 years	Care	Generativity vs. Stagnation	Household, Workmates	Can I make my life count? What can I offer?	Concern for family and society in general	Concern only for self—one's own well-being and prosperity
65–death	Wisdom	Ego Integrity vs. Despair	Mankind, My Kind	Is it okay to have been me?	A sense of integrity and fulfillment; willingness to face death	Dissatisfaction with life; despair over prospect of death

Adapted from Google Images, 2015 Skinnurse. (April 27, 2013). Psychology-Human Development Information to Help Guide Parents, Teachers, and Caregivers. [Online image]. Retrieved from httpd://skinnurse.woedpress.com/tag/8-stage-psychological-theory/.

systems in a child's life that explain how each one is connected and plays a role in individual development. Figure 10.1 illustrates the interaction and impact of each system and the role each plays, as well as how each one influences others. Starting with the microsystem, family is the first influence, then peers and family are influences, then religion, and these factors continue for each system. This can be confusing for some individuals who may feel safe at home and can express emotions, but then at school the teacher does not implement any social-emotional regulation practice. The child can thus be confused as to how to express emotions, which can lead to becoming withdrawn, fearful, and anxious, which are also unhealthy for SEI development.

Unlike the other theorists mentioned, Howard Gardner focuses on multiple intelligences. As seen in figure 10.2, there are many different types of intelligences that can be developed. Learning requires nurturing and support. By incorporating a variety of teaching and learning strategies teachers and parents are simply tapping into the various intelligences a child already has. This will create a diverse learning environment that supports each child's strengths and abilities, which supports growth and development. It is important to focus on the child's strengths because this offers support and encouragement, which also fosters a positive mindset that allows children to believe in their strengths and abilities (self-awareness). When the adults around them offer support and encouragement, the child too begins to believe in themself.

As explained above, many people play a role in the SEI development of a child. Yes, it begins with the parents, but then it transitions to teachers, peers, religious leaders, community member, and so on. The parent's influence is

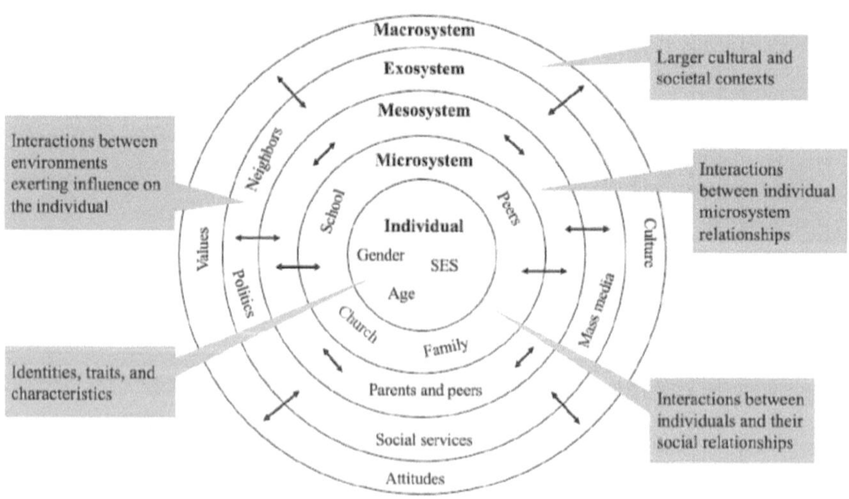

Figure 10.1. Bronfenbrenner's ecological systems. ***https://www.structural-learning.com/post/bronfenbrenners-ecological-model.***

Figure 10.2. Gardner's multiple intelligences. ***Adapted from Google Images, 2015. Escobar, L. (April 14, 2010). Multiple Intelligences and Software (Online Image). Retrieved from http://edel518.wikispace.com//Multiple+Intelligences+amd+Software.***

usually the strongest and children follow in their footsteps. It is important for parents to support SEI, but it is just as important for parents to be aware of what they are role modeling; it is being absorbed by the child whether or not it is intentional.

DEVELOPMENTAL BENEFITS

There are developmental benefits of nurturing and supporting SEI. Historically, SEI was perhaps misunderstood, but researchers have illustrated the important role it plays in the developmental process. Social and emotional development nurtures and supports self-awareness, self-regulation (how to manage emotions), positive relationships, goal setting, the ability to make responsible decisions, and appreciation of the perspective of others.

Behaviors like kindness, empathy, and sharing are said to improve attitudes toward school. When these prosocial behaviors are nurtured, children also have reduced stress and depression, simply because they are in happier moods and therefore motivated and better able to work toward their goals (Yu et al., 2023). Building positive relationships allows them to have individuals around them who also have positive attitudes, and they can support and motivate each other. It is like a chain reaction of positivity and support that connects one aspect to another. Again, this needs to begin in the early years to have the best influence because it becomes part of the child's foundation and does not have to be relearned.

Temperament

There are three types of temperament styles that an individual can develop early in their development and growth years. Each temperament style requires different approaches as emotions are expressed differently and require different responses from the caregiver. According to Martorell and Kruk (2014) three types of temperaments have been identified: easy-going, difficult, and slow-to-warm-up.

An easy-going child, just as the name implies, is simply usually going with the flow. These children can develop and follow routines and adapt to new environments easily. Don't be mistaken that easy-going children do not cry; they certainly do. However, they may not necessarily display intense emotions as in a child with a difficult-temperament-style. These children have a more positive mood, generally, but they too can have a bad day.

Difficult-temperament-style children can be more challenging to deal with personally and socially. They display more negative emotions, as well as intense emotions. These children can also have difficulty when introduced to new environments, which they may find it difficult to adapt to. Developing routines with them can also present challenges, sometimes daily or weekly.

Children with the slow-to-warm-up temperament may exhibit low activity levels and less intense displays of emotions. Children with this temperament exhibit negative moods or display very little emotion.

It is most likely that a child fits into one of the temperament styles described above. When considering SEI, taking temperament style into consideration is beneficial for the caregiver, as it can help with determining the right approach rather than entering a battle daily or weekly. It can also help with regulating behaviors and emotions because the approaches used might be more appropriate than using punishments or rewards.

Is it possible for a child to display more than one temperament style? Absolutely, and it truly depends on the child, their experiences, and the environment they are exposed to. Given this information, it is important to really understand who the child is and what approach works best for the current situation. Once the parent or teacher has gained this understanding, it really can relieve a lot of stress and pressure for the caregiver and the care receiver as well.

Attachment

Attachment is the type of relationship that develops between a child and their parent or main caregiver(s), this also includes the quality of the relationship and can be categorized into four different attachment styles. It begins at birth and continues through childhood, and researchers have indicated that it contributes to healthy brain development (Martorell & Kruk, 2014). A lack of stimulation can lead to underdevelopment and possibly impairments, which is why social-emotional connections are a crucial part of healthy child development. Attachment happens in different stages beginning with an infant crying and the response from the caregiver. As the infant grows and develops, crying changes to verbal language and the parent response continues to play an important role in the type of attachment being developed.

Secure attachment is when a baby has developed a secure, and trusting relationship. This takes place when a parent responds to the child's needs in a caring, consistent, and nurturing manner. There is a secure base in which the child can safely explore their surroundings that also allows for developing secure attachment. This type of attachment helps children develop self-awareness, emotional regulation, and meaningful relationships, and allows them to realize their potential.

Insecure avoidant is when a baby shows insecurity by avoiding the parent or main caregiver. This can happen when the parent shows avoidant behavior toward the child. When feeding an infant, for example, if the parent does not interact, communicate, or make eye-contact with the child an insecure, avoidant attachment will begin to develop. Parents tend to have inconsistent strategies when meeting the child's needs, hence the disorganized and disoriented behavior displayed by the child. Generally, children with insecure avoidant attachment tend to manage distress on their own and do not tend to look for comfort from the parent or other caregiver(s).

Insecure resistant is when a baby clings and resists the parent. The baby might cry or push the caregiver away to resist being comforted. These babies also don't explore the environment when the parent is around and would instead cling to the parent. Parents tend to be inconsistent, dismissing, insensitive, and/or neglectful as a result. Subsequently, these children might display signs of being passive, crying, and failing to seek contact when needed.

Insecure disorganized is when babies display patterns of avoidance and resistance and can sometimes include extreme fearfulness when around the parent. This is a result of the parents not being viewed as a secure base, as is present in secure attachment. The child's needs are not being met, emotion ally, or physically. These children might display signs of depression, anger, or lack of responsiveness. Parents tend to have extremely erratic strategies, like being passive or intrusive when meeting the child's needs, hence the disorganized and disoriented behavior displayed by the child.

The type of attachment developed matters because it sets the foundation for future social-emotional relationships and how they are developed. It can determine who the child will be friends with, how they will allow others to treat them, and how they solve problems. This might be considered the root of lifelong social-emotional behaviors because infancy is the phase where it all begins. Children cry, but parents and caregivers understand that the next thing to do is figure out why they are crying. Once you figure out the why, it is up to the parent to decide how to respond, and each time the child is nurtured, the child is most likely developing secure attachment, which developmentally speaking has many more benefits to the child.

Parents and caregivers have bad days too. The point is to do the best one can each day, recognizing the developing social-emotional needs of each child. Communicate with the child even when they may not be able to verbally respond back. Perhaps the caregivers were not even upset with the child, but if the child witnessed the angry behavior, once the care giver has calmed down, they need to let the child know the reason for their anger. When this is done the caregiver reassures the child that they continue to be the secure base that can always be returned to when there is an emotional issue.

TIPS FOR PARENTS

It can be a challenge to navigate through all the aspects of parenthood. There are so many decisions to make, and some parents are left wondering if the decisions they make are the right ones. There are many ways that parents and caregivers can offer social-emotional support naturally. Here are specific tips that have worked for others:

1. ***Know your child.*** Caregivers are the first point of contact for children, and they really do best know the specific child. If caregivers think they don't truly know the child, then they should simply begin observing them. When caregivers take a few minutes and just watch and listen to children during play, or during dinner, they will learn much about the social-emotional level of the child. It isn't even necessary to have to talk to the child but simply watch their behaviors. This really is the easiest way to see who the child is from a whole-child perspective, because caregivers can learn about likes and dislikes of the child and even the things and people that the child might find frustrating. Through observation it is possible to even determine the child's temperament style, which can be helpful when dealing with their emotions.

2. ***Communicate with children***. This should start during infancy. Even though they are not able to verbally respond, through their coos, cries, and babbles they are responding. During feeding caregivers can make eye contact with the infant while also talking to them. As children continue to grow and go through the various growth and development stages, it is imperative to continue speaking to them during mealtimes and play. This helps to reinforce building social skills while creating a bond and a secure attachment that allows children to feel safe. Intentionally communicating with children also contributes to their emotions as they can begin to learn how to become self-aware and feel comfortable letting others know what they might be feeling as well as feel safe expressing those feelings.
3. ***Have realistic expectations***. Caregivers need to always consider what they are expecting from each child at each of the growth and development stages. This can help with managing emotions and prevent behavior challenges later on. For example, asking a two-year-old child to sit for five minutes and calm down would be inappropriate because at that age they are simply more active. Asking a four- or five- year-old to sit for five minutes while they calm down might be a much better expectation because at this developmental stage they can follow instructions and are much less active compared to a two-year-old.
4. ***Practice self-regulation with children.*** When a child is expressing themselves, allow them to do so as freely as possible, given the context. When they are having those big, intense emotions, allow them to express how they are feeling, and acknowledge their feelings. Remember their feeling is their feeling, no matter how small it may seem to adults at that moment, this is how they genuinely feel. By allowing them to express their feelings and acknowledging those feelings, parents reassure their children, and they can then learn how to better deal with those emotions. Each child is different, so it is imperative to comfort them or allow them to sit and cool down, this varies with temperament style as well as attachment style.

Caregivers can also model the behavior they expect of the children under their care. Adults must always consider the way they speak and act to children under their care and supervision. Children are most likely going to speak and act exactly the way that the caregivers in their life spoke and acted since they were born. They have been watching all this time and absorbing everything, and if an adult thinks they should be acting differently it can become very confusing for children. For example, an adult can be loud at home at the dinner table, but then go out to dinner and be quieter, but a child is not always able to adapt as easily. If such confusing behaviors continue, then a child can become withdrawn and unsure how they are supposed to behave in different environments.

5. ***Communicate with teachers.*** This can be especially helpful because parents and other caregivers can see what might be working at school and adapt it at home. For example, if a parent or caregiver is not sure how to get their child into a bedtime routine, simply ask the teacher how the routines in the classroom are implemented. If the child is able to follow through with the routines at school, bring it home and use it. So, if the teacher is using music to bring calmness, you can do the same. It will send a signal to the brain that the child is familiar with and help them learn to follow the routine at home. Regular consistent routines help manage emotions and reduce stress because it becomes predictable.

TIPS FOR TEACHERS

1. ***Understand each child as an individual.*** When teachers comprehensively understand each child and their unique behaviors and dispositions it allows them to know their learning and social-emotional needs. To plan accordingly, teachers can begin by noting the temperament styles of the children in their learning environment. This allows them to know what strategies, techniques, methods, and materials will work best with each child in the learning context and, consequently, social-emotional-related behavior challenges can become less challenging. Teachers often prepare for various learning styles, but when it comes to SEI, they need to prepare for the various temperament styles of the children in their learning settings.

   When planning and considering these differences teachers are tapping into a child's intelligences, which Robert Sternberg and Howard Gardner discuss in their theories (i.e., Theory of Intelligence and Multiple Intelligences Theory). Children learn differently, and when the different intelligences are supported, it encourages higher-order thinking (Vinney, 2020) and allows the development of different mental strengths and abilities (Barrington, 2004). Vygotsky discusses the Zone of Proximal Development (ZPD), which helps teachers determine the level of support needed for each child. Figure 10.3 displays how scaffolding can be implemented based on a child's needs. The less frustration a child experiences during the independent stage the more likely they will reach the goal of the task being completed. When teachers prepare for various learning styles, and temperaments the level of support only further assists with the learning process.

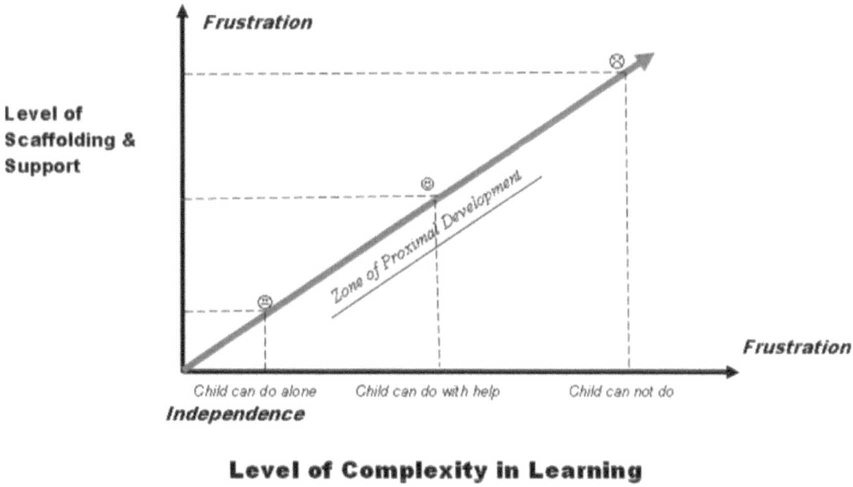

Figure 10.3. Vygotsky's zone of proximal development. ***Developed by McKenna & Patterson, 2015.***

2. ***Practice mindfulness everyday.*** Very often, teachers really have no specific ideas about the homelife experiences of their students However, it can be asserted with a great degree of certainty that not all parents practice mindfulness or are even aware of its importance in relation to SEI. Learning how to calm the mind and how to decompress is important for children too. Children are at various stages of learning as well as various stages of growth and development, and they are learning how to navigate life, which can be more stressful for some children than others, so teaching and practicing mindfulness can be beneficial. Practicing mindfulness can help with self-awareness, self-regulation, empathy, and social skills, as well as simply in in developing SEI, which can also be referred to as Mindful-Based Stress Reduction (Inner-Explorer, 2023).
3. ***Have a clear and consistent behavior-management plan.*** This is something that needs to start early and at the beginning of each school year. It is important to note that a clear behavior-management plan does not mean punishment; it is, rather, just the teacher's expectations for the behavior in the classroom. When that behavior becomes disruptive, challenging, or worse, the consequences for that behavior need to be specific and enforced. Oftentimes when children are aware of the consequences, they are unlikely to engage in unexpected behavior. Behavior expectations should also be modeled by the teacher(s) in the classroom so children can see what that behavior looks like; oftentimes teachers are the main role models.

Classrooms should have a specific area dedicated to self-regulation. This way if a child is feeling frustrated, angry, or sad, they can go to that area and calm down. It should be in a quieter part of the classroom with perhaps a cozy setup. This way, the children can go there and utilize the space as needed.

4. ***Build positive relationships and have an open line of communication with the children***. Good communication will help with developing trust in the children, especially with children who have difficulty with trust. This will allow the children to learn that they can have meaningful conversations and discussions with adults, especially if it is not something they have at home, and can help children start to overcome fears and anxieties, reduce stress, and even become motivated academically.
5. ***Communicate with parents.*** This is important because it creates a bridge between home and school. Teachers should use different ways of communicating, as not every parent can email or speak in person. Teachers need to let parents know how their child is doing based on the needs of each child. Discuss SEI with parents and other caregivers and inform them about how their child is doing in terms of building friendships and socializing in the classroom. Provide parents with tips and techniques.

FLIP YOUR LID

Some teachers, parents, or other caregivers have "flipped their lid." What does this mean? Flipping your lid is when there is a disconnect between the right side of the brain, which is responsible for emotions, and the left side of the brain, responsible for logic. At this point, some caregivers are not able to make smart, sensible decisions, and this is when they may say things to children that they may later regret. When children flip their lid, they too are not able to make logical decisions and they can often say hurtful things, but it is because they are not thinking logically. This is an important part of social-emotional intelligence (SEI) because this is where self-awareness and self-regulation come in. In order to avoid flipping your lid it is important for parents, teachers, and all caregivers supervising children to be aware of how they are feeling (self-awareness) and what to do with those emotions (self-regulation) in order to help children to recognize how they are feeling, what the emotion is, and how to express it, or decompress in a more beneficial and constructive manner.

Allowing children to express their emotions is important because in the early years they are not aware what emotions they are feeling because they are just feeling. When they learn about the different emotions, how to express them, and what behaviors are most appropriate, they can learn how to regulate. This is also taught by the parents and what their behaviors are like, so children will copy what they see, because it is what they have learned in their home environment.

FINAL THOUGHTS

Social-emotional intelligence is an important part of child development. It contributes to healthy relationships and positive mental health. Parents are the first people to interact and stimulate the child both socially and emotionally. It would be unfair to think that a child, especially in the early years, knows better, because the possibility that they don't is very real. They are acting and behaving in the ways they think is best as well as based on what they see from their direct influences (e.g., parents, caregivers, television shows, siblings, etc.). Always keep in mind they are in the learning stages of life.

Every child is different, and it is important to understand each child, ensuring that all the child's caregivers are together choosing the right and most consistent approach. Considering the temperament of the child can be a good starting point. If a chosen approach does not work, then it is imperative try something different. Remaining calm throughout the process will be helpful because it will allow the child's caregivers to continue thinking in a calm and reasonable manner. If some techniques fail, that does not mean the caregiver has failed; it is important to try again. Take a step back and maybe take a few deep breaths and reflect about the interventions tried, sometimes there may be another solution that will occur that can be much easier and more effective.

KEY PRAGMATIC LEADERSHIP TAKEAWAYS

- Get to know and understand the whole child; this includes determining their temperament and attachment style.
- Communicate with children to help build social skills and elevate emotional distress.
- Genuinely acknowledge children's feelings, big or small, as well as positive or negative.
- Practice behavior management and be consistent with rewards and consequences.
- Establish routines for children to follow, especially very young children.
- Recognize that social-emotional intelligence (SEI) contributes to well-being and positive mental health in children, and daily incorporate its concepts and strategies in living and working with children.

- Keep in mind the sage advice of Abraham Maslow, who identified the primacy to individuals of having their physiological needs as well as their need for a sense of safety and belonginess met in their early human growth and development stages.
- Comprehend the significance of SEI in developing a solid basis to succeed in the more advanced stages of Maslow's personal development, consisting of self-esteem and cognitive, aesthetic, and self-actualization needs. Maslow adroitly posits that advancement to the other levels of the Hierarchy of Needs is predicated on success in those initial stages, which are consistent with the significance of SEI to successful human growth and development.
- Frequently reference Maslow's Developmental Needs Pyramid, as provided in figure 10.4, as a key reference for parents and teachers when working with children at all ages but especially the very early years.

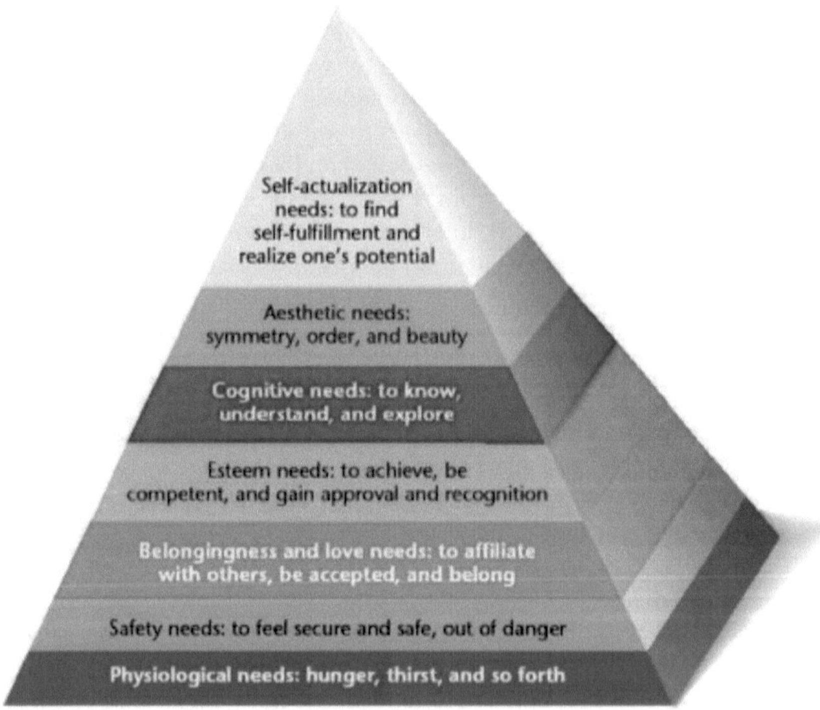

Figure 10.4. Maslow's hierarchy of needs. ***From Google Images, 2015. McMahon, K. (March 2, 2011).*** *Beyond Maslow's hierarchy of needs.* ***[Online image]. Retrieved from http:www.peakoilblues.org/blog/2011/03/02/beyond-maslows-hierarchy-of-needs/.***

REFERENCES

Alwali, J., & Alwali, W. (2022). "The Relationship between Emotional Intelligence, Transformational Leadership, and Performance: A Test of the Mediating Role of Job Satisfaction." *Leadership & Organization Development Journal 43*(6), 928–52. https://doi.org/10.1108/LODJ-10-2021-0486.

Barrington, E. (2004). "Teaching to Student Diversity in Higher Education: How Multiple Intelligence Theory Can Help." *Teaching in Higher Education 9*(4), 421–34. https://doi.org/10.1080/1356251042000252363.

Chandrahasa, R., T. N. S., & Bommanavar, S. M. (2022). Emotional Intelligence in Academic Performance of University Students. *Phronimos 2*(4), 54–66. https://ezproxy.niagara.edu/login?url=https://www.proquest.com/scholarly-journals/emotional-intelligence-academic-performance/docview/2719495760/se-2.

Evans, Olvia Guy. (2024). Bronfenbrenner's Ecological Systems Theory. Simply Psychology. https://www.simplypsychology.org/bronfenbrenner.html.

Inner-Explorer. (2023). "Teaching Mindfulness in Schools." https://innerexplorer.org/mbsel#:~:text=Mindfulness%2DBased%20Social%20Emotional%20Learning,brain%20networks%20associated%20with%20learning.

Mcleod, S. (2023). "Erik Erikson's Stages of Psychosocial Development." Simply Psychology, October 16. https://www.simplypsychology.org/erik-erikson.html.

Martorell, G., & Kruk, R. (2014). *Child from birth to adolescence*. McGraw-Hill Education.

Ontario Ministry of Education. (2014). "How Does Learning Happen? Ontario's Pedagogy for the Early Years." https://www.ontario.ca/page/how-does-learning-happen-ontarios-pedagogy-early-years.

Polka, W., & McKenna, J. (Eds.). (2016). *Confronting Oppressive Assessments: How Parents, Educators, and Policy-Makers Are Rethinking Current Educational Reforms*. Lanham, MD: Rowman & Littlefield Education Publications.

Shillington, K. J., Yates, J., Vanderloo, L. M., Burke, S. M., Ng, V., Tucker, P., & Irwin, J. D. (2023). "'When You Give Kindness Out, You Get It Back Ten Times More': Ontario Adults' Prosocial Behaviour during the First 16 Months of the COVID-19 Pandemic." *PLoS One 18*(7). https://doi.org/10.1371/journal.pone.0288720.

Suizzo, M. (2000). "The Social-Emotional and Cultural Contexts of Cognitive Development: Neo-Piagetian Perspectives." *Child Development 71*(4), 846–49. https://doi.org/10.1111/1467-8624.00191.

Trad, M., Mona, O. A., Rasha, A. K., & Khaddage-Soboh, N. (2022). "Assessing the Influence of Emotional Intelligence on Teachers' Performance in Lebanese Private Education Institutions." *Higher Education, Skills and Work-Based Learning 12*(3), 556–73. https://doi.org/10.1108/HESWBL-12-2020-0268.

University of Central Florida. (2023). "Bloom's Taxonomy." https://fctl.ucf.edu/teaching-resources/course-design/blooms-taxonomy/#:~:text=The%20goal%20of%20an%20educator%27s,scale%20educational%20goals%20or%20guidelines.

Vinney, C. (2020). "Understanding the Triarchic Theory of Intelligence." *ThoughtCo.* https://www.thoughtco.com/triarchic-theory-of-intelligence-4172497.

Yu, R., Perera, C., Sharma, M., Ipince, A., Bakrania, S., Shokraneh, F., Mosquera Sepulveda, J. S., & Anthony, D. (2023). "Child and Adolescent Mental Health and Psychosocial Support Interventions: An Evidence and Gap Map of Low- and Middle-Income Countries." *Campbell Systematic Reviews 19*(3). https://doi.org/10.1002/cl2.1349.

Chapter 11

From Overwhelmed to Resilient

The Role of Artificial Intelligence in Reducing Burnout

Caitlin Riegel and Monica J. VanHusen

In the field of education, teachers play an indispensable role. They are committed practitioners who share knowledge, cultivate skill, and nurture growth. However, their unwavering dedication and passion, coupled with the increasing demands of the twenty-first century classroom, can render them susceptible to burnout. When it comes to education, there is no doubt a system filled with effective educators is the goal. However, recent studies and press highlighting a concerning trend in teacher burnout rates (Madigan & Kim, 2021; Marken & Agrawal, 2022; Ozamiz-Etxebarria et al., 2023) suggest the current landscape is far from this goal. Addressing the escalating burnout rates and concerns related to teacher well-being across the nation has become a pressing priority to ensure a sustainable work environment and thriving education system (Madigan et al., 2023). The escalating worry is the adverse repercussions teacher burnout has on both the teachers themselves and the entire education system. This has prompted a search for innovative solutions that require systemic change acknowledging and addressing the challenges educators are facing, while providing the tools, resources, and appreciation they need to thrive in their essential roles. The intersection of education and technology and the recent growth of artificial intelligence (AI) has given rise to a promising avenue to support teacher well-being and potentially mitigate burnout.

Through an examination of teacher well-being and the rising rate of burnout, this chapter highlights the need to provide teachers with social-emotional support. By exploring the potential role of AI-powered solutions, this chapter aims to shed light on the transformative impact of AI and provide insights that contribute to the ongoing discourse on teacher support and retention. While educators can agree that AI should not replace the human touch in education, and some argue that the integration of AI into education minimizes the human element, this chapter suggests that AI is actually *necessary* to maintain the human element in education.

AI enables teachers to maintain their personal well-being while performing an increasingly stressful job; in turn, this allows them to provide emotional support, motivation, and mentorship for students that AI cannot fully replicate. The strategic and deliberate integration of AI should enhance the teacher's role and free up their time for more meaningful interactions with students. This chapter provides examples from both K–12 and higher education that speak to how AI makes it possible for teachers to transition from a state of overwhelm to one of resilience, and to thrive while nurturing the hearts and minds of the next generation. As AI continues to advance, its role in promoting teacher resilience and combating burnout emerges as a significant opportunity to build a more sustainable future for educators that combines human expertise and technological innovation.

EXPLORING THE ROLE OF ARTIFICIAL INTELLIGENCE (AI)

As technology continues to advance, the integration of AI into various sectors of society, including education, has become increasingly prominent (see figure 11.1). At its simplest form, artificial intelligence combines computer science and robust datasets to enable machines to problem-solve (IBM, 2023). This simulation of human intelligence processes by machines includes carrying out tasks such as learning, reasoning, problem-solving, and decision-making.

In the context of education, the U.S. Department of Education's Office of Educational Technology (2023) outlines how AI continues to transform traditional aspects of teaching. Given that educators today face a myriad of expectations reflecting the evolving demands of society, the need is high to harness AI to address the increased demands that often lead to burnout. By changing the way educators navigate their responsibilities, AI has changed the foundation of a teachers' job, impacting areas such as:

1. **Personalized learning:** Educators are expected to tailor instruction to meet the diverse needs and learning styles of students, providing customized learning experiences. AI can streamline the process of teachers

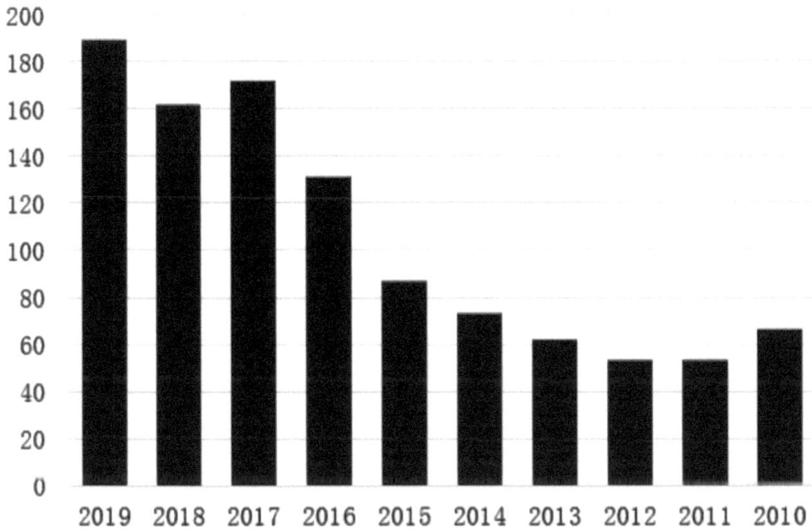

Figure 11.1. Papers in Web of Science and Google Scholar in the last ten years with key words "AI" and "Education." ***From Chen et al. (2020), Figure 1, p. 75266.***

adapting content to individual student needs, providing tailored instruction and pacing.

2. **Differentiated tiered instruction:** Educators are required to differentiate instruction to address the varying readiness levels of students. AI can provide teachers different levels of content complexity and support to accommodate all learners.
3. **Cultivating twenty-first-century skills:** Educators are encouraged to foster skills such as critical thinking, problem-solving, creativity, communication, and collaboration to prepare students for the challenges of the modern world. AI can help foster these skills by providing students with immediate feedback and answers to their questions to continue the learning process.
4. **Incorporating technology:** Educators are expected to integrate technology, leveraging digital tools and resources to enhance learning and engagement. AI can offer teachers options for low- and high-tech technology integration.
5. **Embracing cultural competence:** Teachers are encouraged to be culturally competent, recognizing and valuing the cultural diversity present in their classrooms. AI can offer teachers options for adapting their teaching approaches to the specific and unique cultures present in their classroom.

6. **Assessment:** Educators are responsible for conducting and grading assessments. AI can perform automated grading, which provides students with immediate feedback and saves educators valuable time.
7. **Data-driven decisions:** Educators are expected to analyze student data for performance trends, learning gaps, and areas that require additional attention. AI can process, analyze, and provide insights in large sets of educational data so teachers can focus their time on tailoring their instructional approaches.
8. **Effective classroom management:** Educators must manage student behavior and create a positive and structured learning environment. AI can identify potential learning difficulties or behavioral issues early on so teachers can provide early interventions and timely support to students.

The above examples just begin to scratch the surface of the roles and expectations placed upon educators. It is evident from these examples alone that AI has emerged as a transformative force, reshaping the traditional role of a teacher. By addressing stressors, saving time, optimizing workloads, and providing on-demand support, AI equips educators with the tools and resources needed to build *resilience*. Ultimately, AI-driven interventions enhance educators' ability to cope with challenges, bounce back from setbacks, and maintain a positive and sustainable teaching career. By augmenting educators with these AI-driven capabilities, the educational system is better poised to alleviate teacher burnout and create a more sustainable, effective, and inclusive learning environment for both educators and students alike.

REAL-WORLD VIGNETTES OF AI APPLICATION

Within both K–12 and higher education, the integration of AI has emerged as a transformative force, reshaping the field of education for teachers and teacher educators. As individuals navigate the complex terrain of modern education, AI applications have garnered attention for their potential to alleviate challenges and enhance the learning experience. In this section, real-world vignettes are provided that illuminate the diverse ways AI is being harnessed to manage the ever increasing workload and alleviate symptoms of burnout. These vignettes span elementary, secondary, and higher education and were developed using guidance from Miller (2023) and current AI tools outlined in figure 11.2. They serve as tangible examples of AI's impact, shedding light on its role in supporting teachers and teacher educators by personalizing learning, streamlining administrative tasks, and shaping the future of educational methodologies.

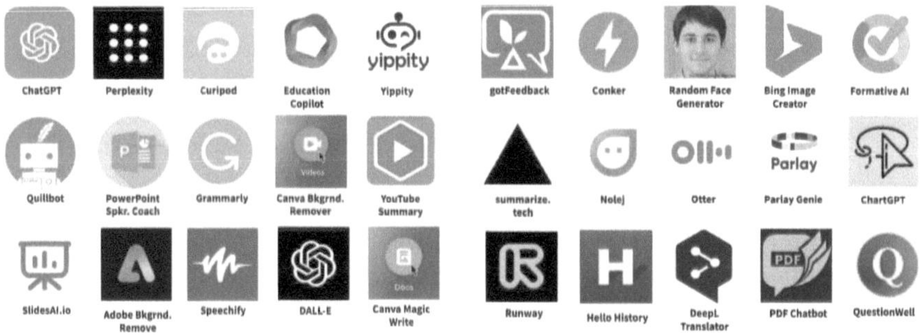

Figure 11.2. 30 AI tools for the classroom. *From Ditch That Textbook (2023).*

Elementary Education Vignette

As a new school year dawned upon Maplewood Elementary, Ms. Johnson, a second year second-grade teacher, braced herself for the whirlwind of tasks that awaited her. With a classroom full of eager young minds and the responsibility of creating engaging lessons and collecting student data related to her objectives, Ms. Johnson knew that the initial weeks could be overwhelming. However, this year brought a transformative addition to her teaching toolkit that she didn't have last year: AI-powered platforms. In an effort to not have to build lesson plans from scratch, Ms. Johnson utilized Education Copilot (https://educationcopilot.com) as a starting point when planning instruction. By providing a few details related to the content she wanted to cover, Ms. Johnson now had AI generated templates for lesson plans, writing prompts, educational handouts, and project outlines that she could adjust with strategically crafted full-up prompts. Ms. Johnson went on to use Curipod (https://curipod.ai) to immediately generate an interactive slide deck for her lessons. Fascinated with how quickly she could generate starting materials for her lessons, she turned her attention to collecting student data so she could differentiate the lessons she was building based on student needs. Ms. Johnson utilized Yippity (https://yippity.io) to automatically convert the text from the e-texts used in her curriculum into quizzes. By submitting specific text, Ms. Johnson instantly had questions and answers she could copy and paste into a flashcard app or quiz tool to gather formative feedback on progress toward objectives without overextending herself outside of school hours to develop assessments. By leveraging AI's capabilities right from the beginning of the school year, Ms. Johnson not only prevented the early signs of burnout, but also laid the foundation for an inclusive and captivating classroom environment.

Secondary Education Vignette

Mr. Ramirez, an experienced history teacher, found himself stretched thin midyear as he endeavored to engage his students in meaningful discussions related to current events. The extensive hours spent watching videos of government meetings, forums, and expert opinions to get caught up on contemporary events were taking a toll on his enthusiasm and energy. Mr. Ramirez overheard a colleague talking about an AI platform that would provide the summary of any video. After asking his colleague for a brief tutorial, Mr. Ramirez used summarize.tech (https://www.summarize.tech) and Glasp.co (https://glasp.co) the next day to summarize the State of the Union address and School Board meeting. He used this information to prepare a classroom discussion related to the similarities and differences in policies within each public forum. Mr. Ramirez was in disbelief that the classroom activities that once seemed too monumental to make a reality were now things that he could put together during his planning period. Diving into the AI world, Mr. Ramirez came across more tools he could use in his class, such as Hello History (https://www.hellohistory.ai) to have his students partake in life-like conversations with historical figures, something he could only have dreamt possible in the past! The AI application not only empowered him to become more knowledgeable in his content area, but also enriched his students' educational experience, showcasing how technology can positively impact secondary education by promoting teacher well-being.

Higher Education Vignette

In a university setting, Dr. Martinez had been grappling with the overwhelming demands of grading assignments and providing timely, personalized feedback. As the semester progressed, she began to feel the effects of burnout, struggling to maintain the energy needed to perform at her best and meet the needs of her teacher candidates. Recognizing the issue, Dr. Martinez decided to try several AI-powered solutions. The first was gotFeedback (https://feedback.gotlearning.com). After uploading student work, gotFeedback helped her provide individualized feedback in a timely fashion focusing on the writing structure, details, claim, evidence, and so on. This not only reduced his grading workload but also offered insightful data on student performance trends. After hearing students discuss the potential of ChatGPT (https://chat.openai.com), Dr. Martinez discovered she could use this platform to provide feedback on discussion boards, something that used to take her hours to draft. Now, in a matter of minutes, she had a summarized version of the class discussion to share, along with targeted themes and developing ideas. Finally, Dr. Martinez utilized Parley Genie (https://new.parlayideas.com) to provide personalized feedback to teacher candidates working on strategic questioning within their instruction. This platform generated higher-order thinking questions for teacher candidates to consider based on the lesson plan they submitted. Typically, these questions would take her hours to develop; now, Dr. Martinez could provide this personalized feedback to each student in minutes. This AI-supported approach not only rejuvenated Dr. Martinez's enthusiasm, but also improved her students' learning experience by allowing the teaching to continue through feedback provided.

CONSIDERATIONS FOR SUCCESSFUL AI INTEGRATION

When integrating AI into education, clear guidelines that ensure that AI complements and enhances the educational process rather than diverging from it and avoiding blocking its potential should be established. Ethical guidelines must also be included to promote responsible AI usage. Privacy and data security should be paramount, to protect students' and employees' data and adhere to data protection regulations. Furthermore, amid these technological advancements, the delicate balance between AI and human interaction must be upheld, acknowledging that they are complementary forces propelling education toward an innovative horizon.

Innovative leadership is the first consideration when creating a successful AI integration within education organizations. Albert Einstein famously stated, "Imagination is more important than knowledge. Knowledge is limited, but imagination encircles the world" (as cited in Nilsson, 2010). This statement resonates with the rapid advancement of AI, which is becoming increasingly integrated into our daily lives. It underscores the importance of fostering curiosity and encouraging the continued development of AI applications in education. The field currently requires innovative leaders who possess the vision and creativity to explore the limitless possibilities that AI offers. Innovative leaders create a nurturing environment where educators can continually imagine how AI can best support our students in preparing for their future workplace. As noted by DuFour et al. (2021), innovative leaders are able to create a shared vision among stakeholders, which is essential for success. A shared vision around AI used in education helps to ensure that everyone is working toward the same goals and is committed to achieving them. An innovative leader actively listens, asks questions, and provides feedback to ensure that everyone understands the vision. This is crucial in the beginning stages when creating organizational guidelines around implementing AI. According to Garmston and Wellman (2009), innovative educational leaders use various strategies to communicate their vision effectively. These include storytelling (e.g., vignettes), metaphors, and analogies, which can help to make complex ideas around AI relatable to stakeholders.

Once an innovative leadership mindset is firmly in place, the next step is to establish a stakeholder coalition that can effectively address ethical and privacy concerns associated with the implementation of AI. These stakeholders should encompass both internal and external participants who can provide diverse perspectives and expertise. Internally, this may involve representatives from various departments, including educators, administrators, IT specialists, and data privacy officers. Externally, it is essential to engage with parents, students, legal experts, and community advocates to ensure a comprehensive and well-rounded approach to ethical and privacy considerations. In uniting these stakeholders, an innovative leader must adeptly steer their collective attention toward the seamless integration of AI. This imperative arises from the likelihood that each stakeholder group may harbor preexisting perspectives on AI, which may lean toward skepticism or even outright resistance. Thus, the role of an effective leader is to summon the courage to both challenge and guide these entrenched mindsets, thereby fostering a shift from reluctance to curiosity. Leaders must exercise a delicate balance of "pushing" to stimulate fresh thinking and "pulling" to elicit valuable insights from stakeholders. This dynamic approach, as articulated by Fullan and Kirtman (2019), is essential in cultivating a receptive environment for change. It enables leaders to effectively challenge existing paradigms while simultaneously harnessing feedback, deepening their understanding, and channeling the collective focus of the stakeholders toward the common goal of AI integration in education.

The State of Virginia provides an example of building a stakeholder coalition around Artificial Intelligence, where Governor Glenn Younkin has taken an innovative leadership approach to help guide the discussions surrounding AI. This specific stakeholder coalition fosters collaboration throughout different organizations within the state around AI integration. In an executive directive, he challenged businesses, educational institutions, and non-profit organizations to come together and create guidelines and procedures for the use of AI within their respective areas of responsibility:

> The Commonwealth of Virginia is home to a rapidly evolving entrepreneurial ecosystem and one of the most innovative workforces in the nation. Virginia's colleges and universities lead the nation in technology research and development, and the most critical national security and military intelligence institutions in the United States are headquartered in Virginia. These unique factors charge Virginia with the responsibility to spearhead a policy environment that drives trust, safety, and security in the development and deployment of AI Technologies. (Commonwealth of Virginia, 2023, p. 1)

In pursuit of these objectives, the initiative aims to galvanize a wide array of stakeholders, including educational organizations. This collaborative effort seeks to leverage AI's transformative potential while ensuring unwavering commitment to the highest standards of ethical practice and privacy safeguards.

To maintain this focus and facilitate meaningful discussions surrounding AI in education, it is essential to adhere to focused topics. As an illustration, consider the adapted Guidelines for AI in Education proposed by the Stafford

County Public Schools stakeholder coalition, known as the Instructional Technology Advisory Committee.

- **Curriculum Relevance:** Using AI in the classroom must be part of an intentional lesson plan and align with curriculum objectives. Educators are encouraged to model the appropriate use of AI and incorporate AI to enhance or differentiate the learning process and not solely for entertainment purposes.
- **Professional Development:** Teachers and staff who use AI tools shall receive training on how to innovate with AI to enhance the curriculum including the ethical use of AI, its limitations, and potential risks, including data privacy issues, before use of AI.
- **Avoiding Misrepresentation and Plagiarism:** Teachers are obligated to educate students about giving appropriate credit when using AI-generated content to avoid misrepresentation and plagiarism. Proper citation and referencing guidelines must be taught and enforced.
- **Digital Citizenship, Ethical Awareness, and Appropriate Content:** Students require proper education about the ethical implications of using AI. Staff will model the ethical and appropriate use of AI. Discussions on bias, fairness, and transparency in AI are encouraged in order to develop digital citizenship skills among students. Students must use content-appropriate prompts when working with AI to avoid generating inappropriate content. Students who intentionally create inappropriate content may face disciplinary consequences pursuant to the student code of conduct.
- **Developmental Appropriateness:** Younger students may be unable to distinguish between AI and human-created content or understand the potential for error, bias, and the risks associated with content created by either source. Accordingly, elementary and middle school students shall only access content from AI when led by their teacher or when using an AI learning assistant in a content-specific software platform.
- **Data Privacy and Security:** Staff must prioritize the protection of student data privacy and ensure that AI-generated content does not reveal sensitive information about individual students. All student data used for AI shall comply with state and federal data protection laws and school board policy.

After guidelines have been put in place, a strategic framework for seamless integrations of AI technologies within an educational setting needs to be developed. This framework must be carefully developed to navigate and balance technology vs. human interactions. Figure 11.3 outlines an example of a framework when implementing AI in education: the Five Big

Ideas in Artificial Intelligence (Artificial Intelligence for K-12 initiative [AI4K12], 2020).

This framework is a collaborative endeavor, jointly sponsored by the American Association for Artificial Intelligence (AAAI) and the Computer Science Teachers Association (CSTA). The Artificial Intelligence for K–12 initiative [AI4K12] is diligently working on several key components to enhance AI education in K–12 settings. These ideas form the cornerstone of a strategic framework for the seamless integration of AI technologies within educational settings, all while emphasizing the maintenance of a delicate equilibrium between technology-driven advancements and essential human interactions. With innovative leadership, a stakeholder coalition, and a framework, the foundation for successful AI integration is set in place.

FINAL THOUGHTS

This chapter has focused on the potential of artificial intelligence (AI) to support teacher well-being and mitigate the issue of teacher burnout. We began by highlighting the factors contributing to teacher burnout and the adverse consequences it has on educators and the education system. The urgent need for proactive interventions and the impact of burnout on the teacher shortage crisis in the United States was emphasized.

The discussion then explored how AI can serve as a powerful tool in creating sustainable work environments and supporting teachers as they face

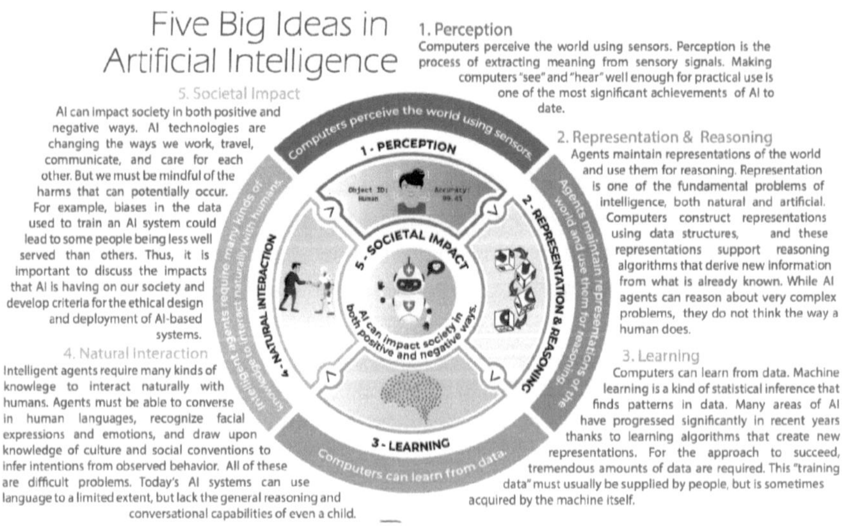

Figure 11.3. Five big ideas in artificial intelligence. ***From AI4K12 (2020).***

increasing demands, high workloads, and emotional strain. We examined AI's potential to alleviate workload burdens, promote personalized learning, and provide educators with valuable tools for enhancing instructional effectiveness. Ethical considerations, practical implementation strategies, and the responsible use of AI were also addressed, advocating for the responsible integration of AI to increase teacher resiliency.

The topic of AI in education is rapidly evolving. As AI technologies find their way into educational organizations, the landscape of AI will consistently be changing to meet the needs of students, educators, and families. Articles and chapters like this must be read with the awareness that the strategies, examples, and suggestions discussed may have evolved since publication. It is essential that educators, policymakers, and stakeholders stay up to date with the latest developments and research to make informed decisions and leverage AI's full potential in the educational setting.

KEY PRAGMATIC LEADERSHIP TAKEAWAYS

The intersection of education and technology, particularly the growth of artificial intelligence, offers a promising avenue to address teacher burnout and enhance the teaching profession. As we move forward, it is crucial for educational institutions, policymakers, and stakeholders to take action:

- *Invest in AI education:* Ensure that educators receive the necessary training and resources to effectively utilize AI tools and platforms in their classrooms.
- *Ethical AI guidelines:* Develop and implement clear ethical guidelines for the use of AI in education to protect student data, ensure fairness, and uphold privacy standards.
- *Support innovative leadership:* Foster a culture of innovative leadership that encourages exploration and experimentation with AI technologies to benefit both educators and students.
- *Stakeholder collaboration:* Establish collaborative coalitions that include diverse perspectives from within and outside educational organizations to address ethical and practices AI integration challenges.
- *Sustain teacher well-being:* Prioritize the well-being of educators by utilizing AI to alleviate workload pressures, provide personalized support, and create a positive work environment.
- *Continuous research:* Encourage ongoing research and evaluation of AI's impact on teacher well-being, student outcomes, and educational practices to refine and optimize its implementation.

- *Advocate for policy support:* Advocate for policies that support the responsible and equitable use of AI in education, ensuring that it aligns with broader educational goals and values.

By taking these actions, we can harness the transformative potential of AI to support teachers, reduce burnout, and create a more resilient and effective education system for the future.

REFERENCES

Artificial Intelligence for K–12 Initiative [AI4K12]. 2020. *5 Big Ideas in AI.* https://ai4k12.org/wp-content/uploads/2022/01/AI4K12_Five_Big_Ideas_Poster_3_19_2021.pdf.

Chen, L., Chen, P., & Lin, Z. (2020). "Artificial Intelligence in Education: A Review." *IEEE Access 8*, 75264–75278. https://doi.org/10.1109/ACCESS.2020.2988510.

Commonwealth of Virginia. (2023). *Recognizing the Risks and Seizing the Opportunities of Artificial Intelligence*. Executive Directive Number Five. https://www.governor.virginia.gov/media/governorvirginiagov/governor-of-virginia/pdf/ed/Executive-Directive-No.-5---Recognizing-the-Risks-and-Seizing-the-Opportunities-of-Artificial-Intelligence.pdf.

Ditch That Textbook. (2023). "30 AI Tools for the Classroom." https://ditchthattextbook.com/ai-tools.

DuFour, R., DuFour, R., Eaker, R., Mattos, M., & Muhammad, A. (2021). *Revisiting Professional Learning Communities at Work®: Proven Insights for Sustained, Substantive School Improvement*. Second Edition. Bloomington, IN: Solution Tree.

Fullan, M., & Kirtman, L. (2019). *Coherent School Leadership: Forging Clarity from Complexity*. Association for Supervision & Curriculum Development.

Garmston, R. J., & Wellman, B. M. (2009). *The Adaptive School: A Sourcebook for Developing Collaborative Groups.* Second edition. Norwood, MA: Christopher-Gordon Publishers, Inc.

IBM. (2023). "What Is Artificial Intelligence?" https://www.ibm.com/topics/artificial-intelligence.

Madigan, D. J., & Kim, L. E. (2021). "Towards an Understanding of Teacher Attrition: A Meta-Analysis of Burnout, Job Satisfaction, and Teachers' Intentions to Quit." *Teaching and Teacher Education 105*, 103425.

Madigan, D. J., Kim, L. E., Glandorf, H. L., & Kavanagh, O. (2023). "Teacher Burnout and Physical Health: A Systematic Review." *International Journal of Educational Research 119*, 102173. https://doi.org/10.1016/j.ijer.2023.102173.

Marken, S., & Agrawal, S. (2022). "K–12 Workers Have Highest Burnout Rate in U.S." Gallup. https://news.gallup.com/poll/393500/workers-highest-burnout-rate.aspx.

Miller, M. (2023). *AI for Educators: Learning Strategies, Teacher Effectiveness, and a Vision for an Artificial Intelligence Future*. N.p.: Dave Burgess Consulting, Inc.

Nilsson, J. (2010, March). "Imagination Is More Important Than Knowledge." *Saturday Evening Post*. https://www.saturdayeveningpost.com/2010/03/imagination-important-knowledge/.

Office of Educational Technology (2023, May). *Artificial Intelligence and the Future of Teaching and Learning*. Washington, DC: U.S. Department of Education. https://www2.ed.gov/documents/ai-report/ai-report.pdf.

Ozamiz-Etxebarria, N., Legorburu Fernnadez, I., Lipnicki, D. M., Idoiaga Mondragon, N., & Santabárbara, J. (2023). "Prevalence of Burnout among Teachers during the COVID-19 Pandemic: A Meta-Analysis." *International Journal of Environmental Research and Public Health 20*(6), 4866. https://doi.org/10.3390/ijerph20064866.

Chapter 12

The Necessity to Develop, Implement, and Navigate Proven Social-Emotional Learning Practices, NOW!

John E. McKenna, Walter S. Polka, and Monica J. VanHusen

> *The single most common finding is that children who end up doing well have had at least one stable and committed relationship with a supportive parent, caregiver, or other adult.*
>
> —Center on the Developing Child, Harvard University

The editors of this book, as reflected by all of the chapter authors, enthusiastically agree that empathy, caring, and understanding are needed in our schools and across our society now more than ever! Developing and maintaining effective social-emotional learning practices in schools is all about developing and maintaining relationships, relationships, and more relationships between people!

CURRENT URGENT NEED FOR SOCIAL-EMOTIONAL LEARNING

"People don't care how much you know, until they know how much you care." This often quote has been attributed to Theodore Roosevelt but has been used by many others to emphasize the importance of empathy and taking a personal interest in the well-being of others.

Our schools today need caring and compassion now more than ever. According to the National Association of Secondary School Principals (NASSP) 2022 Survey of America's School Leaders and High School Students, "3 out of 4 of school leaders (73%) and students (74%) report they needed help with their mental and emotional health" (survey.NASSP.org/2022). These statistics are alarming and represent a crisis that must be directly addressed, *now*!

Recent findings from the CDC stress the importance of "school connectedness." Their research highlights that a sense of being cared for, supported, and belonging at school is critical for students' emotional well-being (CDC, 2022). To combat this current crisis, school districts across the country have been exploring methods, and searching for programs and practices to provide additional social-emotional support to their students, staff, and families at present time and well into the future.

Future Approaches to Increasing the Frequency and Quality of Social-Emotional Learning

Various visionaries of the future have developed different mindset orientations in projecting future options for organizational leaders to consider related to the people, things, and ideas in the ever-evolving global landscape. However, one future-thinking approach, the *Three P's of Future Thinking* that the editors of this book contend is very appropriate for educational leaders at both the building and districtwide levels to consider when projecting the future of social-emotional learning in schools is a three-tiered progressive paradigm initially adopted and promulgated by the Hudson Institute's *Visions of the Future Project.*

The *Three P's of Future Thinking* paradigm initially developed by noted futurist, Herman Kahn, is based on a theoretical framework related to force-field analyses of the impacts and results of both planned and unplanned changes in society throughout history (Melnick, 1984). Kahn illustrated that educational leaders need to facilitate their own as well as their respective stakeholders' thinking and analysis of multiple options to be employed in order to mitigate the negative influences of changes in their context and maximum positive outcomes. His paradigm is based on using a systematic and structured three-tiered approach based on the collection and analysis of comprehensive context data related to the impacts of the change challenges and to select the most appropriate organizational responses to them using deductive analysis procedures.

Accordingly, educational leaders, when designing programs, projects, and activities with their stakeholders to confront the personal, professional, and organizational challenges of changes should always include in their visionary orientations and problem-solving approaches the following three key *Visions of the Future* scenarios: *Possible Future, Probable Future,* and *Preferable Future.* Leaders who employ such a heuristic must be prepared to present specific pragmatic examples related to their organizational missions to their respective stakeholders in order to explain the impacts of both planned and serendipitous future changes. See figure 12.1.

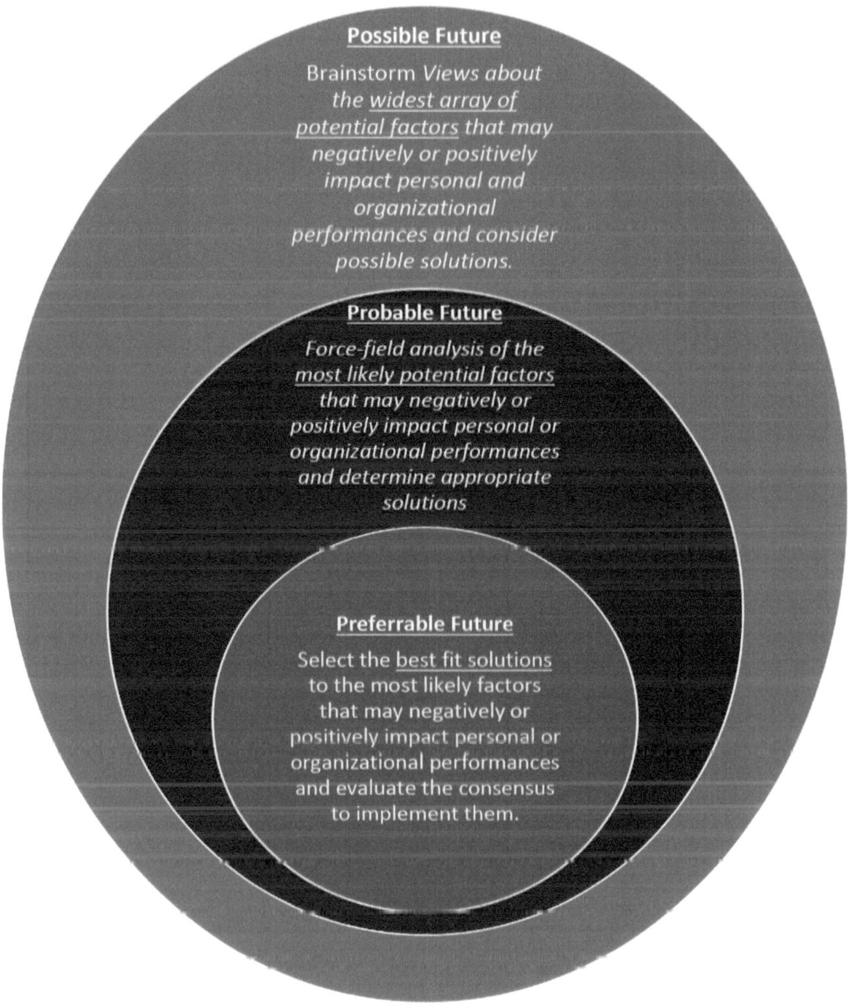

Figure 12.1. Visions of the future: three P's of future thinking. ***From Polka (2023).***

The following brief descriptions of each of the visions of the future scenarios should be presented by school leaders to their teachers, support staff, and community members to facilitate comprehension of the impacts and potential outcomes of educational changes including curriculum and instruction modifications. Educators promoting major instructional changes such as incorporating more social-emotional learning programs, projects, and activities into the school curricula need to consider each of the three following future scenarios and provide examples for each relative in their respective contexts.

- *Possible future*—This vision of the future requires leaders to include a comprehensive analysis of all of the potential events or operational changes that could happen, either planned or unplanned, in their various contexts in both the short term (within one year) and long term (more than one year) including: (a) events or changes at the micro level such as those events that are limited to their respective context and may impact only their schools and school districts such as curriculum and instructional changes to better meet student needs; (b) events or changes at the macro level such as those that may impact their regional or statewide institutions such as new operational policies; (c) events or changes at the mega or international level that impact our global village like COVID-19.

Subsequently, organizational leaders who think with such a visionary mindset encourage those within their supervisory purview and span of control to brainstorm the perceived impacts of changing situations and discuss "best-fit" options to abate the deleterious effects on people, things, and ideas (Polka & VanHusen, 2023). Such future thinking leaders encourage their followers to comprehensively reflect about and articulate the many potential benefits that may accrue to all of the organizational stakeholders due to changes provoked by the context changes, such as incorporating more frequent and higher-quality social-emotional programs, projects, and activities into their respective school curricula. Ranking all of the potential impacts and benefits that may occur helps to develop a realistic and "Possible Vision of the Future" (Melnick, 1984).

It is imperative that school leaders be acutely aware and overtly emphasize their perspectives about social-emotional learning and its benefits to students, faculty, parents, and community members as well as current information regarding the breadth and depth of planned curricular changes. The educational leader must professionally motivate not only their faculty and staff but also their students, student care-givers, and community members to comprehensively analyze the diverse impacts and multiple opportunities that embracing social-emotional learning has on all stakeholders. The entire school community must be energized by their school leaders to pragmatically act, in the best personal interests of their students, according to the continuously evolving micro-, macro-, and mega-changes that may occur and force urgent changes in the school curriculum, such as the current need to institute more social-emotional learning in education.

School leaders must encourage fidelity to those new social-emotional curriculum programs, projects, and activities and hold their faculty and support staff accountable to implement them as best as possible for maximum impact on the people, things, and ideas of their school context.

- *Probable future*—This vision of the future is based on collecting and comprehensively evaluating credible information about the anticipated realities associated with implementing any significant curricula changes in classrooms, school buildings, and school districts. Leaders must employ this vision of the future paradigmatic approach using historical information about the people in their context and their acceptance or rejection levels of implementing new programs, projects, and activities. Thus, information associated with past implementation events in this context provides leaders with the ability to make accurate and more focused predictions about the "best fit" probabilities for new social-emotional curriculum adaptations.

However, educational leaders should be cautious in encouraging their faculty, staff, and community members to brainstorm, rank-list using "force-field analysis" the most probable future impacts of major changes in curriculum and instructional practices because some of the individuals involved in this process may not have access to all the information necessary to appropriately plan for implementation without focused leadership.

Intentional leaders with a comprehensive historical contextual perspective and fortified with current accurate data about the urgent need for quality social-emotional changes in their respective contexts can assess the willingness and degree of usage of their faculty and staff to implement the various programs, projects, and activities associated with social-emotional learning. Such intentional transformational leaders will be able to articulate their visions of the probable future for SEL based on their knowledge of previous similar curricula and instructional changes in their respective contexts. Thus, having more widespread support for their vision.

However, it should be noted that there is no template or ready-made plan that is applicable in making changes in any organization due to due external events because change events are unique and unpredictable, and, at times, the outcomes may be unexpected (Melnick, 1984). However, acute educational leaders will always try their best to make appropriate changes to improve the learning experiences for the students under their supervision.

- *Preferable future*—This vision of the future is based on the desires of the individuals implementing necessary changes in organizations that go beyond the credible information provided in the probable future paradigmatic approach. However, using the information gathered in the "probable future" scenario, this desired level of change perspective requires input from the people who are experiencing the realities of the need for significant changes in their specific operations. Thus, the people involved with the change must be able to comprehensively and specifically identify and evaluate how the changes contemplated for implementation incorporate their views of the most preferrable way to make and apply such needed changes in the most efficient and effective manner.

Accordingly, intentional educational leaders can facilitate their faculty, staff, students, parents, and community members to further envision their preferable future for themselves, their family, and their organizations and institutions by using the data collected during possible and probable visions of the future discussions and focusing on the most valued human wants and needs of the people associated in their organizational contexts including: micro-, macro-, and mega-settings (Polka & VanHusen, 2023).

Educational leaders employing this preferable future paradigmatic approach can help their school community realize their preferable future for urgently implementing more quality social-emotional curriculum and instruction by strategically planning, collaboratively reviewing, and making focused choices in the "best interests" of students. This preferable future may never be completely realized, but it's that "reaching and stretching" to achieve this preferable future that provides a visionary goal for the school community to recognize as their optimum and to continuously work on trying their best to come as close to it as possible.

Futurists like Herman Kahn recognized that it is unlikely that all individuals will agree about their expectations for the preferable future, but futurists also agree that educational leaders can encourage groups and organizations to a more desired state by focusing their energy and time on the preferred state of change for people, things, and ideas in their contexts (Polka & VanHusen, 2023). However, this is a very time-consuming and may even become an acrimonious experience because arriving at consensus regarding a preferable future is a very personal and quite challenging introspective exercise.

School leaders who possess such a visionary mindset consisting of the above three visions of the future: possible, probable, and preferable, are able to manage curriculum and instructional changes, such as those associated with social-emotional learning, in their context in a more focused and, consequently, effective fashion. Margaret Mead, famed anthropologist, reinforced the significance of collective focus on preference goals when she reinforced the power of a group of focused individuals to promulgate significant changes, "Never doubt that a small group of dedicated people can change the world. In fact, it's the only thing that ever has."

However, futurists also contend that it is necessary for all effective and meaningful changes to occur, especially in schools, for leaders to employ intentional and bold visionary mindsets. In terms of incorporating more effective and quality social-emotional learning programs in today's schools the following admonishment of a recognized futurist should be heeded: "Not everything in the future comes under your control, but to sit back and take no action to create your preferred future is neither reasonable nor responsible" (Melnick, 1984, p. 6). It is imperative at this time for educational leaders to take bold yet intentional actions to incorporate more social-emotional learning in our schools for the sake of our children and their teachers and parents.

FINAL THOUGHTS

"It takes a village to raise a child" is a proverb that has been attributed to African cultures. It means the entire community must come together and interact positively to provide support and nurture a child to ensure they grow up in a safe and healthy environment. This concept is needed now more than ever! In our post-COVID world it has become evident that communities must come together to provide social-emotional support to our students and help them navigate through these trying times.

The chapter authors have emphasized that schools must work together with families and community organizations to provide a "full court press of services" to impact the social-emotional wellness of our students. Figure 12.2 illustrates some of the people and entities that need to come together to provide quality support and meaningful social-emotional learning services to children. Where all three areas intersect is the SEL "Power Zone." These are the areas that will have the greatest impact on students.

Where the three areas cooperatively join together and intersect is the "sweet spot" where all groups intentionally work for the benefit of the child. When everyone works together with a common purpose to ensure that all children receive individual attention and support, it is a game changer in the lives of students. As previously mentioned in a study by the Center on the Developing Child at Harvard University (Walsh, 2015), "the single most common finding is that children who end up doing well have had at least one stable and committed relationship with a supportive parent, caregiver, or other adult" (p. 1).

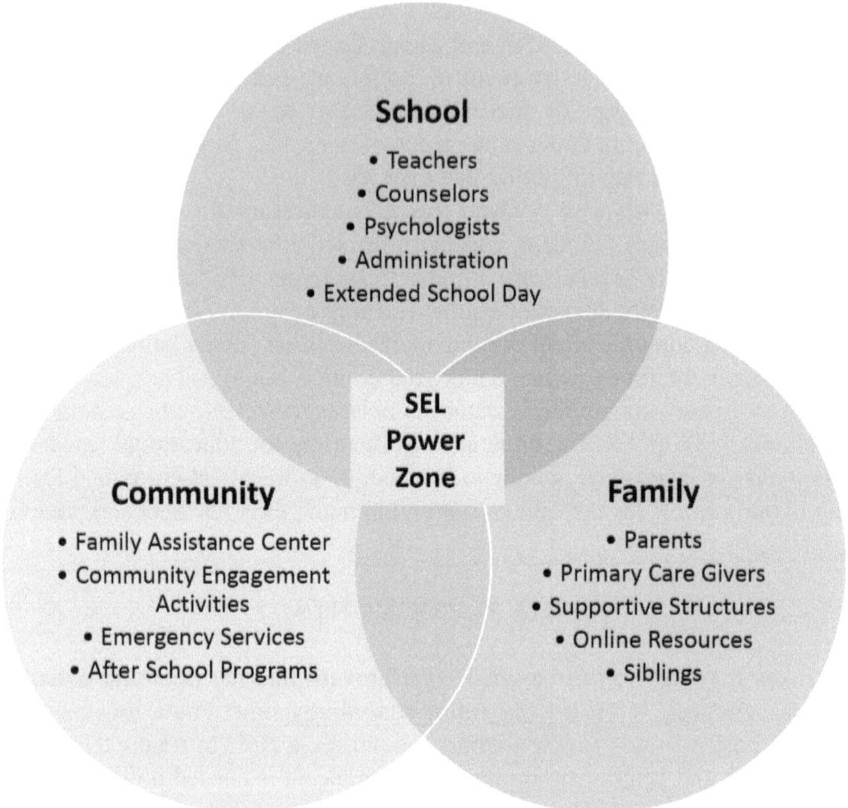

Figure 12.2. SEL power zone. ***From Polka, W., McKenna, J. & Vanhusen, M. (2024).***

The following poem illustrates the significance of all stakeholders coming together to make a positive difference in the lives of students:

UNITY

I dreamed I stood in a studio and
watched two sculptors there.
The clay they used was a young child's
mind and they fashioned it with care.

One was a teacher
the tools that were used
were books, music, and art.
The other, a parent,
worked with a guiding hand
and a gentle, loving heart.

Day after day,
the teacher toiled with touch
that was deft and sure.
While the parent labored close nearby
and polished and smoothed it o'er.

And when their task was done,
they were proud of
what they had wrought,
For the things they had molded into a child
could neither be sold nor bought.

And each agree they would have failed
if each had worked alone.
For behind the parents stood the school
and behind the teacher stood the home.

—*Author Unknown*

The chapter authors of this book have identified multiple strategies, methods, and programs that school leaders can utilize to address the various needs, problems, and issues they are facing regarding the social-emotional well-being of their students, staff, and communities. The following is a summary of the best practices presented in this book.

KEY PRAGMATIC LEADERSHIP TAKEAWAYS

1. Begin by establishing and officially articulating consensus "Visions of the Future" for this educational organization with an emphasis on "Moral Purpose" and "Mindset" of the School Community.

The chapter authors all emphasized the importance of immediately addressing the social-emotional well-being of their students, staff, and parents. The data and statistics presented by the authors clearly show that there is a mental health crisis not only across the country but throughout the world. Key findings from Mental Health America show that over 2.7 million youth are experiencing severe major depression and 17 percent of youth report suffering from at least one major depressive episode in the past year. The report also indicates that 21 percent of adults are currently experiencing some form of mental illness and 15 percent of adults are struggling with a substance-abuse problem. A startling statistic from the report is that over

60 percent of youth and 55 percent of adults receive no treatment for their conditions (MHA, 2023).

Mental health is the moral imperative of our time and school leaders must embrace this and intentionally engage their staff to understand "why" integrating social-emotional wellness strategies into their daily routines is of critical importance. In "Leading in a Culture of Change," Fullan explains that to successfully lead any significant change initiative begins with "moral purpose" (Fullan, 2020). If a leader does not take the time to educate their staff on the importance or "why" of an issue or program it will falter and not be successful. If people are not connected or see the purpose of an initiative they will never "buy in" and do the bare minimum; they will soon become disengaged from the process.

It is imperative that educational leaders present to their respective stakeholders the vision of the future that they possess and encourage them to, via consensus, formulate strategic plans and tactical activities to incorporate and better quality social-emotional learning into their teaching-learning settings using the *possible future, probable future, and preferable future* heuristic or deductive planning paradigm illustrated in this chapter.

Establishing a "moral purpose" is the foundation for creating a positive mindset associated with the preferable vision of the future in the staff. This is what allows and inspires the staff to embrace an initiative. When the staff "believes" in the "preferable vision" and the importance of a project and sees the value to themselves and others they welcome the initiative and willingly support the work. Dweck (2018) affirms this concept and describes the importance in establishing a "growth mindset" in people. She explains that a growth mindset is key to a positive attitude, motivating others to view challenges as opportunities and find inspiration in helping others.

Leaders must take the time to lay the foundation of a strong moral purpose and establish a positive mindset with their staff before they begin implementing any initiative or program. The administration and staff should be role models and examples of what they would like to see in students. Kindness, caring, empathy, and respect are non-negotiable and must be clearly understood by all staff. This is a foundation for developing a culture that supports the social and emotional well-being of everyone in the school community.

2. Embed Social-Emotional Wellness and Learning into the Strategic Plan

Social-emotional wellness and learning must be intentionally embedded into every program and practice throughout the school community. The best way to ensure this happens with fidelity is to make it part of the strategic planning process as well as developing specific SEL-PLCs at all levels of the context. Leaders must address social-emotional learning in their district mission and vision of the future pronouncements. They must also write specific district-wide goals directly related to social-emotional wellness.

A district-wide "Social-Emotional Learning and Wellness Committee" should be formed. This committee should have members from all buildings, grade levels, and subject areas. It should also contain members from all major community stakeholder groups. It is important to have input from as many voices as possible to address the wide array of needs throughout the community. This committee needs to develop district-wide goals, identify district-wide programs and practices, and write action plans with specific timelines.

The strategic plan should also address a committee structure at the building level. Each school building should have a building-based "Social-Emotional Learning and Wellness" committee who have members that sit as representatives on the district-wide committee. This committee is responsible for implementing the programs and practices identified by the district committee. Building committees tailor programs and individualize practices to meet the unique needs of the students and staff in each building. They also develop building-based goals and action plans that include specific building initiatives, timelines, and people responsible for implementation.

Building-based "Social-Emotional Learning and Wellness" committees report to the Building Leadership Team (BLT) as well as the District Social-Emotional Wellness Committee. Usually, BLT's meet monthly while District Committees meet three times per year at the beginning, middle, and end of the year.

This is a basic communication structure between the district and building levels that needs to be clearly articulated in the district strategic plan. Each district must design their own plan that meets their needs, but a specific plan to ensure that district and building goals align is essential.

3. Collaborative Teams and Staff Engagement

It is imperative to get everyone involved and engaged in the process of implementing best practices in social-emotional learning. It is important to establish a culture where social-emotional wellness is a top priority in the school. Part of the strategic planning process is to set up building teams in all subject areas and curriculum areas to ensure that social-emotional learning practices are implemented across all areas consistently. Schools should set up a "Professional Learning Community" structure that includes vertical and horizontal teams to articulate consistent practice across and between grade levels (DuFour, DuFour, & Eaker, 2020). Each district must determine their specific building team structure based on their own unique needs.

Each team should include a social-emotional learning component as part of their action planning process. This will actively engage the entire staff in a consistent process of goal setting, program implementation, and evaluation specifically targeted at social-emotional learning and wellness. The building "Social-Emotional Wellness Team" should provide support and guidance to the building teams and be available as a resource to help them implement the programs with fidelity. The administration should have the committees share best practices and report results periodically at grade level and faculty meetings. This will maximize engagement, allow the staff to support each other, and keep the information at the forefront of the school (DuFour, DuFour, & Eaker, 2020).

4. Embed Explicit Social-Emotional Learning and Wellness Activities into Curriculum and Daily Instruction

After the collaborative structure has been established to engage the staff and ensure communication across and between grade levels exists, a district can begin the process of developing and adopting social-emotional learning programs and practices to embed throughout the curriculum.

The chapter authors have emphasized the importance of developing explicit instruction and using evidenced-based practices on a daily basis throughout the school. One of the main programs that was identified for embedding social-emotional learning into the curriculum was the *Collaborative for Academic, Social, Emotional Learning* (CASEL) program. This program includes five core social-emotional competencies that serve as a framework to integrate instruction into all curriculum areas. These competencies include self-awareness, self-management, responsible decision-making, relationship skills, and social awareness (Casel.org 2023). The CASEL framework and five competencies provide a consistent curriculum structure to develop explicit instruction (CASEL, 2023).

Hanover Research (2019) also reported that school districts should provide explicit instruction in SEL skills, behaviors, and attitudes to promote social-emotional development. Their research recommends that districts integrate SEL skills into the curriculum of all core academic subjects; design instructional practices that promote SEL, such as project-based learning and cooperative learning; and integrate explicit SEL skills instruction in the classroom through coaching, modeling, and practicing specific SEL skills on a regular basis.

Their research identified two researched-based programs that have been successfully implemented across the country that provide a clear and viable curriculum, explicit instruction, individual lessons on SEL skills, general practices that can be utilized by students and staff throughout the day, and a home component to extend support to families. Those programs are the Promoting Alternative Thinking Strategies (PATHS) program developed by researchers at Penn State University and the Recognizing, Understanding, Labeling, Expressing, Regulating Emotion (RULER) program developed by the Yale Center for Emotional Intelligence (Hanover, 2019).

Their research further recommends that when school districts develop or select SEL programs they should do so using cooperative teams that represent all stakeholders, only adopt evidenced-based practices with proven results of success, and must consider the local contextual factors and unique demographics of the school (Hanover, 2019).

Hanover researchers (2019) also suggest two other areas that should be embedded into the daily routines of a school to promote social-emotional wellness in students and they are Restorative Practices and diversity, equity, and inclusion (DEI) activities. Restorative practices are an alternative to traditional disciplinary procedures used in schools. A restorative approach implements practices that proactively build healthy relationships and a sense of community to prevent conflict. These practices allow an individual who may have committed harm to positively address the person they harmed and take full responsibility for their behavior. They must acknowledge their behavior and understand how their behavior affected others. Most importantly, they must take action to repair the harm they caused by their actions and ensure they learn from the situation so that no further harm comes in the future (Schott Foundation, 2014). For restorative practices to be successful they must be implemented consistently throughout the school. When implemented with fidelity they can create a culture of caring and establish an environment that proactively promotes empathy and respect (Walker, 2020).

It is also important to incorporate diversity, equity, and inclusion practices and culturally responsive teaching into daily routines. The Wake Forest School of Professional Studies emphasizes the importance of embedding DEI in a school's daily practice: "It is the responsibility of a school's leadership team to spearhead diversity, equity, and inclusion (DEI) initiatives to ensure everyone—from students and families to teachers and staff members—feels valued and heard. Diversity in schools is an important component to make a learning environment truly thrive" (Nagl, 2023).

The New York State Education Department's Culturally Responsive Sustaining Education Framework (2021) further expounds on the importance of making culturally responsive teaching part of a school's daily repertoire. It identifies Four Principles that they claim should be incorporated into the daily routines of all schools. They are: a welcoming and affirming environment, high expectations and rigorous instruction, inclusive curriculum and assessments, and ongoing professional learning (NYSED, 2021).

Our schools today are more diverse than ever before. A student's culture is connected to their social and emotional well-being. School leaders must intentionally address these issues and embed practices that make all students feel welcome and cared for.

5. Develop School-Wide Systems and Structures to Provide Services and Evaluate Effectiveness

To effectively implement SEL programs and evaluate effectiveness, a school must develop a consistent structure to deliver instruction and monitor progress (Jones et al., 2021).

The chapter authors recommend that every school must have a fully functioning Student Support Team (SST) or Child Study Team (CST) that meets regularly to review and address the social-emotional and academic needs of all students. These teams should have a wide variety of professionals including but not limited to classroom teachers, social workers, psychologists, counselors, speech therapists, reading and math specialists, special area teachers, and building administrators. These teams review quantitative data and qualitative information on students and make recommendations for interventions and programs to support students in need.

Once the Student Support Team is in place it is imperative that the team develop a multi-tiered system of support (MTSS). MTSS is a comprehensive schoolwide framework to provide academic, behavioral, and social-emotional support to all students based on their individual needs (Fredrick, 2023). Typically, a MTSS framework consists of three tiers of support. Students move up the tiers and gain access to the support they need through progress monitoring by the Student Support Team. The tiers are usually identified as: Tier 1: Universal supports for all students. Tier 2: Targeted supports for some students who need extra help. Tier 3: Intensive supports for the few students who need extensive services (figure 12.3).

An MTSS is a framework that diagnoses student needs, moves them up the tiers, and provides the specific support they need in three areas: academic, social-emotional, and behavioral.

Academic supports are provided through a Response to Intervention (RTI) model. Students who are falling behind academically are reviewed using multiple measures both quantitative and qualitative. The Student Support Team thoroughly reviews and discusses the data and recommends academic interventions to provide support. The team will apply the interventions and monitor the progress on a regular basis. They will provide additional interventions and more intensive support based on data and observations. The goal is to provide the individual support necessary for each student to be successful.

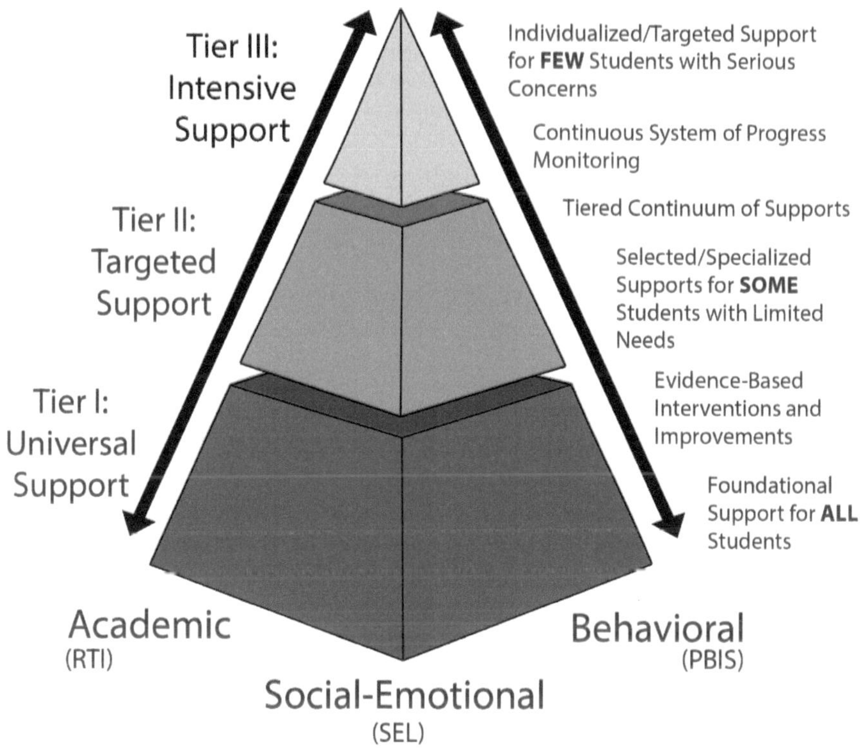

Figure 12.3. MTSS framework. ***Developed by McKenna and McKenna (2024).***

The process to provide behavioral support is called Positive Behavior Intervention Supports (PBIS). This follows the same three-tiered system to provide individualized support to students. PBIS should be implemented consistently schoolwide and the following practices put into practice: schoolwide rules and expectations; classroom management plans that acknowledge appropriate behavior and respond to negative behavior, establish structure, and routines; and foster ways to maximize student engagement in positive ways (PBIS.org. 2023).

The system to provide social-emotional (SEL) support follows the same three-tiered MTSS model. Teachers need to be trained in best practices in providing social-emotional learning and embedding SEL into their daily practice. They also need to be taught to proactively observe what signs and behaviors to look for in students who may be experiencing social-emotional trauma.

The Center for Health Care Strategies (2021) recommend that every school and district incorporate trauma-informed care training into their multi-tiered support system to ensure that all staff know and understand how to recognize and provide support to students experiencing trauma.

An essential element of a successful MTSS is an evaluation component to diagnose needs and monitor progress. A school must establish a system to collect quantitative and qualitative data in all areas in a multi-tiered support system including academic, behavioral, and social-emotional. All areas are intertwined so it is important to review all aspects of a student when making any decisions about applying interventions. It is imperative to review data to develop the appropriate interventions and place a student on the correct tier.

6. Develop a Comprehensive Plan for Professional Learning and Training

Training for social-emotional learning is not a one and done initiative but must be constant and ongoing over time (Panorama, 2023). It is imperative that schools and districts develop a strategic plan for implementing social-emotional learning across and throughout all grade levels. Professional learning must be comprehensive and planned for all stakeholder groups in a school community. School leaders must develop clear plans around the individual needs of schools and districts. They must also tailor training sessions to intentionally target specific staff populations and parents who work with students in different capacities (Hanover, 2019).

According to the Wallace Foundation, teachers traditionally receive very little training to promote SEL skills and deal with conflict or the trauma that many students have experienced. Teachers generally receive some behavior management training but little to none regarding the social-emotional needs of students. Staff members other than teachers receive even less. Cafeteria monitors, secretaries, bus drivers, aides, and athletic coaches who spend a great deal of time with students rarely get any training and support to deal with the social-emotional issues our students are facing (Jones et al., 2021).

School districts must develop intentional plans, policies, and protocols to address the social needs of their students, staff, and community. The authors of this book have offered many specific suggestions. The following is summary of ideas a district should consider when developing a SEL professional learning plan:

- Create a district-level SEL team of all stakeholders to research and identify best practices that meet the needs of the schools.
- Create building-level SEL teams to work in conjunction with the district team.
- Review the current practices and resources to determine needs and capacity to deliver programs.
- Review outside programs that contain curriculum, lessons, coaching, and training components.

- Bring in outside trainers and consultants.
- Make site visits to other schools who have utilized programs and see them in action.
- Hire a special SEL coordinator who has specialized training and expertise to guide your efforts.
- Hire SEL coaches for each building to provide ongoing support to the staff.
- Identify mandatory and optional training sessions.
- Identify onetime and recurring sessions.
- Develop a catalog with various training sessions that run throughout the year for continuous opportunities for learning.
- Use a Professional Learning Community (PLC) model to deliver training and embed learning into existing team structures in schools.

These are some of the strategies our authors recommend when developing a professional learning plan for social-emotional learning. Each district or school must find unique programs and develop an individualized plan that meets their specific needs. It is imperative that whatever plan is decided it is developed with stakeholder involvement and implemented with fidelity.

7. Work with Families and Extend SEL beyond the Classroom

Social-emotional wellness and support is necessary both in and outside of school. Collaborative communication between schools, families, and community partners is essential to provide the services and support that students need to be successful (Hanover Research, 2019). Schools should also develop extended-day and extracurricular activities that form positive relationships and enhance the social-emotional well-being of students. School leaders need to develop intentional plans, programs, and strategies to extend SEL support beyond the classroom. These programs connect students to school, help them build positive relationships with peers and adults, tap into their interests, and enhance their learning experiences. Extended-school-day activities can take many forms including:

- **Specialized SEL programs** to address specific areas such as problem-solving skills, restorative strategies, coping skills, relationship building, leadership skills, anti-bullying, diversity, equity, and inclusion and other customized programs based on the individual needs of the students and aligned with the mission of the school.
- **Curriculum extension programs** such as homework clubs, writing clubs, science experiments, coding, robotics, book clubs, art activities,

music programs and physical education activities. These programs provide academic support and enhance areas of interest for the students.
- **Family engagement activities** are designed to bring families together and provide support or just enjoy a fun activity at school. These include but are not limited to specialized workshops, family fun nights, cultural celebrations, DEI activities, games, carnivals, or special presentations.
- **Community engagement activities** can take many forms including community service projects, career nights, safety programs sponsored by local police and fire departments, volunteer opportunities in local agencies, and nonprofit organizations.
- **Create a Family Assistance Center** to provide counseling support and crisis intervention services to families. These centers also work with families as a liaison to help them access other community services related to food, clothing, and shelter.

School district leaders should also establish partnerships with community organizations to help provide wrap-around services to provide continuous support to students and families. According to Hanover Research these partnerships should include:

- Nonprofit organizations that provide prevention services, counseling, DEI training, after-school youth programs, and staff training.
- Mental health and crisis networks, such as a suicide prevention network, substance abuse counseling, a sexual assault network, family therapists, hospitals, and psychiatric clinics.
- Local universities that provide resources on SEL and offer staff training in trauma-informed care, anti-bullying, and asset building.
- Local government agencies, including the public health department to provide suicide prevention training, and police department to provide resource officers and victim intervention programs (Hanover Research, 2019).

The authors of the chapters emphasized the importance of school districts extending programs beyond the school day and forming explicit partnerships with community organizations to provide a full-court-press approach to provide extensive support to students, staff and families.

8. AI Initiatives to Support and Enhance SEL Practices

Chapter authors researched and examined the use of artificial intelligence in supporting teacher well-being and reducing burnout among school personnel. Studying the programs, practices, and possibilities for the use of artificial intelligence in supporting the academic and social-emotional well-being of students and staff is an emerging and important field of study. We acknowledge that more research needs to be done in this area; however, our authors identified some compelling areas where the use of AI could be very beneficial to supporting teachers' and students' social-emotional and academic needs. Our authors identified eight specific ways that AI could directly support and enhance teachers in the classroom. They include: personalized learning, differentiated, tiered instruction, cultivating twenty-first-century skills, incorporating technology, embracing cultural competence, assessment, data driven decisions, and effective classroom management.

The authors stressed the importance that school districts must embrace an "Innovative Leadership Mindset," embrace a collaborative philosophy, and create a "Stakeholder Coalition" that includes all major community groups as partners to develop programs, practices, and ethical policies. The possibilities are endless regarding AI and safeguards must be put in place to ensure it is utilized productively. Our authors recommend that districts make AI education a priority and implement the following practices: invest in AI, develop ethical AI guidelines, support innovative leadership, support stakeholder engagement, continuously research best practices, and advocate for responsible policies that enhance teaching and learning.

9. Power of Direct Involvement and Direct Connections

The authors of the chapters emphasized the importance of forming positive relationships and described many programs and practices to provide support to students and adults. Programs are necessary but even more important are the direct relationships that people form with each other.

Whitaker in his book, *What Great Principals Do Differently* emphasizes the point that it is "people—not programs" that make the biggest impact on the lives of students (Whitaker, 2020). It is imperative now more than ever for educators to make intentional efforts to directly connect with students in individualized and personalized ways.

As previously mentioned, research from the CDC (2022) stressed the importance of "school connectedness" and that schools must develop practices to positively connect students to school. Research from the National Scientific Council on the Developing Child at Harvard University (2015) emphasizes the point of "direct" connectedness and states that "the single most common finding is that children who end up doing well have had at least one stable and committed relationship with a supportive parent, caregiver, or other adult" (p. 1).

The challenge becomes, "how can educators directly connect with students regarding their social-emotional wellness?" School personnel have traditionally held an indirect role in the lives of their students, but there are many specific strategies they can implement daily that directly impact students and the culture of the school.

In "The Fundamental 5 Revisited," Cain and Laird provide some easy concepts that teachers and principals can implement to foster direct connections with their students. Two key strategies they highlight are, "Recognize and Reinforce" and "Work in the Power Zone" (Cain & Laird, 2021).

Recognize and Reinforce: This concept refers to the recognition and reinforcement of individual students for specific reasons. Most educators engage in what Cain and Laird (2021) refer to as "positive talk." These are general, nonspecific positive statements. When recognition and reinforcement is individualized with specificity it becomes a powerful tool to motivate students.

Work in the Power Zone: Teachers need to directly interact with their students and get to know their individual needs, problems, and interests. In relation to building administrators, this refers to the concept that you need to get away from your desk and spend your time directly in areas where your students are. In classrooms, in the lunchroom, and on the buses. This allows you to have personal conversations with your students, get to know their interests, and recognize and reinforce them individually. Educators must take the time and make the effort to get to know their students personally. Forging individual relationships connects students and staff with the school, creates a positive culture, and, most importantly, lets people know that you care about them.

REFERENCES

Cain, S., Laird, M., Cotton, S., & Ellspermann, J. (2021). "The Fundamental 5 Revisited: Exceptional Instruction in Every Setting." https://survey.nassp.org/2022/.

CASEL. Fundamentals of SEL. (2023). https.//casel.org/fundamentals-of sel/.

Center for Health Care Strategies. (2021). *Trauma Informed Care Implementation Resource Center: What is Trauma Informed Care?* https://www.traumainformedcare.chcs.org/what-is-trauma-informed-care/.

DuFour, R., Dufour, R. & Eaker, R. (2020). *Revisiting Professional Learning Communities at Work*. Bloomington, IN: Solutions Tree.

Dweck, C. (2018). *Mindset: Changing the Way You Think to Fulfill Your Potential.* N.p.: Robinson Pub.

Fredrick, L. (2023). "A Comprehensive Guide to MTSS." Panorama. https://www.panoramaed.com/blog/mtss-comprehensive-guide.

Fullan, M. (2020). *Leading in a Culture of Change*. Hoboken, NJ: John Wiley & Sons.

Jones, S. et al. (2021). *Navigating SEL from The Inside Out: Looking Inside and across 33 Leading SEL Programs: A Practical Resource for Schools and OST*

Providers. Cambridge, MA: Wallace Foundation, Harvard Graduate School of Education.

Melnick, R. (1984). *Visions of the Future: A Textbook on the Past, Present, and Future.* Pelham Manor, NY: Hudson Institute/Indiana & International Center for the Development of Thinking Skills.

Mental Health America. (2023). "The State of Mental Health in America." https://mhanational.org/issues/state-mental-health-america.

Nagl, S. (2023). "How Education Leaders Impact Diversity, Equity, and Inclusion in Schools." Wake Forest University School of Professional Studies. https://sps.wfu.edu/articles/how-educational-leaders-impact-dei-in-schools/.

National Association of Secondary School Principals. (2022). "NASSP's Survey of America's School Leaders and High School Students." https://survey.nassp.org/2022/#intro.

National Scientific Council on the Developing Child. (2015). "Supportive Relationships and Active Skill-Building Strengthen the Foundations of Resilience." Working paper no. 13. Center on the Developing Child at Harvard University. www.developingchild.harvard.edu.

New York State Education Department. (2021). *The Culturally Sustaining Responsive Framework.* https://www.nysed.gov/sites/default/files/programs/crs/culturally-responsive-sustaining-education-framework.pdf.

Panorama Education (2023). "SEL Playbook for Superintendents: 18 Superintendents Share Their Best Social Emotional Learning Leadership Advice." https://go.panoramaed.com/sel-playbook-for-superintendents.

Polka, W., & VanHusen, M. (2023). "Managing Yourself during Crises: Surviving and Thriving in the Education's Ever-Evolving Open Social System of People, Things, and Ideas." In W. Polka, J. McKenna, & M. VanHusen (Eds.), *Managing Yourself and Others during Crises: Key Leadership Visions, Approaches, and Dispositions to Survive and Thrive.* Lanham, MD: Rowman & Littlefield Education Publications.

Schott Foundation. (2014). "Restorative Practices: Fostering Healthy Relationships and Promoting Positive Discipline in Schools: A Guide for Educators." https://schottfoundation.org/wp-content/uploads/restorative-practices-guide.pdf.

Walker, T. (2020). "Restorative Practices in Schools Work: But They Can Work Better." NEA.org. https://www.nea.org/nea-today/all-news-articles/restorative-practices-schools-work-they-can-work-better.

Walsh, Bari. (2015). *The Science of Resilience: Why Some Children Thrive Despite Adversity.* Cambridge, MA: Harvard Graduate School of Education.

WASA School Information and Research Service. (2019). *Best Practices in Social Emotional Learning.* Hanover Research. www.hanoverresearch.com/.

Whitaker, T. (2020). *What Great Principals Do Differently: Twenty Things That Matter Most.* Third edition. New York: Routledge.

Afterword

"Casserian Engeri"

Michael Cornell

"And How Are the Children?"

In October of 2022, administrators and service providers from every agency, clinic, and facility that provides mental and emotional health support to school-aged children in Erie County, New York, had an opportunity to join together with leaders from all of the county's schools in conversation about how we can serve this critical need for social-emotional support in a more coordinated way. As one of the two founders of this event, I had the honor of speaking to the 130 or so people who attended this very first of four such gatherings for the 2022–2023 school year. I used that occasion to speak about the Masai tribe in Africa. Among the many tribes of Africa, no tribe was considered to have warriors more fearsome or more intelligent than the mighty Masai. It may be surprising, then, to learn that the traditional greeting passed among the Masai warriors when they encountered each other was *Casserian engeri*, "And how are the children?"

This is still the traditional greeting of the Masai, acknowledging the high value the Masai placed on the children's well-being. Even warriors with no children of their own would always give the traditional answer, "All the children are well." This meant, of course, that the priority of protecting the young and the powerless was in place, and that the Masai people had not forgotten their reason for being, their proper function, and their responsibilities.

"All the children are well" means life is good. It means the daily struggles for existence, even among poor people in difficult survival contexts, include the proper care of the young and defenseless. "And how are the children" has become the critical question of this current moment in our history, and one that should dominate the conversations in every school everywhere.

I asked the group that morning if someone walked by any of us on the street, or in a school hallway, and asked "And how are the children," what would our answer be? Could we say honestly that all of the children are well? Our current response might be, "Some of them are, but many clearly are not."

Anyone who has been paying attention to what happens in our nation's schools knows that every one of society's challenges walks in the schoolhouse door every day. The homelessness crisis, the scourge of substance use, food insecurity, our culture of violence, the impact of social media, and many other more localized challenges weigh heavily in the lives of school children everywhere. Chief among them, and perhaps a common thread woven though the others, is the mental and emotional health of the children we serve.

Since early in the 2010s, we have known that 20 percent of all school-aged children will experience some type of mental or emotional health need while they are in school. We also know that the onset of substance abuse in the majority of cases involving adolescents and young adults is caused by undiagnosed or untreated mental illness. Finally, we know that schools today are often the first, and most readily accessible source of mental and emotional health support for school-aged children.

However, making the mental and emotional well-being of children the most important priority in a school district isn't as easy as one might think. The tough questions in a typical school normally center around district rankings of graduation rates, state assessment scores, and AP/SAT/ACT scores rather than the most important questions like "And how are the children." It takes courage, persistence, and conviction from school leaders to keep the mental and emotional health of students, and of our adult staff, at the forefront of our service to children.

The scope of work for every person who works in, or on behalf of, a school of any kind has broadened dramatically in the past twenty years. It is no longer about just reading, writing, and arithmetic. School leaders and teachers today must also ensure that all students experience significant amounts of joy, value, and connection as a feature of their school day. Without joy, value, and connection every day in school, the children are not well. There is an ancient proverb that says, "A child who does not feel the warmth of belonging from the village will burn it down to finally feel its warmth."

As a school superintendent who has served in my role for nearly a decade, I appreciate the practical perspective offered by the editors of this book, Polka, Mckenna, VanHusen, and the chapter contributors they've assembled. Each chapter is written by a practicing educator or team who shares real-life examples and contains a "Pragmatic Leadership Takeaways" section that highlights the key actions that school leaders may take to improve social-emotional learning in their schools. Every school leader every day must ask herself/himself the question, "And how are the children?" We all want to employ every tactic and practice at our disposal so that we can honestly answer, "The children are well. They are all well."

About the Authors and Contributors

Dr. Olasumbo O. Adelakun, originally from Nigeria, is a Canadian citizen who completed her PhD in leadership and policy at Niagara University (2020) in Lewiston, New York. She completed her BS in environmental chemistry at Lagos State University in Nigeria. She also completed an MPhil in analytical chemistry at Anglia Ruskin University, Cambridge, England, and an Advanced Diploma in food hygiene and safety from the Royal Institute of Public Health and Hygiene in the United Kingdom. In addition, she earned a Bachelor of Applied Sciences in occupational, public health, and safety from Ryerson University, Toronto, Canada.

Dr. Olasumbo Adelakun conducted her dissertation study via phenomenological field studies related to the high incidents of infant mortality in Nigeria and possible gaps in government policies and leadership practices that contributing to it. She currently works as a community educator with a not-for-a-profit, multiservice, organization that provides comprehensive services to children and families in the Milton area of Toronto, Canada. In addition, she is currently an adjunct professor in global leadership at St. Bonaventure University, Olean, New York.

Dr. Roselle C. Aranha is presently a graduate student in the PhD program in leadership and policy at Niagara University, New York. In her professional journey as an educator, Roselle has taken on many roles. She began as a secondary school teacher in India, then she worked as an assistant professor at the University of Mumbai, where she taught teacher-candidates such courses as: Educational Psychology, Action Research, and Math Pedagogy. She also served as the quality assurance lead and accreditation coordinator at the College of Education, where she previously worked. Since moving to Canada, Roselle has worked in K–12 schools within the private sector.

She has extensive knowledge of the Ontario Ministry curriculum and the International Baccalaureate (IB) curriculum. Roselle is an IB examiner for math in the diploma program (Grades 11–12) and she has also had successful stints as the IB middle years program coordinator and IB personal projects coordinator at her previous school. Roselle has a PhD in education from the University of Mumbai and additional certifications from the University of Toronto and the International Baccalaureate Organization. A passionate educator, Roselle finds her joy in working on curriculum enhancement processes and systems-thinking efforts for teacher and student well-being thus endeavoring to make schools happier places for students and teachers.

Dr. Lisa Condino has been a special education teacher for over twenty-six years. She began her career working for Orleans-Niagara BOCES and has served students with various types of special needs in several of the local school districts, including Niagara Wheatfield and Lewiston Porter. She is currently employed as a sixth- and seventh-grade consultant teacher, providing instruction and support for students with specific learning disabilities, other health impairments, autism spectrum disorders, and speech and language impairments. In her position as a special education teacher and liaison, she has attended many CSE and 504 accommodation meetings, as well as other meetings concerning the education of students with special needs.

Since 2012, Dr. Condino has served as the special education liaison on the Executive Council for the Wilson Central School District, where she is presently employed. She is an advocate for students and their families, as well as her special education colleagues. Dr. Condino works closely with the district's administration and with parents to ensure that students with special needs are receiving the instruction and support that will enable them to be successful.

Michael Cornell, "Afterword" author, is currently the superintendent of the Hamburg Central School District in Western New York. He is also the president of the Erie/Niagara School Superintendents Association, where he and his team represent and support thirty school districts in a wide array of policy and advocacy initiatives. Mike is one of the most respected educators across the state and has been honored by the School Administrators Association of New York State Region 12 with the "Principal of the Year Award" and the Buffalo/Niagara Chapter of Phi Delta Kappa bestowed upon him the prestigious "President's Distinguished Administrator Award" for his outstanding service and contributions to the education profession. As a fierce advocate for students, and a leader in promoting social-emotional learning and wellness programs for students, he was the first superintendent in Western New York to require all school-based adults to receive a full-day Youth Mental Health First Aid training in 2018. This requirement of all employees remains in place today.

Dr. Salvatore Curella is a former teacher and current school administrator with over fifteen years of educational experience. As a teacher, Dr. Curella served as a middle and high school teacher in the Rye City School District in Westchester County, New York. As a high school administrator, he has worked in the East Aurora Union Free School District and Williamsville Central School District in Erie County, New York. Dr. Curella holds a BS and MS from Buffalo State University, an MEd in educational leadership from Manhattanville College, and earned his EdD in educational leadership and policy from the University at Buffalo.

Mr. Pete Dobmeier has worked in education for nearly twenty-five years, beginning with graduate study at the University of Denver and time as a content analyst for McREL. After returning to Western New York and working as a high school English teacher, he served as an assistant principal and principal for twelve years at a suburban middle school and currently works as a principal at an elementary school in a semirural area. He is also the cofounder and vice president of Root-Ed Learning & Leadership, an organization that provides professional development and consulting for educators and leaders in the areas of burnout, building intrinsic motivation, effective leadership practices, and nurturing a positive school culture. Over the course of his work at all levels of K–12 education, he has learned about the value of intentionality in building relationships through an explicit focus on interaction over transaction. This has driven his focus on attending to the social-emotional needs of adults and students in schools in order to build communities where all feel safe to learn.

Dr. Gregory A. Fabiano is a professor of psychology at Florida International University. His interests are in the area of evidence-based assessments and treatments for children with ADHD. He is author on over one hundred peer-reviewed publications and book chapters, and he has written two books on effective school-based interventions. Dr. Fabiano is also the developer of a Massive Open Online Course entitled "Everyday Strategies for ADHD" that has been completed by over 6,500 online students across six continents. A cross-cutting theme throughout his work is developing intervention programs that are effective for children and families within the contexts of their everyday environments. Dr. Fabiano's work has been continuously funded by federal agencies and foundations since 2006. In 2007 Dr. Fabiano was nominated by the US Department of Education and invited to the White House to receive the Presidential Early Career Award for Scientists and Engineers, the nation's highest honor for early career investigators.

Dr. Paul M. Fanuele is the superintendent of schools for the Spackenkill Union Free School District located in New York. He has over twenty-eight years of experience in education serving as a coach, teacher, assistant principal, house principal, principal, executive principal, and, most recently, superintendent. Dr. Fanuele has served in districts both large and small and understands the unique challenges of both. He served on the Board of Directors for the National Association of Secondary School Principals (NASSP) after serving as New York State coordinator for NASSP. He also is a past president of the School Administrators Association of New York State (SAANYS).

Leadership and learning have always been his passion. Dr. Fanuele has presented at national and state conferences and written numerous articles. His most recent academic presentation, "Staying Positive and Refreshed to Counteract Negativity," integrated his core beliefs on the topic as espoused in past articles. Dr. Fanuele's dissertation, titled, "Addressing New Challenges: A Framework for Educational Leadership," analyzes effective leadership in the school setting. All of his roles have been rewarding, including, most importantly, being a husband and father of two.

Sophia Frontale graduated with an MPS in clinical psychological science from the University of Maryland (UMD) College Park in November of 2022. She also graduated from the George Washington University (GWU) with a BA in psychology in the spring of 2021. She worked previously in the social psychology lab at GWU, where she conducted studies and assisted doctoral students with their research. She has also coauthored a sociology publication in *Deviance Today Journal*. She started working as a research coordinator for the TPAC program (UMD ADHD Lab) in July of 2022. In January of 2023 she also took on the role of clinic assistant and executive functioning coach for college students with ADHD in the SUCCEEDS clinic (UMD ADHD Lab). In July 2023, she started a research coordinator position at Florida International University's (FIU) Center for Children and Families of Western New York. Her research interests include parental and family influences on youth with anxiety and ADHD, and she hopes to pursue a PhD in clinical psychology in the future.

Dr. Alan Ingraham is a former teacher and current school administrator with nearly two decades of educational experience, fourteen years as a secondary mathematics teacher and the last five as a school administrator. As a teacher, Dr. Ingraham has served as a middle school and high school teacher in Buffalo Public Schools and Lewiston-Porter Central School District in Youngstown, New York. Dr. Ingraham was recognized as a New York State master teacher during his tenure teaching mathematics at Lewiston-Porter

High School. Dr. Ingraham currently works as the high school principal at Starpoint Central School District in Lockport, New York.

Dr. Ingraham holds an MEd in educational leadership from Niagara University and holds a BA in mathematics, an MS in mathematics education, and earned his EdD in educational administration from the State University of New York at Buffalo.

Dr. Joshua Janese is currently the principal at North Tonawanda Middle School, where he serves on the district's strategic planning committee, safety team, and capital project committee. At North Tonawanda Middle School, much of his work has centered around improving scheduling efficiencies within the academic program to ensure instructional equity for all students as well as creating elective course offerings for historically marginalized students. Dedicated to developing the whole child, he has created schoolwide student professional development days, established Liberty Partnership Programs with local colleges, and expanded student career awareness opportunities through the district's local BOCES. Prior to his tenure as a principal, Dr. Janese was an assistant principal at North Tonawanda High School and a special education teacher at Amherst Middle School. In the community, he serves on a local village planning board.

Lori Jonas emphasizes that possessing cultural awareness, unwavering determination, and resolute perseverance are essential attributes for effective leadership. She believes that when individuals are placed under a leader's positive guidance, they hold the power to significantly influence the course of many lives. With a diverse background spanning two decades in education, Mrs. Jonas has transitioned from being a classroom educator to assuming roles as an assistant principal and eventually as a principal, overseeing elementary and middle school campuses on both coasts of the United States. Her contributions to education were acknowledged in 2021 when she was honored with the prestigious Principal of the Year award nomination from her California school district. Beyond her role as a building leader, she played a pivotal role in guiding numerous district-wide initiatives, including the Strategic Goals Committee, Equity and Racial Justice Task Force, Curriculum Council, and Administrators Evaluation Manual. Her involvement in these initiatives significantly shaped the visions of several districts. Currently, Mrs. Jonas is actively pursuing a PhD in leadership and policy at Niagara University, while serving as the PhD assistant in the same program.

Alix Printup is an Indigenous scholar from the Haudenosaunee Peoples with a BA in both psychology and philosophy from the College of Wooster. His previous work has focused on the utility of alternative culturally/

contextually relevant diagnoses and treatment interventions within psychopathology. Furthermore, his interest in the utilization of culture as both a protective factor and treatment intervention regarding perceived racial group discrimination-based anxiety and depression for Indigenous peoples has resulted in a project which has garnered attention for presentation at the annual Society for Personality and Social Psychology conference in 2024. He is dedicated to promoting the inclusion of culturally/contextually relevant diagnoses and treatment interventions to better support and care for minoritized populations within clinical psychology.

Carolina Ramirez is a doctoral student in the Clinical Science in Child and Adolescent Psychology Program at Florida International University (FIU), with a keen interest in researching child ADHD in the Hispanic community, emphasizing the need for culturally sensitive approaches. As an undergraduate, she played a key role in creating the Mindful Peer Exchange Program, aimed at reducing the stigma around mental health for middle and high school students. Having earned her BA at FIU, her academic journey led to a postbaccalaureate research assistant position where she analyzed the effects of early language and behavior intervention in kindergarten and first-grade students with ADHD symptoms and in the English as a Second or Foreign Language program. Additionally, she's contributed to clinical work as a referral and enrollment specialist at FIU's Center for Children and Families, assisting families seeking services and handling safety planning and reporting. Her experiences have strengthened her commitment to advancing mental health understanding, particularly in the Hispanic culture.

Daniel Reichard is the coordinator of New Teacher Support for Stafford County Schools, where he coaches lead mentors and new teachers as part of the Mentor 360 induction program. Dan began his professional teaching career in Stafford County at Kate Waller Barrett Elementary in 2012 teaching third and fifth grade. Dan attended Indiana University of Pennsylvania earning his bachelor's in elementary education K–6 and his master's in educational leadership K–12 from George Mason University. Dan has received numerous awards and accolades, notably being named the 2018 Stafford County Schools, *Washington Post*, and the 2019 Virginia Region III Teacher of the Year.

Melanie Rengel-Isea is a doctoral student in the Clinical Science in Child and Adolescent Psychology Program at Florida International University (FIU). Previously, she received her bachelor's and master's degrees in the field of psychology and early child childhood education. Her experience as a counselor in programs such as the Summer Treatment Program that focuses on tailored interventions for children with ADHD led her to pursue a career in child clinical psychology. In her prior baccalaureate and graduate student years, she has been involved in projects concerning language and spatial development in the hippocampus and active involvement in treatment programs targeting ADHD and comorbid disruptive behaviors in the classroom and home settings. Her interests center around the increase in quality and span of evidence-based interventions for children with externalizing and internalizing problems. She is interested in the development, evaluation, and dissemination of early interventions across multiple domains to promote school readiness and socio-emotional functioning. She aspires to develop and deliver evidence-based treatments to improve parent and child behaviors and understand the mental health problems affecting children by learning effective implementations of school-based interventions to improve daily life functioning. More specifically, her focus includes investigating the practice of tailored interventions to increase the effectiveness and efficacy of treatments in children experiencing externalizing and internalizing challenges.

Dr. Caitlin Riegel is an assistant professor in the Department of Teacher Education at Niagara University, where she serves as the program coordinator for their graduate elementary and secondary education programs. She earned a BA degree in education with a concentration in adolescent mathematics, an MS degree in special education, and a doctorate in leadership and policy where she focused on developing an instrument to measure how often teacher candidates model and apply the International Society for Technology in Education (ISTE) Standards in teacher preparation programs.

Dr. Riegel was the recipient of the International Society of Educational Planning (ISEP) Glen Earthman Outstanding Dissertation Award in 2020 and the *Journal of Research in Technology in Education* Reviewer of the Year in 2023. She was elected in 2023 as the president of ISEP and also serves on the Board of Directors of the Association for Independent Liberal Arts Colleges for Teacher Education (AILACTE). Dr. Riegel serves as an assistant editor for the *AILACTE Journal* and on the review board for the *Journal of Research on Technology in Education* (JRTE) and *Educational Planning Journal*. When not working in the field of teacher education, Dr. Riegel spends her time on the ice as a US Figure Skating Association (USFSA) figure skating coach.

Jennifer Sikov is a doctoral student in the Clinical Science in Child and Adolescent Psychology Program at Florida International University (FIU). After graduating with a BA in psychology from Brandeis University, she completed an MA in psychology from Boston University. Prior to graduate school, she served as a research coordinator at Boston Medical Center (BMC) Department of Psychiatry REACH 4 ADHD lab, conducting multiple mixed methods and intervention projects aimed at addressing barriers and disparities in the diagnosis and treatment of ADHD among socioeconomically disadvantaged and minoritized families. She also served as a research coordinator on the Kids FACE FEARS multisite implementation-effectiveness trial of digital vs. face-to-face cognitive behavioral therapy (CBT) for pediatric anxiety.

She currently works under the mentorship of Dr. Gregory Fabiano at the Center for Children and Families at FIU. Her research interests focus on augmenting existing school and community-based services to mitigate disparities in access and promote resiliency among youth with normative and atypical developmental challenges. She aspires to develop and implement evidence-based practices in youth-serving contexts to scaffold adjustment and independence among youth and adolescents with ADHD. Jennifer has worked in schools, summer treatment programs, and clinical and research settings with children, adolescents, and young adults with ADHD and other mental health diagnoses.

Sharon Singh is currently a PhD candidate in the PhD program in leadership and policy at Niagara University and is in the final dissertation stage of the program. She has been in the education field for over fifteen years. She started as an early childhood educator, then became an elementary teacher which led to teaching at the college level, where she is currently a professor of education at Sheridan College, Ontario, Canada. Her research areas of interest include: diversity in education and mental health in childhood. Diversity in the classroom is something she continuously ensures, and she does her best to maintain inclusivity for all her students. Mental health is another important aspect that she focuses on and highlights as much as possible to help with students' overall well-being. These two areas are what she will continue to advocate for to help those in the education field.

Emily Sutton received a BA in both psychology and law from SUNY University at Buffalo. As of July 2023, she works at the Center for Children and Families of WNY as a research assistant. In this position she aids in school and home ADHD interventions, works with children and parents directly, and organizes and codes collected data. She also continues to pursue projects within social psychological attitudinal research and sexual risk-taking of marginalized adolescents. Her work utilizes a feminist perspective to better represent the experiences of marginalized women and youths.

Dr. Jennifer Young Wallace, "Foreword" author, is a tenured associate professor/coordinator of the doctoral program of Educational Leadership for the College of Education and Human Development at Jackson State University. Dr. Wallace was recently elected president 2025 for the Association of Teacher

Educators, where she served as a Board member (2019–2022) and chair of the Legislative Government Relations Committee (2022–2025). She serves on a national research team with college professors across America, researching K–12 teachers' perceptions of their own pedagogy. She was selected as a national evaluator of education programs in colleges and universities in the United States, where she travels to evaluate colleges' performance on educational standards. She consults with educational agencies and organizations on issues and trends in education that lead to building and improving educational frameworks, policies, principles, standards, and professional development.

Julie Zook is the leadership and talent development coach for Stafford County Public Schools, Virginia. She has thirty-four years of K–12 experience as a classroom teacher, assistant principal, and principal. She recently became certified as a leadership coach and works with more than twenty leaders in the school division. Julie received her bachelor's degree in Spanish and secondary education from James Madison University and her master's in educational leadership and policy studies from the University of Virginia.

About the Editors

Dr. Walter S. Polka is currently a tenured full professor in the Department of Leadership and coordinator of the PhD program in Leadership and Policy at Niagara University, New York. Previously, he was an associate professor of educational administration and coordinator of the doctoral program at Georgia Southern University, Statesboro, Georgia. Seventy-eight doctoral candidates have successfully defended their research dissertations under his guidance at three different universities including Addis Ababa University, Ethiopia. He also served for over thirty-five years as a public school teacher, curriculum coordinator, school district administrator, and superintendent of schools in New York. He has authored or coauthored over seventy-five book chapters and peer-reviewed research articles and book chapters. His eight books about educational leadership, curriculum improvement, and managing change include:

- *Coping with Crises: Approaches from School Leaders Who Did It!* (2023) with McKenna and VanHusen.
- *Managing Yourself and Others during Crises: Key Leadership Visions, Approaches, and Dispositions to Survive and Thrive* (2023) with McKenna and VanHusen.
- *Fatal Attractions in the Digital Age: The Impact of Dire "High-Tech" and "High-Touch" Indiscretions in Our Global Village* (2020) with Adelakun and DeSimone.
- *Very Good to Despicable: The Impact of the Seven Deadly Sins on Contemporary Leaders* (2018) with Mete.
- *Confronting Oppressive Assessments: How Parents, Educators, and Policy-Makers Are Rethinking Current Educational Reforms* (2016) with McKenna.
- *Living on the Horns of Dilemmas: Superintendents, Politics and Decision-Making* (2014) with Litchka and Calzi.

- *Superintendents and the Professional Victim Syndrome* (2008) with Litfchka.

Dr. Polka has presented his research in forty-seven states of the United States and in over twenty-five countries worldwide. In 2013, he received the prestigious Distinguished Alumni Award from the College of Education of the State University of New York at Buffalo. Dr. Polka completed his doctorate at State University of New York at Buffalo in 1977. The title of his dissertation is, "Curriculum Planning for the Individualization of Instruction."

Dr. John E. McKenna is an award-winning educator and national speaker from Western New York. He is currently an assistant professor of Educational Leadership at Niagara University. In his career that has spanned over thirty-five years, he has served as an acting superintendent, assistant superintendent, principal, assistant principal, and teacher. For his contributions he has been honored with several honors and awards including the New York State Outstanding Educator and the Friend of Education Award by the School Administrators Association of New York State; the Presidential Distinguished Elementary Principal Award from the Buffalo/Niagara Chapter of Phi Delta Kappa International, the Distinguished Service Award from Kappa Delta Pi, the Honorary Life Award and the Advocate in Action Award by the New York State PTA, the Special Service Award from the Niagara Region PTA for Outstanding Leadership and Contributions, a Proclamation and Resolution from the New York State Senate for Leadership and Distinguished Service, a resolution from the Erie County Legislature for Dedication and Contributions, and two prestigious Distinguished Alumni Awards by the State University of New York at Buffalo Graduate School of Education in 2014 and the University at Buffalo Alumni Association in 2021. He is a former president of the School Administrators Association of New York State (SAANYS), where he led approximately five hundred school districts across New York State. He has also served as president of Phi-Delta Kappa at Buffalo State College, the Committee for Identifying and Developing Educational Leaders (CIDEL), and the SUNY at Buffalo Graduate School of Education Alumni Association.

Monica J. VanHusen earned her BS in public communications at Buffalo State College, an MS in education from Niagara University, and an MA in educational leadership/administration from William and Mary College. She taught social studies at the middle school level in Stafford, Virginia, for eight years and was the Heim Middle School Teacher of the Year in 2011. She was appointed as high school instructional technology resource teacher in 2011 and became the districtwide coordinator of instructional technology resource teachers in 2018. During COVID-19 she played a key role in facilitating the development and implementation of both online and hybrid courses to facilitate learning for more than thirty thousand K–12 students at Stafford County Schools. She was highlighted in a 2022 State University of New York College at Buffalo Athletics Publication celebrating fifty years of Title IX and female collegiate athletics as she was a 2010 inductee for both her interscholastic volleyball and basketball achievements. Monica's research interests relate to integrating technology in curriculum, differentiating instruction, and school leadership. She has served as a coeditor of three books and coauthored ten book chapters and peer reviewed journal articles.